The
Killer Book
of True Crime

Incredible Stories, Facts and Trivia from the World of Murder and Mayhem

Tom Philbin and Michael Philbin

SOURCEBOOKS, INC.®
NAPERVILLE, ILLINOIS

Published by Sourcebooks, Inc.
P.O. Box 4410, Naperville, Illinois 60567–4410
(630) 961-3900
Fax: (630) 961-2128
www.sourcebooks.com

© 2007 by Tom Philbin and Michael Philbin

ISBN-13 978-1-4022-0829-4
ISBN-10 1-4022-0829-4

Printed in Canada
WC 10 9 8 7 6 5 4 3 2 1

Contents

Introduction:
Welcome to Gore Galore v

Chapter 1:
Robbery 1

Chapter 2:
Organized Crimes and Gangs 25

Chapter 3:
Prostitution 39

Chapter 4:
Serial Murder 51

Chapter 5:
Mass Murder 95

Chapter 6:
Criminal Investigation 141

Chapter 7:
Rape .153

Chapter 8:
Sexual Perversions 163

Chapter 9:
Terrorism 177

Chapter 10:
Auto Theft 187

Chapter 11:
Death Row 191

Chapter 12:
Prisons 199

Chapter 13:
Stalking 217

Chapter 14:
Female Killers 223

Chapter 15:
Arson .243

Chapter 16:
Celebrities and Crime 255

Chapter 17:
Kids Who Kill 265

Chapter 18:
Miscellaneous 273

Chapter 19:
Mostly Gore (Not Al) 295

Index 329

About the Authors 345

Introduction:

Welcome to Gore Galore

This book is designed to serve up a potpourri of delectable information about crime in a manner that's entertaining, informative, and satisfying. It should be right down the average crime lover's gurney—or rather, alley.

This book serves up crime in a variety of ways. There are Notable Quotables (quotes from people involved in crime in one way or another), straight facts and factoids, match games (such as matching the correct mafia nicknames to the correct mobster), Q & A's, "Who Am I?" brain teasers, and many lists—everything from the characteristics of a serial murderer to characteristics of kids who murder their parents. Also included is the jargon that particular groups of criminals use (such as prisoners, who say "family style" to describe the missionary position for sodomy in prison).

But not all the entries have a serious side. Crime Can Be Funny, and entries so marked describe encounters New York cops have had with criminals; many of these stories describe criminals who were just plain dumb. These pieces came from the book *The Funniest Cop Stories Ever*, by Tom Philbin and Scott Baker.

Most of what's served appears in short form—snacks, if you will—but there are also some longer pieces: full-course meals such as in the "Mass Murder" chapter, which recounts stories such as the night in Chicago when Richard Speck perpetrated one of the most abominable crimes of the twentieth century.

While words can be great, there's nothing like illustrations, and this book contains a variety—everything from pictures of some of the worst maniacs of the twentieth century to crime scene art; from notes given to bank tellers during bank robberies to the graphic autopsy report that details the brutal slaying of Nicole Brown Simpson. If you follow true crime, some of the material presented here will be familiar to you. But most of it likely will not be familiar, because it wasn't even familiar to the Brothers Philbin when we researched this book, and we are both self-proclaimed card-carrying ghouls. (Ah, yes: there's nothing like the smell of decomposing flesh in the morning!)

We have, though, exercised some discretion and excluded some material (such as photos showing JFK's head after being shot with a high-powered rifle. This is because while true crime can make one's eyes dilate with interest and pleasure, sometimes it can also be just too much to bear: the subject matter walks a fine line between intensely interesting and outright disgusting. Where is the line that separates the two? We don't know, but we think it's probably somewhere in the stomach.

We hope you enjoy this book. We are sure you will learn some things from it (like the fact that abysmal childhoods often produce murderers), but that's not our main goal. Our main purpose is to entertain, and we hope you decide that we've succeeded.

—Mike and Tom Philbin

Chapter 1
Robbery

Notable Quotable

"It's where the money is."

—Bank robber Willie Sutton, when asked why he exclusively robbed banks.

Make My Day Law

Burglars intent on a home invasion—taking over a house when the occupants are home—should probably think twice before doing it in the state of Colorado. In 1985, Colorado passed the controversial Make My Day law, which states, "Citizens of Colorado have a right to expect absolute safety within their own homes . . ." and that a homeowner/occupant is justified in using "any degree of physical force, including deadly physical force" on an intruder, if the intruder has made an unlawful entry into the dwelling and the occupant feels physically threatened. In July 2006, a man in Aurora, Illinois, who had been burglarized several times

(New York Public Library Picture Collection)

before, used his 12-gauge shotgun to shoot and kill an intruder who had pushed in an air conditioner to gain access to the intended victim's one-story bungalow. At the time of this book's writing, the Make My Day law was being cited, but the outcome was pending.

A Very Dangerous Little Boy

In South Bend, Indiana, in 2002, an eleven-year-boy and his grandmother were alone in their home when someone came to the door. The grandmother knew the man was a drug dealer, but he was also a friend of her daughter, who was in jail on drug charges. Against her better judgment, and in trying to be civil to her daughter's friend, the grandmother allowed the man into her home. While the man initially acted friendly and appeared concerned about the imprisoned daughter's well-being, the man's demeanor changed radically after a few minutes. Knowing there were guns in the house, the man pulled out a carpet cutter and held it to the grandmother's throat, demanding to know where the guns were. The young boy ran from the room, upstairs to the gun cabinet and grabbed a shotgun and a loaded Spanish Llama .45 automatic. The boy's father had died three years earlier of a heart attack, and what the drug dealer didn't know was that by the time the boy was eight years old, the boy's father had taught his son all about guns and shooting. The boy came down the stairs and threw the shotgun onto the floor, distracting the man, and the boy then assumed a two-handed, straight-armed combat position known as the isosceles stance. The drug dealer tried to swing the grandmother around for more protection, but it was too late. The boy saw the man's exposed side and fired off a round, hitting him squarely in the upper chest. The drug dealer managed to run out the door, but he collapsed and died in an alleyway about forty yards from the house. The child's expertise and fast action had certainly saved his grandmother's life. The court's ruling on the incident came as no surprise—justifiable homicide.

The Most Prolific Burglar

Bernard C. Welch Jr. may be arguably the most prolific burglar of all time. This forty-year-old man—whom cops nicknamed "The Standard Time Burglar" because he liked to work in winter, when nights are longer—packed thirty-three hundred burglaries into his life and also committed three at-gunpoint rapes and one murder.

Most of the time, Welch, who later took the name Norm Hamilton, lived an ordinary life in Great Falls, Virginia, and worked as a collectibles dealer (a great job for a thief). But eventually the police sniffed him out. After arresting him, when they searched Welch's house, the police found an astonishing thirteen thousand stolen items in the basement worth approximately $7 million and which took police six days to inventory. Also found in the search were two smelters that Welch used to melt down gold and silver.

In 1981, Welch was sentenced to nine consecutive life terms, but it wasn't the burglaries that earned him the heavy sentence. One night while Welch was robbing a house in Washington, D.C., the home's owner, Michael Halberstam (forty-eight-year-old brother of the famous writer David Halberstam) startled Welch. Welch panicked and shot Halberstam, who died.

Welch was on the fourth year of his long sentence when he escaped from prison, but he was recaptured. An interesting side note to Welch's burglaries is that, after he was captured, some four thousand victims came forward attempting to reclaim their stolen property.

How Desperate for Cash Are Some Drug Addicts?

I [Tom Philbin] have a friend—let's call her Jenny White—who spent three years in a woman's institution in Framingham for burglary. She gave me a good idea of just how desperate drug addicts can be.

"I was involved," she said, "in eighty-seven burglaries, and many of them took place in broad daylight, while the people were home. In Massachusetts that goes from plain burglary to home invasion, and there is much heavier time involved. But we didn't give a fuck. Getting money or things we could fence was all that mattered.

"Let me put it this way. On more than one occasion, we would snake into a house while the people were in the back-yard having a cookout, and me and this guy Mikey went though the front door and hit the pocketbooks in the living room. At any moment someone could have walked in. We didn't have any intention of hurting anyone, but you never know.

Panic Rooms: Not New

Most people were probably surprised by the movie Panic Room, in which Jodie Foster and her son retreat into an impregnable room while home invaders try to break through to get into the room. But people might also be surprised to learn that such rooms have existed for a long time. Corporate executives in fear of being kidnapped, people in sensitive government situations, or ordinary people who just want to protect themselves and/or their valuables—say, against an abusive or vengeful spouse—are common users of these types of "panic rooms."

The walls may be built of concrete or some other semi-impregnable material, the door made of solid wood or metal and opening outward so that its edges are resting on metal jambs or framework that can't be pushed in easily. But unlike the room in the movie, real safe rooms are not built to withstand hours of assault, but rather they are constructed to give the person inside enough time to summon help. Experts also recommend stocking the room with weapons, food, and water, and, of course, a means of communication with the police. Experts also say that the room should blend in with the rest of the house. The best defense is for intruders not to know you're in there.

Q&A

Q: How much do retail stores lose to theft each year?

A: A survey in 2002 found that retail stores suffered between .7 percent and 2.2 percent retail inventory loss of gross sales due to theft, with the average being about 1.7 percent.

Q: What is "crotch walking?"

A: (No, it's not walking on your crotch!) It's a technique used by female shoplifters wearing full skirts and dresses. The shoplifter places an item between their thighs and then exits the store. Walking in a natural manner is the trick, and shoplifters who are good at this technique have been known to walk out of stores with very large objects between their legs—even typewriters and hams!

Crime Can Be Funny

Why Shotgun Teams Were Disbanded

In New York in the 1960s, in locations where robberies were common, cops would deploy "shotgun teams" to provide an unpleasant surprise for robbers. This would give police an advantage over the robbers, and an arrest would follow. But shotgun teams were disbanded as the result of the actions of one overzealous shotgun team, whose members hid behind a vent in a liquor store that had been held up five or six times earlier.

What happened was recounted the next day by the perpetrator, who spoke from his hospital bed.

"I came into the joint," he says, "and put the heat on the dude, and tell him to give me all the bread in the register. As he's doing that I hear a little noise to my right and then I hear someone yell, though I can't see anyone: 'Goodbye motherf——r!' And the next thing I know I wake up here."

Q&A

Q: Are males or female shoplifters more common?

A: Female shoplifters outnumber males by about twenty to one. Nine out of ten shoplifters are under the age of thirty.

Q: How do shoplifters beat electronic security systems?

A: To defeat the RFID (Radio Frequency Identification) security system in department stores (where the item contains a small transponder that sends signals to the alarm system), shoplifters bring in bags or boxes that they have lined with aluminum foil. If they can successfully get the pilfered item into the bag or box unobserved, they will be able to simply walk out of the store. The aluminum blocks the alarm signal. Underwear lined with aluminum foil is another shoplifting trick.

Q: How are shoplifters taking advantage of modern technology?

A: More sophisticated shoplifters are taking advantage of high quality printing and digital technology. They will purchase low cost items at a department store. Once home, they remove the low cost bar codes and print multiple copies of them. Returning to the store, they cover the bar codes of higher priced items with one of their own. The item scans at the lower price and, assuming the cashier doesn't notice, they get away with it.

Q: How do shoplifters beat cashiers?

A: The shoplifter will put the item she wants to steal under the folded baby seat of a shopping cart or conceal it under a sales leaflet. Having other merchandise in the cart for which she intends to pay, she seeks out a cashier who seems slow or inexperienced and who will often not notice the semi-hidden item.

Check Washing

Check washing is a document-altering scam that's disturbingly simple. Thieves will look for a mailbox with the flag up and snatch the outgoing mail before the mailman arrives. They look for mail containing personal checks made out to utilities, credit card companies, and so forth. Then they use chemicals to erase all the information on the checks except your signature.

How? A number of common household chemicals are capable of dissolving ink. The most widely used chemical is acetone. A mixture of Isopropyl alcohol, benzene, bleach, carbon

7

tetrachloride, and a few other chemicals (don't you try this at home, now!) will also do the trick. Once all the original information is erased, they rewrite the check to themselves (for hundreds or even thousands of dollars), go to a bank, give the teller phony identification which matches the name on the check, and they walk out with your cash.

According to The National Check Fraud Center, hundreds of millions of dollars are stolen each year in the U.S. as a result of check washing. While this is mostly perpetrated by street criminals, occasionally a "bad-apple" postal worker has been known to pull this stunt. Fortunately, check manufacturing companies are very aware of the problem and are always improving their security measures; they even make some stock wash-proof now, but the federal authorities still offer the following advice.

- Try to bring your mail directly to the post office or a collection box or, if that's not possible, hand the mail to the letter carrier personally. If you must put outgoing mail in an old fashioned mailbox, don't put up the flag, and put the mail out just before the postman arrives. Also, don't leave outgoing mail in the box on Sundays or holidays when the letter carriers aren't working.

- To protect yourself further, writing checks out in gel ink instead of regular (dye-based) ink makes it much harder (if not impossible) for thieves to do their dirty work. Also, find out from your bank what security measures are contained in their documents to protect against check washing. Examine your bank statements closely. If fraud is not reported within thirty days of you receiving your statement, the bank does not have to reimburse you for your loss.

Two Wallet-Stealing Tricks

1. Two pickpockets will often work in tandem to steal a wallet. One such technique is known as the "Pile-Up-Pick." Poised near a crowded escalator, they will spot a potential male victim. One pickpocket gets on the escalator in front of the victim and the other pickpocket stands on the escalator behind the victim. Just as the escalator ride is ending, the front man will drop something on the escalator stairs and clumsily bend down to pick it up, creating a football-style pile-up of people. The victim, sandwiched between the two thieves, doesn't feel a thing, and the pickpocket in back steals the man's wallet.

2. One trick of female thieves is to follow a lone woman with a pocketbook into the ladies' room. They know many women hang their bags on the hook on the inside of the stall. Once they know the victim is sitting on the toilet, the thief will simply reach over and grab the bag off the hook. Sometimes, just before the purse is stolen, an accomplice drops change in the adjacent stall to create a distraction.

Q&A

Q: Should you let a robber take your purse?

A: That's a decision you have to make on the spot, and a lot of different factors influence the decision. In some situations, women decide to give up their purse to get the person to leave. If that's the decision that you make, experts recommend throwing the purse as far away from you as you can, on the assumption that the criminal is much more interested in your money than in you. Once you've thrown the bag, run as fast as possible in the other direction.

9

If you decide that you want to fight for your purse, you should first make sure your attacker is not armed, and then you should know effective ways to fight and defend yourself. There are also some advance steps you can take to minimize the impact of any potential theft or robbery, such as not carrying much cash, making sure you have copies at home of the favorite photos you carry, and knowing the procedures for reporting stolen credit cards. If you take these precautions, it might be easier to give up the purse without a fight and you can potentially avoid any physical harm.

Q: What is Inventory Shrinkage?

A: Inventory shrinkage is a term used to describe a combination of employee theft, shoplifting, vendor fraud, and administrative error, and it is the single largest category of larceny in the U.S. According to the National Retail Security Survey, it cost U.S. retailers over 31 billion dollars in 2002.

Robbery Jargon

1. **Bunko:** A con game. The term may stem from the Spanish word banca, a card game similar to Three Card Monte. It has been in use since the nineteenth century. A crime report in the July 6, 1875, issue of the Chicago Tribune said, "The fugitive is the same person who bunkoed a stranger of seventy-five dollars recently." Today many police departments still have Bunko Squads to handle such swindles.

2. **Check Kiter:** Someone who writes bad checks. Check kiters run the gamut from the basically honest citizen trying to make ends meet to the calculating, trained thief who lives on kited checks.
   Check kiting can also involve big-time sums of money. For example, in 1985, E. F. Hutton and Co., Inc., a stock brokerage,

pleaded guilty to federal charges that involved check kiting and were fined $2 million plus the cost of the government investigation ($750,000). In addition, they had to pay back $8 million they had defrauded from banks. The government said the scheme had lasted from July 1980 to February 1982, a time when interest rates were very high. In one aspect of this scheme, Hutton managers would write checks for more money than they had on account, using money that in effect didn't exist—just like an ordinary individual would do.

The term "check kiting" probably derives from the action of a kite: It is up in the air temporarily before it comes to rest to launder money.

3. **Money laundering** is the process of making a currency transaction for the sole purpose of reducing a larger amount of money into negotiable instruments of less than $10,000. (Any amount in any form over $10,000 is automatically reported by banks to the IRS.) The people who actually convert the money are nicknamed Smurfs after the energetic little blue cartoon characters of the mid-1980s. Chuck Sapphos, a lawyer in the Department of Justice, was explaining the process of laundering money to his young daughter, and explained that the people who did the work had to run from bank to bank to do it. "Oh," his daughter said, "they're like Smurfs." And the name stuck.

4. **Dip:** A pickpocket. This term is primarily used by bunko squads and likely derives from the physical action involved: the hand dips into the pocket and extracts the valuables. In 1888, the St. Louis Globe Democrat reported that no one is immune from a skillful pickpocket: "A dip."

5. **Fallen off a truck:** A stolen item, the product of a burglary, a hijacking, or bought "hot."

   The phrase is usually associated with the mafia, and from time to time one hears a version of it in popular media. In the movie, Married to the Mob, for example, the wife of one Mafioso tells him that she is tired of living the mob lifestyle, where "everything we own fell off a truck."

Q&A

Q: Do shoplifters work alone?

A: Sometimes. But they also often work in pairs or groups. With pairs, one member of the team distracts the employee with questions while the other does the stealing. In groups, several members enter the store at the same time and then disperse to all areas of the store. They know employees cannot watch everyone at once.

Q: How do kids help shoplifters?

A: One way is that mothers will hand items to children to put in their pockets. If the security system is triggered as they are leaving the store, the mothers will act as if the child took the merchandise on their own. Knowing the store will not arrest a child, she acts shocked and scolds the child, making him "put it back." Another technique is using a stroller or baby carriage as a stash. They hide items in the blankets and sometimes even put merchandise under the infant. Carriages with false bottoms also are used. Another way, as seen in the movie The King of the Gypsies, is for a child to swallow a valuable gem and later excrete it.

A Human Bomb

High on the list of bizarre ways to rob a bank is turning someone into a human bomb. On August 28, 2003, as near as authorities can determine, a man named Wells, who delivered for Mama Mia's Pizza Parlor, was called to deliver two pepperoni pizzas to what turned out to be a bogus address in Erie, Pennsylvania.

Forty minutes later, Wells walked into a bank and told them that he had a bomb around his neck and that he wanted $250,000. It is unclear if the bank gave him any money, but they did alert the police, who were waiting for Wells when he emerged from the bank. Wells screamed that he was innocent, but they forced him to sit down in the road and members of the bomb squad were called.

But help did not arrive soon enough. Wells said that the bomb around his neck was set to go off in twenty minutes and, true to his word, the bomb exploded, killing Wells instantly.

Q&A

Q: How can an umbrella help a shoplifter?

A: On rainy days, an umbrella that is closed but not snapped makes a good catch-all. With the umbrella hung on the forearm, shoplifters push or drop items into the upside-down umbrella. It's a common technique.

Crime Can Be Funny

Just Being Helpful

Two officers in a squad car near Houston Street in downtown New York received a report over the police radio of a robbery near them. The officers got a description of the perpetrator and shortly thereafter, the officers saw the perpetrator on the street. The perpetrator noticed the cops and he started to run. The cops caught up to him and started to handcuff the man, and the suspect looked around in total bewilderment.

"Hey," he said, "whatcha doin'? Whatcha doin'? What's going on?"

"You robbed a lady back there," one of the cops said.

"I didn't rob no lady! I didn't rob no lady."

"Then why you running from us?"

"I was running after the guy who did it! I was trying to help you catch him! Come on—follow me before he gets away!"

Q&A

Q: When are most burglaries committed?

A: During daylight hours, when apartment or home dwellers are not likely to be home. The most common month is August, when people are most likely to be on vacation. According to Burglars on the Job, by Richard Wright and Scott Decker, the first place a burglar searches for valuables is the dresser in the master bedroom, followed by the bedside table, shoe boxes in the closet, under the mattress, and then the refrigerator and freezer.

King of the Pickpockets

Thomas "Butterfingers" Moran is considered the king of pick-pockets. In a career that spanned sixty-five years, Moran had an estimated 50,000 scores and, amazingly, he worked without the help of a "framer" (someone to distract the victim). To ply his trade, he frequented subways, racetracks, buses, and one of his favorite places, union meetings—where, of course, no one would suspect a union brother of theft.

Bank Robbery at a Glance

1. Bank robberies usually occur on Friday mornings between the hours of 9 and 11 a.m. Monday is the second most frequent day for bank robberies. (Credit Union magazine)
2. The average bank robbery haul is five thousand dollars. (AP Online)
3. On average, one out of ten bank robbers will be caught.
4. Metropolitan Los Angeles has more banks robbed than any other area in the U.S. It averages about one thousand robberies a year. One important reason: the freeway networks allow easier escape. (FBI)

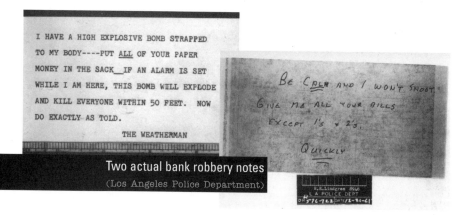

I HAVE A HIGH EXPLOSIVE BOMB STRAPPED TO MY BODY----PUT ALL OF YOUR PAPER MONEY IN THE SACK__IF AN ALARM IS SET WHILE I AM HERE, THIS BOMB WILL EXPLODE AND KILL EVERYONE WITHIN 50 FEET. NOW DO EXACTLY AS TOLD.

THE WEATHERMAN

Be CALM AND I WON'T SHOOT GIVE ME ALL YOUR BILLS EXCEPT 1's + 2's, QUICKLY

Two actual bank robbery notes
(Los Angeles Police Department)

The Brink's Job

One of the best planned and best executed crimes of the twentieth century was the robbery of a Brink's, the monetary transportation company. On January 17, 1950, seven armed thieves in Boston made off with $1,218,211.29 in cash and $1,557,183.83 in checks, money orders, and other securities. The haul weighed over twelve hundred pounds. The job took seventeen minutes and the FBI spent $29 million investigating it.

The architect of the job was Anthony "Fats" Pino, a career criminal who, with the other thieves, studied and planned the job for a year and a half. The object of their affection was the Brink's Counting Room, where money flowed from various sources at the rate of $10 million a day. Over the eighteen-month planning period, the thieves made twenty-seven nighttime trips to the complex of buildings that comprised Brink's. To get into the Counting Room, they had to go through five locked doors. Over the months, they removed each of the lock cylinders, made a key, and returned the cylinder to the door before it was noticed.

Pino and his cohorts entered the Counting Room very easily thanks to the keys and the criminals' appearances—wearing chauffeurs uniforms and bizarre comic masks both disguised their identities and terrorized the Brink's workers.

It all would have gone unsolved except for one thing. One of the robbers, "Specs" O'Keefe, entrusted $90,000 of his share of the loot to a fellow thief, and when he asked for it back, the other man would not give it to him. O'Keefe threatened to go to the cops if he wasn't paid. Pino and others reacted by getting Elmer "Trigger" Burke, a notorious New York hitman, to "clip" O'Keefe, but Burke was unsuccessful and O'Keefe went to the authorities. They were all arrested—only five days before the six-year statute of limitations on the crime would have expired. Everyone in the gang was sent to jail.

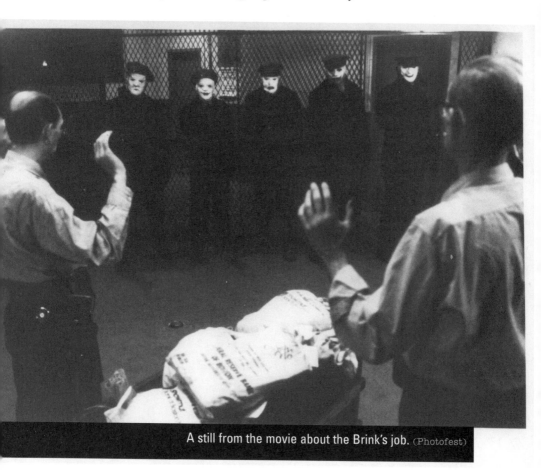

A still from the movie about the Brink's job. (Photofest)

Characteristics of Burglars

There are two kinds of burglars: house burglars and cat burglars. House burglars are criminals who are only interested in stealing from a house or business; they will usually enter a house in the daytime. Cat burglars, who tend to rob houses at night, are a whole different animal.

House Burglars	Cat Burglars
• Burglars usually don't carry weapons.	• According to cops, cat burglars are crazy. Anyone who would prowl around a house while the occupants are asleep is a mental case.
• Professional burglars are much smarter than most criminals. Everything they do is carefully planned. Junkies looking for money for a quick fix usually are not smart enough to be burglars.	• A cat burglar can become violent if confronted—or become a rapist when he peels back bedclothes to look at a woman whose house he's burglarizing.
• Burglars usually net about one third of the worth of what they steal after fencing or selling it. So, for example, if the burglar steals $1,000 worth of property, he can only expect to get $300 or so out of it. Burglars prefer to fence their stuff at bars. There's no paper trail like there is when someone sells something to a pawn shop.	• Cat burglars defecating on the floor or bed are very common. Some cat burglars will even defecate on a bed where occupants are sleeping. One found a detective's shield, defecated on the dining room table, and stuck the shield into the feces.

Thieving Home Improvement Contractors

In Missouri, ex-Assistant Attorney General Peter Lumaghi tells the story of an elderly woman living in the southeastern part of the state who had no understanding of home improvements and contractors. So when a contractor slapped a lien on her home, despair set in and she eventually set the house on fire, and stayed inside—a suicide.

Robbery

This is, admittedly, a horror story that is atypical. However, it's just an extreme result of a common problem. There are many, many smaller horror stories about the financial and emotional perils people face when hiring carpenters, plumbers, roofers, and other home-improvement contractors.

The Council of Better Business Bureau's records indicate that home repair complaints across the country have increased 40 percent or so in the last five years. Additionally, The National Association of Attorney Generals says its annual, nationwide survey of consumer complaints shows that home repair and/or construction is always in its top ten. And those numbers are sure to rise because of homeowners victimized in gulf states hit by Katrina and other hurricanes. Repair predators quickly smelled blood. Richard Mitchell, president of the New Orleans BBB, says the first of this type of scammer has already arrived—and they're ruthless. One lady had four trees on her property and contractors took them off—then presented her with a bill for $14,000.

Q & A

Q: How Many Home Improvement Contractors Are Thieves?
1 of 2
1 of 5
1 of 10
1 of 20

A: The answer to this has never been scientifically measured, but Fred Gorman, a big-time contractor who spent fifty years in the trade, says he believes 1 in 10 were "highbinders."

19

Beware the Williamsons

The Williamson gang is the ultimate example of contractors who rip people off. They are known to every consumer protection agency in the U.S. because they travel all over the country, usually showing up in the warm months. They may be into anything now, but they are famous for one asphalt-driveway scam. William Webster, ex-attorney general of Missouri, calls them "asphalt gypsies."

They wear clean uniforms and drive around in new trucks until they spot a driveway with a few hairline cracks or other defects. They point out the problems to the person who answers the door (they usually arrive midday, when, they hope, only a woman is home), then offer to seal the driveway for what seems like a good price, say a five-gallon can for $60. If they get the go-ahead they'll be back a half hour later, finish, and ask for $600. Naturally the consumer will point out that the agreed-upon charge was $60.

> ### Sticky Fingers
>
> Don't leave valuables lying around when you have home improvements done—such items can be an open invitation to sticky fingers. And you never know the background of anyone coming into your home.

"That's right," says the scamster. "Sixty dollars for a five-gallon can; we used ten cans." He expects the person to argue and is prepared to settle for less—say, $400. The consumer offers a check, but the gypsy won't take a check; when the person says he doesn't have that kind of cash in the house, the gypsy says he'll take a check—but only if the person goes to the bank with him to cash it. If the consumer agrees and leaves the house, the gypsy's confederates may rob it while he is gone. And the driveway won't be properly sealed either. These swindlers may use low-quality sealer, but they've also been known to swab on used motor oil or cheap black enamel paint. It looks good until you drive on it—and take it with you into the street. (Some consumer experts call the Williamsons the "crankcase-oil brigade." They are also known as "The Travelers" (which also was the name of a movie about them starring Bill Paxton).

Crime Can Be Funny

And I'll Be On My Way

During Mayor Dinkins' Administration in the early 1990s, it was like the wild west in New York City—twenty-one hundred homicides a year. The city government came up with a brilliant plan to rid the streets of crime—the Buy Back plan. The administration announced they would buy guns from anyone, no questions asked—even if the gun had no serial numbers or was used to commit a murder. The goal was just to get guns off the street. During this period, two cops were out on foot patrol, and a passerby pointed to a man who was walking down the block and said, "He's got a gun!" The guy who allegedly had the gun was heading down a one-way street, so the cops radioed to headquarters to get a car to block the other end of the street. This worked, and when the guy saw the squad car coming down the one-way street, he turned and ran—almost right into the cops' arms.

The officers searched the man and pulled a gun out of his waistband.

"Where you going?" they asked him.

"I'm goin' to the precinct for the Buy Back program. Handing in my gun."

"Then why are you runnin' from us?"

"Got to get there quick! But now that you here, why don't you give me the money and I'll be on my way!"

Scamming the Elderly

The elderly are particularly vulnerable to the rip-off artist. A man named Harold Bartlett, for example, specialized in victimizing elderly black women in East St. Louis, conning them into signing deeds of trust to their homes and then threatening to foreclose if they didn't pay for improvements.

ABC's *Home Show* featured a story about an alert bank manager who saved an elderly client before she was victimized too badly. The manager had noticed that the woman had transferred large amounts of money from her savings to her checking account and was writing fairly large checks to someone the bank manager had not heard of. Suspicious, the manager contacted the Los Angeles bunko squad. An investigating detective found that the woman was having an old shed reroofed, a job later determined to be worth perhaps $700. The woman had already paid the roofer $5,000 of the overall asking price of $58,000.

"Spiking" a home improvement job.
(Author's Collection)

Another scam: "spiking" the house, which is starting the job by ripping down the siding. Then, no matter what, the homeowner is forced to have the job finished, either by the spiker or by someone else.

Robbery

Crime Can Be Funny

"They Almost Got Me"

A detective on the Bunko Squad was fortunate enough to arrest some of the Williamson gang, a notorious group of traveling home improvement thieves. He was visiting his older aunt in Queens and the doorbell rang. A solicitor started talking to the aunt, and the cop sneaked up and listened while the solicitor explained why she needed her roof done. He was good. In fact, he was so convincing the officer was tempted to come out from behind the door and say: "Where do I sign?"

But instead the cop came out with his shield—the contractor didn't have a license, so he was locked up.

There are many other kinds of construction scams. One of the most damaging is contractors who take down payments on a job and never start work. Also, there are those who start work and then never finish. And the amounts that the consumers are defrauded are not small—usually they're in the thousands of dollars, many times in the tens of thousands. Sue Nichols of the Connecticut Consumer Affairs Department says they had one "contractor" who made a livelihood of this. "That's all he did: go from job to job giving estimates, taking advances, and never coming back. He got around eighty thousand dollars before he blew out of town."

This, of course, is felonious behavior. The district attorney will be happy to take your complaint, and to pursue it; but usually only after he or she has gone after the perpetrators of the other complaints on the desk—the robberies, burglaries, assaults, rapes, and murders.

23

Crime Can Be Funny

With Friends Like These, Who Needs Enemies?

Figure this one out. One day two cops responded to a burglary in progress; when they arrived at the location, a neighbor explained that the homeowners were away but that he had seen a man enter through the back door. They entered the house, guns drawn—it was clear downstairs, so they headed up. They checked the rooms and found a guy in one of them, lying under the covers in one of the beds. One cop stripped off the blanket while the other kept him covered with a gun. The man was fully clothed, boots and all.

"Hey, what's the deal?" one cop said.

"Hey, what you all doin' in my house?"

"This ain't your house."

"Well," he said, "it's my best friend's house, I'm watchin' it for him."

The cops nodded and started to cuff him. "What about all the electronic equipment in the garbage bags?"

"Oh," he says, "that's my boy's stuff. I'm gonna take it to the repair shop tomorrow."

"But tomorrow is Sunday," one cop said.

The man replied, "Well, my other friend gots a shop. He opens for me only on Sunday!"

The officers took the man to jail, and once in, he starts pleading his case to two other guests there. They were sympathizing with him, and one of the cops overheard him say in a high, plaintive voice:

"They locked me up because I was in my cousin's house!"

The cop couldn't help but say: "But you told me that it was your best friend's house."

The man looked at the cop with a mystified look on his face. "Yo five-o, my cousin is my best friend!"

Chapter 2
Organized Crime and Gangs

The Most Feared Mafioso

One of the most feared men ever in the New York Mafia was a pudgy man named Roy DeMeo. He was a made member of the mafia, a murderer, loan shark, and car thief who hung out with other thugs in the Gemini Lounge in Brooklyn. He created an "assembly line" for murder. The potential victim was lured to the Gemini Lounge Clubhouse, where he was shot and then stabbed in the heart. Next came the butcher knives and bone saws to cut him apart and package him in little pieces, which were then thrown in the dumpster for pickup. It was estimated that DeMeo was responsible for murdering over two hundred people and he liked "having the power of God, deciding who lives, who dies."

DeMeo eventually ran afoul of the Boss of all Bosses, Paul Castellano, and Castellano, fearing that DeMeo would cooperate with the government, ordered his death. One frozen January day, DeMeo was found in the trunk of a car, shot seven times. One bullet had gone through his frozen hand, which he had held to his face to protect himself, and there was a pool of blood—frozen. They also found a recorder wire, a message that anyone who crossed the mafia would also end up in the trunk of a car.

Match Game
Mafia Deaths

Match each Mafioso with the way he met his fate.

1. Vito Genovese ———
2. Bugsy Siegel ———
3. Joe Adonis ———
4. Paul Castellano ———
5. Carlo Gambino ———
6. Albert Anastasia ———
7. Lucky Luciano ———
8. Meyer Lansky ———
9. Louis "Lepke" Buchalter ———
10. Carmine Galante ———

11. Joey Gallo ———
12. Joe Profaci ———
13. Sam Giancana ———
14. Abe Reles ———
15. Joe Columbo ———
16. John Gotti ———
17. Dutch Schultz ———
18. Raymond Patriarca ———
19. Frank Nitti ———
20. Joe Bonanno ———

A. Died of a massive heart attack in a Providence hospital

B. Assassinated in his basement kitchen while preparing a bedtime snack

C. Took three bullets in the head while sitting in his girlfriend's living room

D. Murdered while getting a haircut in the barbershop of a Manhattan hotel

E. Died of heart failure while in federal prison

F. Assassinated on his birthday at a clam house in Little Italy

G. Died of lung cancer in Miami Beach

H. Died of a heart attack while at a Naples airport

I. Committed suicide by putting a pistol to his head

J. Thrown from a sixth-floor window at a Coney Island hotel

K. Died of throat cancer while in prison

L. Had a fatal heart attack while being interrogated by the police

M. Died of peritonitis after being shot in a New Jersey chop house

N. Passed away at age ninety-seven from natural causes

O. Killed by three gunmen in the outdoor courtyard of a Brooklyn restaurant

P. Executed in the electric chair at Sing-Sing

Q. Succumbed to liver cancer while still boss of the Brooklyn family

R. Died of cardiac arrest while watching a Yankees game in his home

S. Shot by multiple gunmen outside a Manhattan steakhouse

T. Died after lingering in a coma for seven years following an assassination attempt

Gang/Organized Crime Jargon

1. **Put out a contract:** This is one of the most common names for a mob murder, used both by law enforcement personnel and mobsters. The threat of death is the ultimate weapon used by organized crime to control people. The rule is simple: Do it my way or be killed.

   For years, if you were going to be hit by the family you could expect that a certain decorum would be observed: for example, they wouldn't kill you in front of your wife and kids. That has changed. The most dramatic example was the killing of Joey "Crazy Joe" Gallo, a renegade Mafioso who was shot by two gunmen while dining with his wife in Umberto's Clam House in New York City.

   The time to worry about being hit is when you are aware of having committed a fatal offense (such as stealing drugs) and are subsequently invited somewhere by a close friend. This is frequently the way a mob hit is achieved: a friend is forced to set up a friend.

Today, the various gangs also are much more violent than in the past. Indeed, the level of violence is mind boggling, and perhaps most shocking are the Colombians. They not only don't care about your family seeing you being killed, but will kill them all because of your transgressions.

"Hit" first showed up in print in America in 1971 in Sleep is for the Rich by D. McKenzie: "I got scared and called the whole thing off. Someone else must have made the hit."

2. **Do a piece of work:** This is the most common phrase mobsters use when they are going to murder someone.

3. **Button man:** A soldier in a mafia family.

Button men do the dirty work for the mafia—collecting for loan sharks or from people paying extortion money, acting as enforcers, bodyguards, runners—whatever they are ordered to do. The button man may or may not be a "made man" (one formally inducted into the mafia) but is connected to the family nonetheless. Button men are considered the low men on the mafia totem pole but are highly regarded within the criminal community because of their mafia affiliation. One said the term comes from the idea that a button man acting as a "hit man makes buttonholes, or bullet holes, in his victim.

4. *Capo di tutti di cappi:* Italian for "boss of all bosses."

5. **Consigliere:** Chief counselor to the head of a mafia family; from the Italian consiglio, meaning advice or counsel.

Consigliere is a revered position in the mafia; the man who holds it is regarded as very wise in the ways of the mob. Consiglieres tend to be older men.

6. Wire man: Anyone skilled in placing a recording device.

Most law enforcement entities have wire men, and these days they play a crucial role, particularly in the war against organized crime.

The public consciousness of what it takes to wiretap a telephone is erroneous. The popular conception is of a quick, furtive placement in a phone or on a wire close by; in fact, the wire man can tap a wire far from a subject's house.

In other instances, placing the wire must be quick and furtive and carries some risk of the wire men being discovered. One of the classic wires was placed one windswept, rainy night by New York State Police officers, who succeeded in placing a bug in the Jaguar of the subject, a big-time Mafioso named Anthony "Tony Ducks" Corrallo, who at the time was attending a wedding reception. Corrallo, feeling perfectly safe in his car, talked naturally and lugubriously about mafia business to his driver, his conversation spiced with uncomplimentary references to some of his compatriots.

At one point in the operation, the bug, powered by the car's failing battery, started to fail as well. Corrallo brought the vehicle in for servicing—which would have meant discovery of the bug. But agents were able to get to the car and remove the bug, then replace it after the car was serviced. Thanks to that bug, Corrallo died in jail.

Police also have placed bugs in parked cars to listen to street conversations. In one Portland neighborhood, for example, police noticed that the bad guys they wanted so much never talked in an incriminating way inside a building. But each day they would stand on a certain street corner and speak openly. The creative solution was to park a car on that corner and leave it there: A tiny hole had been drilled in the trunk and the conversations were captured by sensitive recording equipment inside the trunk.

7. **Colombian necktie:** A murder in which the victim's throat is cut and the tongue is pulled down through the opening to resemble a tie.

Colombian drug dealers engage in this gruesome practice, and they normally reserve it for a snitch. Though everything is relative, the Colombians are generally regarded as the most brutal of all drug-dealing gangs. Perhaps their reputation is most fearsome because it is well known that they will kill not only someone who has crossed them, but that person's family as well. In fact, that is an implicit threat when dealing with Colombians.

8. **Pulling Train:** Gang rape. It is also known as "training" and is the fate of many women who join street gangs or criminal motorcycle gangs.

9. **Doin' the Houdini:** Cutting a body into pieces, then discarding them to make the body disappear. (See also the later entry on the Westies.)

Q&A

Q: Who was the big-time 1920s mobster who the government couldn't convict for gang activity, but who eventually got arrested for tax evasion?

A: Al Capone. Brooklyn-born Capone moved to Chicago and rose to run a vicious mob in the 1920s and 1930s that controlled beer and liquor trade during Prohibition. He made a reputed $100 million a year, little of which he reported. The government got him for not paying $231,000 in income taxes, and he was sentenced to eleven years in jail and a $50,000 fine. He ultimately died of syphilis.

Al Capone's Scar

Al "Scarface" Capone always claimed that his prominent facial scar was a result of action in World War I. The truth is that he was never in the army and received it from a hood that slashed him for making a pass at his girlfriend.

Al Capone (Photofest)

Match Game
Mafia Nicknames

1. Carmine Persico	A. Momo
2. John Gotti	B. Joe Batters
3. Jimmy Fratianno	C. The Bull
4. Tony Accardo	D. The Mad Hatter
5. Albert Anastasia	E. The Dapper Don
6. Benjamin Siegel	F. Lucky
7. Frank Nitti	G. The Prime Minister
8. Al Capone	H. The Chin
9. Sam Giancana	I. Bugsy
10. Sammy Gravano	J. Three Finger Brown
11. Frank Costello	K. The Gent
12. Vincent Gigante	L. Scarface
13. Charles Luciano	M. The Weasel
14. Jimmy Burke	N. The Snake
15. Thomas Lucchese	O. The Enforcer

ANS: 1-N 2-E 3-M 4-B 5-D 6-I 7-O 8-L 9-A 10-C 11-G 12-H 13-F 14-K 15-J

Mafia-Endorsed Weaponry

The weapon of choice for Mafia hitmen is the .22. While not an overly powerful gun, when the trigger is pulled while the gun is against someone's head, the bullet smashes through the skull but is not powerful enough to exit the skull. Rather, it ricochets like a pinball, doing massive damage to the relatively soft tissue of the brain.

To make it appear as if someone has died of natural causes, Mafia hitmen use a technique known as the Ice Pick Kill. In this scenario, two or three men hold the victim still while the killer drives an icepick through an eardrum into the brain. Externally this produces only a tiny puncture and little bleeding, but it causes massive internal bleeding, which looks like a cerebral hemorrhage.

Artist's sketch of Louis Eppolito, a NYPD cop who was convicted of being a mafia hit man. (Photofest)

Q&A

Q: In 2002, which two cities reported the most gang-related homicides?
1. Detroit
2. Chicago
3. New York
4. Miami
5. Los Angeles

A: Chicago and Los Angeles

Street gang being searched. (Dave Green)

Jimmy Coonan's Red Ears

Head of the notorious New York Irish gang the Westies, Jimmy Coonan was a fearsome individual throughout the 1960s and 70s. But his closest ally and enforcer, Mickey Featherstone, said you could tell when Coonan was at his most dangerous, his angriest, because Coonan's ears turned red. One night a man named Harold Whitehead was sitting at a bar ranting to Coonan—whose ears had turned red—about how Coonan was fine but his brother was a "dirtbag." Shortly thereafter, the two went downstairs to the bathroom, and while standing side-by-side at the urinal, Coonan took out a Derringer and shot Whitehead in the base of the skull, killing him.

The Westies were the first gang to dispose of bodies by cutting them into small pieces and discarding them in the river. They learned how to do this from one of the gang's members, Eddie Cumminsky, who had learned butchering in prison. They called the practice "doin' the Houdini."

Jimmy Coonan was a protégé of Ruby Stein, and for many years, the two men were buddies—like father and son. Indeed, Stein paid cash for Coonan's house in Hazlett.

But in the world of gangs, over drinks on Tuesday you can be sincerely promised undying loyalty, and on Wednesday you can have your brains blown out. The only thing that matters is a member's own survival and profit, and as these are people who have been trying to survive in a brutal world all their lives, they are particularly attuned to threats to either.

So it was that Coonan lost his loyalty to Ruby Stein and set him up for a hit. Ostensibly Stein had ordered the hits of a couple of Westies, but the real reason seems to be that Coonan owed Stein $70,000 and a number of other Westies were also indebted to Stein for big money. What better way to clear the books than to eliminate the creditor and eliminate the debt.

Coonan and his fellow Westies knew that this had to be done very carefully—they would be

> Drugs and Crime
>
> In 2002, in a survey of convicted property and drug offenders, 25 percent said they committed their crimes in order to obtain money for drugs, compared to 5 percent for violent and public order (victimless) criminals.
>
> In 2004, law enforcement agencies across the United States arrested approximately 1.7 million people for drug violations and 1.4 million for driving under the influence.

putting a hit on Stein without permission from the Mafia. And the Mafia has a golden rule: no one they're involved with gets clipped without their permission. More than this, Stein had long relationships with the Mafia and, most important of all, he was a big moneymaker.

On the morning of May 5, 1977, Coonan left his home in New Jersey, stopping to pick up some knives and large plastic trash bags. He contacted Stein and told him he wanted to meet with him in the 596 Club at 10th Avenue and 43rd Street.

In his court testimony, Mickey Featherstone remembered finding out that they were going to "do a piece of work"—as Coonan described a hit—on Stein, and Featherstone raced to try to find and possibly warn Stein. Featherstone liked Stein. But Featherstone was too late. What happened to Stein was later described in court testimony.

Coonan led him into the 596 Club. It was midmorning, and the bar was officially closed, but this was not an unusual place for gang people to meet. (They also frequently met at the Market Diner on 43rd Street and 11th Avenue.) Stein was standing at the bar when Danny Grillo, a Mafia hit man, came out of the back, and Stein asked, "What are you doing here?" There was no answer, but, Stein suddenly understood what was about to happen and said, "Oh, my God"—then the first bullet plowed into his skull.

Then, in turn, each of the four people there took the gun and shot Stein one more time. There was method in this collective killing: everyone knew there would be retribution if the wise guys found out, so in this way, everyone would be equally responsible and would not talk for fear of incriminating themselves.

Coonan's idea for Stein was like his idea for so many others: do the Houdini. They put his body in a laundry sink and proceeded to cut him up—one gang member got sick and couldn't help—and put the parts in the bags Coonan had bought, then brought the bags outside. They drove to Ward's Island and dumped the parts in the East River. After a while, the wise guys sent out word looking for Stein, but no one could find him.

Then a legless, armless torso was hauled out of the East River, and the cops were able to identify it as the torso of Ruby Stein. It seems that he had had a heart attack at some point, and when they superimposed the X-ray of the torso over an X-ray that had been taken of Stein when he was alive, the scars matched up. Jimmy Coonan was furious that Stein was able to be identified, and he vowed that the next time they would grind up their victims so fine that no one would be able to identify them.

The recovery of Stein's torso had repercussions, and before long Jimmy Coonan was summoned to Tommasso's Restaurant, a regular Mafia hangout, to talk about Stein. Coonan and Featherstone went to Tommasso's, and they

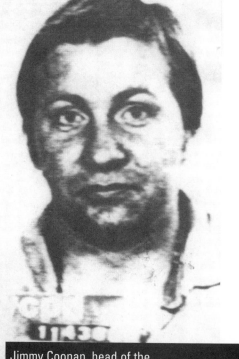

Jimmy Coonan, head of the Westies. If his ears got red, run.
(Author's Collection)

denied any involvement in the killing—and amazingly, they got away with it.

Chapter 3
Prostitution

The Most Famous Prostitute of All

Pearl "Polly" Adler (1900–1962) was a Russian-born madam and author—and the most famous prostitute who ever lived. She was the oldest child of a large family. She emigrated to America from Yanow, Russia, near the Polish border, at the age of fourteen, just before World War II. The war stopped her family from joining her. She worked in clothing factories and sporadically attended school. At the age of nineteen, Polly began to enjoy the company of theater people in Manhattan and moved into the apartment of an actress and showgirl in the upscale neighborhood of Riverside Drive, New York.

She opened her first bordello in 1920. She was under the protection of mobster Dutch Schultz, a friend of Lucky Luciano. In the early thirties, Polly was called as a witness of the Seabury Commission investigations into police and government corruption, and she spent a few months in hiding in Florida to avoid testifying. When captured, she refused to give up any mob names or names of those in power, then she went into hiding again. For over twenty years, Adler avoided prosecution by moving her brothel from apartment to apartment. She officially retired from prostitution in 1944.

Polly went to college at the age of fifty and collaborated on a bestselling book, ghosted by Virginia Faulkner, with a great title: A House is Not a Home. The book was published in 1953 and Adler lived off the proceeds until her death in Los Angeles in 1962.

A few great quotes from Polly Adler:

"My home is in whatever town I'm booked."

"Your heart often knows things before your mind does."

"It's not the college degree that makes a writer. The great thing is to have a story to tell."

"I am one of those people who just can't help getting a kick out of life—even when it's a kick in the teeth."

"The only difference between them and my girls is that my girls gave a man his money's worth."

A Unique Weapon of Choice

From 1964 to 1965, someone murdered seven young prostitutes in London's East End. That information in and of itself it not so out of the ordinary, but what made these murders so bizarre was that evidence pointed to the murder weapon being a penis. All of the women were asphyxiated, and while there was no definitive evidence that a penis had been used, there were indications.

For example, one of the women, twenty-one-year-old Mary Fleming, had been choked or suffocated—as opposed to strangled—and her dentures were missing from the scene. Another victim, twenty-seven-year-old Bridget O'Hara, was found with her front teeth missing, and pathologists determined that she had died on her knees. Some of the other women literally had their front teeth knocked out. The lead detective, John duRose, thought that at least six of the seven victims had been literally choked to death by a penis.

40

There were three suspects: an ex-heavyweight boxer named Freddie Mills; an ex-policeman who killed himself in 1965; and a private security guard, who also killed himself. After those two suicides, the killings stopped. To this day, no one has ever definitively identified the killer, who was dubbed "Jack the Stripper."

Movies Featuring Prostitutes

Hollywood has long had a fascination with prostitutes of both genders. While there have been dozens of productions featuring prostitution as a main or underlying theme, here are some of the better known offerings:

American Gigolo (1980)—Richard Gere and Lauren Hutton star in this crime/romance/thriller where Gere plays a high-priced Beverly Hills "escort" for hire and winds up being the target of police when one of Gere's clients is found murdered.

Midnight Cowboy (1969)—naive male prostitute (Jon Voigt) and his sickly friend (Dustin Hoffman) struggle to survive on the streets of New York City.

Whore (1991)—Filmed in a psuedo-documentary style, this film features Theresa Russell as a Los Angeles streetwalker dealing with the harsh realities of this brutal business.

Pretty Baby (1978)—Brooke Shields stars as a twelve-year-old prostitute's daughter being raised in a New Orleans Brothel in 1917.

Pretty Woman (1990)—Romantic comedy in which businessman Richard Gere hires prostitute Julia Roberts to be an escort for social events and winds up falling in love with her.

Best Little Whorehouse in Texas (1982)—Musical comedy with an all-star cast, including Dolly Parton as the madam of a Texas brothel and Burt Reynolds the sheriff, Parton's character's love interest.

Working Girls (1986)—An honest documentary which follows a typical day in the life of hookers working in an upscale brothel in New York City (this film was based on extensive interviews with real-life prostitutes).

Who Am I?

1. I am one of the more famous Hollywood madams. I made millions, storing most of it under my bed.

2. I had a variety of beautiful women working for me in posh spots in Los Angeles, London, St. Tropez, and New York. We serviced the elite and I was sure to take my 40 percent cut from every girl's earnings.

3. Eventually, as I suspected, I got caught and went on trial in 1997. The trial became a media circus because of the scope of my operation and the celebrities in my little black book. Actor Charlie Sheen was caught in the web and testified against me.

4. I don't know why I became a Madam. If you look at my background it seems normal. I was raised in Los Angeles, the daughter of a respected Hollywood pediatrician, and I characterized my parents as "intellectual hippies." My holidays were spent camping around the United States.

5. I had a tumultuous relationship with actor Tom Sizemore, star of Blackhawk Down, and this included his getting arrested for assaulting me.

6. Money rather than sex motivates me, and today I do nothing—including being interviewed by the media—without getting a fee.

7. A number of films have been made on my life. I make a living as a publisher.

A. I am Heidi Fleiss.

Heidi Fleiss, Hollywood Madam
(Photofest)

Q & A

Q: What percentage of men solicits prostitutes on a regular basis?
   1. 2 percent
   2. 5 percent
   3. 3 percent
   4. 1 percent

A: 1 percent

Q: How many "johns" will street prostitutes service on an average night?
1. 1-2
2. 3-5
3. 6-10
4. More than 10

A: 3-5

Prostitution in America—Facts

1. The Department of Justice estimates that pimps take between 60 and 70 percent of their prostitutes' earnings.

2. Crack-addicted prostitutes have been known to have sex with a client for the cost of a single rock of crack (which can be as low as $10).

3. Street prostitutes generally charge between $20 and $50 for oral sex and between $50 and $100 for sexual intercourse. The average time for an encounter to take place is about ten minutes in a vehicle (usually for oral sex), and twenty-five minutes for an indoor tryst.

4. In the spring of 2006, the Illinois legislature proposed a bill which would allow prostitutes to sue their pimps in court without the fear of being prosecuted for solicitation. The bill also included the right to seek damages from abusive clients who had inflicted bodily harm. Advocates of the bill felt it could help some prostitutes start new lives and help end the cycle of victimization.

5. One million women and girls work as prostitutes.

6. There are one hundred thousand arrests for prostitution annually. Of all women, 7.1 percent of them have worked as prostitutes at some point, with four years being the average length of their careers.

7. More than 90 percent of prostitutes lose their virginity through sexual assault. Two-thirds of all prostitutes have

been sexually abused between ages three and sixteen, with the average age of victimization being ten.

8. Of the prostitutes who started their careers as juveniles, 96 percent were runaways. They stated they had no other options for making money. Most children entered prostitution at around the age of fourteen.

9. Of the prostitutes who were sexually abused as children, 91 percent told no one.

10. Four of five prostitutes stated that customers used pornography and photographs to demonstrate in which activities they wanted to engage.

Prostitution Jargon

1. **Chickens:** Young male prostitutes. The term has had a long history, signifying something young, tender, and defenseless. Young male prostitutes are a part of the underbelly of most big cities, and, like most prostitutes, they usually become prostitutes just to survive. They are more like streetwalkers than call girls because they stand on a corner in the red light district and wait to be picked up; the procedure is repeated many times a night.

Like women streetwalkers, a steady diet of illicit sex, fast food, drugs, and the stress of having to survive causes burnout fairly quickly. Once they lose their

Wanderlust

As a prostitute's fortunes decline (as she gets older and less desirable, something that can occur rapidly even to the youngest of women in this trade), her neighborhood changes: she leaves good, safer areas and goes to higher-crime areas where predators abound and existence is precarious.

looks, their street value is much lower and their burnout accelerates. It is not surprising that male prostitutes look years older than they are and that they die much younger than they should, particularly in this age of AIDS and other sexually-transmitted diseases. And of course, some have the misfortune of being murdered.

2. **Lot Lizards:** Name given to prostitutes who specialize in working truck stops. These women will often proposition truckers on a CB radio from their own vehicle parked in another area of the truck stop.

3. **Whore Stroll:** In the Midwest, this is a name for an area where prostitutes ply their trade.

Child Prostitution at a Gruesome Glance

1. Hundreds of thousands of children have been lured or forced into prostitution. Though girls are more widely publicized, boys are also exploited.

2. When kids become prostitutes, the impact is both immediate and long-term. Most immediate is the physical, mental, and emotional violence these children experience at the hands of pimps, madams, and customers. Long-term dangers include health problems, drug addiction, adverse psychological effects, and death. The most tangible consequence for children involved in prostitution is the extremely high probability of being assaulted—not only by pimps, but by street people and

customers. Violence from pimps tends to be more frequent, while violence by customers is more sporadic but also more likely to be fatal.

3. Kids become prostitutes because of homelessness, poverty, intolerance of their sexual orientation, educational and vocational failure, and other major problems at home. They exchange sex for survival.

4. More than three quarters of child prostitutes use alcohol as a temporary escape. The drug culture in street life is truly a double-edged sword: being sexually exploited through prostitution may result in a higher risk of substance abuse, and abusing substances places children at a higher risk for prostitution. Prostituted children may internalize feelings of guilt for their participation in sexual acts, which may lead to additional promiscuity or engaging in other reckless behaviors.

5. Children on the streets are not only more likely to be clinically depressed, but they are twice as likely to have serious mental health problems and almost twice as likely to be actively suicidal or to have previously attempted suicide. In one group of youths involved in prostitution, who were interviewed in shelters, 71 percent reported thinking about suicide, 33 percent had a plan, and 14 percent reported a previous attempt at ending their lives.

6. Many child prostitutes are only eleven or twelve years old, and some are as young as nine. The average age at which they enter prostitution is reported as fourteen, and the median age is fifteen and a half years. These children come

from inner cities, suburbs, and small towns, and there appears to be an increase in the recruitment of middle-class youth from schools and shopping malls in the suburbs. The vast majority of youth involved in prostitution are girls, although there is an increase in the number of boys. Some attribute this to a greater willingness by boys to disclose their sexual activities.

7. Larger cities are more likely to have a higher proportion of boys involved in prostitution, but it is increasing in smaller cities as well.

8. Prostitution is mainly a seasonal problem, more prevalent during the warmer months and in cities with warmer climates. During the peak seasons for prostitution in the larger cities throughout the United States, there can be as many as 500 prostitutes on the streets.

9. Children who become involved in prostitution may be dealing with anger and low self-esteem. They may engage in delinquent or criminal activity, causing others to view them more as offenders than as victims. And they are very likely to have—often with good reason—a distrust of adults, even adults who want to help them.

10. Child prostitutes crave attention, affection, and love. This can make the child vulnerable to manipulation by a pimp, a madam, or any other person or group seeking to exploit the child. Initially, a pimp seduces the child by providing comfort, protection, and understanding. As he gains the child's trust, he works to alienate the child from a normal and safe existence, increasing the child's dependency on

him. Once the child is financially and emotionally dependent on the pimp, he introduces the child to the world of commercial sexual exploitation. Pimps control 80 to 90 percent of prostitution and can be men or women.

11. A common trend in the prostitution of children involves taking the child far from home, both to

Gold in Prostitution

Prostitution flourished in Gold Rush-era San Francisco, where there were 65,000 men and only 2,500 women.

avoid immediate detection and to decrease the chances of the child returning home. The child's exploiter may travel with the child to many cities, following tourist or event traffic.

12. The prostitution of children is the most overlooked form of child exploitation in the United States. The issue is often treated as a nuisance crime by local law enforcement. There is also the misconception that juveniles are willing participants in their own victimization. To the contrary: having experienced unimaginable exploitation, child prostitutes are truly victims and in desperate need of help.

Chapter 4
Serial Murder

John Wayne Gacy's Incapacitation Technique

The most dangerous situation for young boys to be in with serial murderer John Wayne Gacy—he murdered at least twenty-one boys in the Midwest—was at his home (now torn down, it stood at 8213 West Summerdale Avenue in Chicago). Once he got a young boy (usually age fifteen or sixteen) into the house using one ruse or another, he would incapacitate him by approaching the boy from behind and holding a cloth filled with chloroform over the boy's face.

Gacy would then handcuff the boy—and that was it. Or, Gacy would produce what he said were toy handcuffs, and challenge the boy to put them on and free himself. Of course he couldn't. Then he would proceed to torture him—one of his favorite implements being an 8-inch wooden dildo, which was encrusted with blood and feces for more than half its length when police found it. It's a mystery as to why neighbors didn't hear the screams, or smell the victims' bodies, most of which Gacy had buried under his house in shallow graves.

Q&A

Q: What is the homicidal triangle?

A: The three kinds of aggressive behavior that serial murderers exhibited in childhood are predictions of sociopathic behavior and homicide: enuresis (bedwetting), cruelty to animals, and fire setting.

Some psychologists say that when a child exhibits all these behavioral characteristics, he (they occur mostly in males) is far more likely to eventually commit homicide than someone without these characteristics. Even if just two of the characteristics are present, it is a dangerous sign.

The backgrounds of a number of serial murderers show extreme cruelty to animals, as well as pyromania. For example, Henry Lee Lucas, perhaps the worst serial murderer of all, skinned small animals alive when he was ten. Robert Hanson, who killed prostitutes in Alaska, set many fires as a youth in Pocahontas, Iowa. Edmund Kemper, who killed six coeds in northern California, was also very cruel to animals.

The first observers of this triad were D. S. Hellmann and N. Blackman in the article "Enuresis, Fire setting, and Cruelty to Animals: A Triad Predictive of Adult Crime," which appeared in the June 1966 issue of the American Journal of Psychiatry. Many law enforcement personnel feel that these three behavioral activities are very accurate predictors.

The .44-Caliber Killer

For those who are killers, an examination of their childhoods almost always reveals that their problems stemmed from something that happened in their youth. Not much is known about the childhood of David Berkowitz, but there are definitely hints that he didn't grow up in a household reminiscent of The Brady Bunch.

Shortly after Berkowitz's birth, the waitress and business-man who were his birth parents put him up for adoption, and he became the son of a childless couple named Nat and Pearl Berkowitz. The family lived in the Bronx in Co-op City, a huge cluster of apartment houses where many Bronx residents had moved in the 1960s. Exactly what happened in their apartment is not known, but from it emerged a young boy who had some serious mental maladies, at the center of which was an overrid-ing question: "Who was he?" He developed a variety of phobias and constantly felt rejected and worthless. The death of his adoptive mother when he was fourteen seemed to confirm it all. He thought that she died because he wasn't worthwhile.

As so often happens when a person feels this way about themselves, Berkowitz started to become what one psychiatrist has called a "builder of a fantasy world." This world was not the world of reality where Berkowitz felt worthless, but rather it was one where he was successful and accomplished. It was a world he could bear to live in, where he was handsome—a romantic figure adored by women. It was also a world he controlled.

Sometimes Berkowitz could live completely inside this world, but sometimes reality intruded, and then something even scarier began to happen. He started, as psychiatrists reported, to have other fantasies that were hardly of lightness and love. Berkowitz thought that demons were ordering him to kill people, and as time went by, he developed one particular demon who, he thought, took the form of a neighbor's dog named Sam. Berkowitz started to think of himself as Son of Sam, a son who would faithfully execute what the demons desired. And the demons were a bloodthirsty pack.

By the fall of 1975, when Berkowitz was twenty-two, the "demons" were controlling him, and on Christmas Eve of that year, he went on his first hunt in an area near Co-op City. His

Q&A

Q: What Happened at These Locations?
- 2860 Buhre Avenue, Bronx, New York
- 33rd Avenue, 159th Street, Queens, New York
- 83–31 262nd Street, Queens, New York
- Station Plaza, Continental Avenue, Queens, NY
- Dartmouth Avenue, opposite Forest Hills Gardens, Queens, New York
- One block from 1950 Hutchinson River Parkway, Bronx, New York
- 45–39 211th Street, Queens, New York
- Shore Road, near Bay 17th Street Park, Queens, New York

A: Son of Sam killer David Berkowitz shot his victims with his .44 caliber Bulldog revolver.

prey was to be young girls. His weapon of choice was a knife, because movies he had seen made it seem like a quick, clean way to kill someone. But that was not to be. He encountered a fifteen-year-old girl named Michelle Forman on a bridge near Dreiser Loop that traversed the New York State Thruway. He stabbed her repeatedly, but she didn't die and she continued to scream, and he finally fled in bewilderment, deciding he must fine-tune his methods.

Because he needed a better, easier, and more deadly method, Berkowitz decided he would use a gun. Some months later, he drove to Houston, Texas, and bought a Charter Arms .44-caliber Bulldog, a big, powerful gun that was to become one of the most infamous weapons in New York City history.

The Shootings Begin

On July 26, 1976, Donna Lauria, a pretty, petite woman of eighteen, sat in an Oldsmobile with her friend Judy Valenti. The car was parked in front of Donna's apartment building at 2860 Buhre Avenue in the Bronx, one of a number of apartment buildings that lined the quiet street in the middle-class neighborhood. At about 1:00 a.m., Donna's father, who had been out, returned to the building and spotted Donna and Judy in the car. He suggested Donna come in soon, and she said she would be right up.

Less than a minute later, the two women were distracted by the appearance of a dark-haired man wearing a denim jacket and jeans and carrying a paper bag. They watched as he calmly walked to the passenger side of the car where Donna was sitting. Donna turned to Judy.

"What does he want?"

Suddenly a pistol emerged from the bag and the man dropped into a semi-squatting position, the gun held in both hands. He was in the classic combat shooter's pose and fired five shots through the passenger window, shattering it—and hitting Donna Lauria with gunfire. Upstairs, her father was startled by the rapid-fire crescendo and thought a car was backfiring. Then he went downstairs to find the horrendous sight of his daughter covered with blood, while Valenti, Lauria's friend, shrieked hysterically.

Soon Donna Lauria would be dead, the first victim of the Son of Sam, a name Berkowitz used to identify himself in a letter he sent to New York City detectives some months after the shootings began.

Donna Lauria's killing had a calming effect on David's demons. But gradually the demands of the demons in David's head began again. The demons wanted more blood, more shooting, more death. Soon the demands were so strong that Berkowitz, who fought them, could no longer refuse.

On October 23, 1976, Berkowitz went to Queens, again on the hunt. In the Flushing area, Berkowitz spotted a red Ford Galaxie and followed it in the white Ford he drove. Berkowitz saw there were two people in the car, but he couldn't tell if they were male or female. One had long, dark hair, a favorite of the demons. Soon the couple parked the car near the corner of 33rd Avenue and 159th Street. Berkowitz parked behind them.

Inside the car was Carl Denaro, a young man who was to soon enter the Air Force. Driving the car was Rosemary Keenan, eighteen, whose father was a New York City cop. Berkowitz approached the car, concealing the heavy gun under a denim jacket. He went to the passenger side of the car and fired five times through the window.

Denaro was shot in the head, but miraculously Rosemary Keenan was not hit and she bolted from the car screaming. Berkowitz watched calmly, admiring the aftermath of his five-shot assault. Amazingly, Denaro survived, requiring a metal plate in his head to replace the bone fragments blown away in the shooting.

More Blood Demanded

Less than a month later, the demons in Berkowitz's head were howling for blood again. On the chilly, windy night of November 26, 1976, Berkowitz was back in predatory mode. Two girls, sixteen-year-old Donna DeMasi and eighteen-year-old Joanne Lomino, had returned to Queens after seeing a movie in Manhattan. They got off a bus at 262nd Street and Hillside Avenue and started walking home. Joanne had a 12:30 a.m. curfew and it was almost midnight.

As they walked, they noticed a man starting to follow them. They were worried and walked faster. But by the time they got to 83–31 262nd Street, Joanne's home, he was not in sight. Then they saw him coming toward them, and Joanne searched her bag for her keys. The girls were nervous, but the man—dark-haired, stocky, wearing a denim jacket—didn't seem terribly threatening.

In the next instant he was firing at them—and he hit them both. Then the man was gone. The girls survived, but Joanne Lomino paid a terrible price: one of the bullets had severed her spine and she was paralyzed from the waist down.

No Connection

Unfortunately, the police did not connect any of the assaults with one shooter, simply because they didn't have any physical evidence that tied the crimes together—these assaults were in the days before computers were in common use, which now help immensely in making connections between apparently unconnected cases.

The next shooting resulted in another death. A young couple—Christine Freund, twenty-six, and John Diel, thirty, who were engaged to be married—had gone out to see the movie Rocky. They returned to their car, which was parked at Station Plaza on Continental Avenue near the Long Island Railroad line in Queens. In fact, they had to walk under a railroad bridge to get to the car, a blue Pontiac Firebird.

It was a bitterly cold night, just five or six degrees above zero, and they had just gotten into the car when out of nowhere shots smashed through the passenger side window. Christine Freund was shot twice in the head and once in the chest, but miraculously, Diel was not hit at all. Someone called 911, and within four minutes the emergency service team was on the scene. But it was too late for Freund. She never regained consciousness, and she died at St. John's Hospital the following morning.

Panic Begins

Around this time, panic set in, at least for the police. Police put out the word across the city to see if there were any similar homicides. It was then that police determined that the separate random shootings were related: a large-caliber revolver was involved in them all. Police formed a homicide task force.

On March 8, 1977—a little over a month from the time Christine Freund was killed—there was another shooting. Virginia Voskerichian, an honor student at Barnard College, was returning to her home in Queens, walking along Dartmouth Avenue near 71st Street, when she spotted a man coming toward her. No one will know what she thought, but it might have been that he was overdressed for the day: it was unseasonably warm and he was wearing a ski coat.

For his part, Berkowitz had been in the area for the past hour in search of a pretty girl to shoot and kill, as the demons inside him ordered. Virginia Voskerichian filled the bill. She was slim and pretty. When Berkowitz was within twenty-five feet of Voskerichian, he pulled out his gun. Instinctively, Virginia pulled up to her face the books she was carrying, so as to shield herself. Berkowitz fired once, the bullet entering Virginia's head above the lip. She fell into the bushes that flanked the road.

Virginia was rushed to St. John's Hospital, but she never regained consciousness, and she died at 4:00 a.m. Her family was heartbroken, not only for their personal loss but also for the community's loss of Virginia. She had great potential that would never be allowed to flower.

If the police had any doubts as to whether there was a psycho loose in the city, those doubts were erased during the investigation into Virginia Voskerichian's death. A .44-caliber bullet was recovered, and the NYPD Ballistics Unit matched it up with one of the bullets used to kill Donna Lauria only six months earlier. Commissioner Michael Codd called a press conference on March 10, 1977, and announced to the world that a crazy man was on the loose, and women—particularly pretty girls with dark hair—were at risk. Panic spread, then it deepened. The .44-caliber killer was front-page news, and more shootings—and a frightening letter—whipped those fears into a frenzy.

On April 17, a young couple, Alexander Esau, twenty, and Valentina Suriana, eighteen, were shot dead while parked just a block short of 1950 Hutchinson River Parkway in the Bronx— only three blocks from where the killing of Donna Lauria had occurred. The killer was getting more efficient—fewer shots, more deaths. Only four shots had been fired this time, two into each victim. There was another chilling development with this shooting—along with the bodies, police found the following letter (misspellings and other errors have been left as is):

Dear Captain Joseph Borrelli,

I am deeply hurt by your calling me a wemon hater. I am not. But I am a monster. I am the 'Son of Sam.' I am a little brat.

When father Sam gets drunk he gets mean. He beats his family. Sometimes he ties me up to the back of the house. Other times he locks me in the garage. Sam loves to drink blood.

'Go out and kill,' commands father Sam.

Behind our house some rest. Mostly young—raped and slaugh-tered—their blood drained—just bones now.

Papa Sam keeps me locked in the attic too. I can't get out but I look out the attic window and watch the world go by.

I feel like an outsider. I am on a different wavelength then every-body else—programmed too kill.

However, to stop me you must kill me. Attention all police: Shoot me

first—shoot to kill or else keep out of my way or you will die!
Papa Sam is old now. He needs some blood to preserve his youth. He
has had too many heart attacks. 'Ugh, me hoot, it hurts, sonny boy.'
I miss my pretty princess most of all. She's resting in our ladies
house. But I'll see her soon.
I am the 'Monster'—'Beelzebub'—the chubby behemouth.
I love to hunt. Prowling the streets looking for fair game—tasty
meat. The wemon of Queens are prettyist of all. It must be the
water they drink. I live for the hunt—my life. Blood for papa.
Mr. Borrelli, sir, I don't want to kill anymore. No sur, no more but I
must, 'honour thy father.'
I want to make love to the world. I love people. I don't belong on
earth. Return me to yahoos.
To the people of Queens, I love you. And I want to wish all of you a
happy Easter. May God bless you in this life and in the next.
I say goodbye and goodnight. Police, let me haunt you with these
words: I'll be back! I'll be back! To be interrupted as—bang, bang,
bang, bang, bang—ugh!

"Yours in murder Mr. Monster."

And so the papers had an official name for the killer: the Son of Sam. On June 26, two months after the killings of Esau and Suriana, the killer struck again, this time shooting Judy Placido, seventeen, and Salvatore Lupo, twenty, who had been to a dance club called the Elephas and whose car was parked opposite 45–39 211th Street. Ironically, the young couple was talking about the Son of Sam and was not that concerned, when suddenly there was a booming echo inside the car. Almost unbelievably they survived the shooting, though Placido was shot in the temple, near the spine, and in the shoulder. Lupo was hit in the arm.

Getting Personal

Son of Sam's next foray touched on this author (Tom) personally, and in a chilling way. On July 31, 1977, my two young daughters wanted to go to a teen club in the mall in the town of Huntington, Long Island, where I lived. I discussed the possible danger of Son of Sam with my wife, Catherine, who was worried that the killer might go there. I pooh-poohed her fear, but the end result was that the girls didn't go out. Later, when Son of Sam was captured, it turned out that he had gone to Huntington on July 31, planning to kill someone, but as reported in Son of Sam by Lawrence D. Klausner, he decided not to do it because the place didn't seem right—his demons demurred.

Small World

In fact, on that night of July 31, he also went to Brooklyn still looking for someone to shoot, and he found them—a young couple, Stacy Moskowitz, a pretty twenty-year-old blonde, and her date, twenty-year-old Robert Violante. The couple had parked on the Shore Parkway, next to a cyclone fence, after another very lucky couple had pulled out of the area just moments before. It was at 2:35 a.m. when Son of Sam fired five shots into the car. The shots caused Robert Violante to go blind. The shots killed Stacy Moskowitz.

The shooting of the young couple brought more fear to a city already near hysteria. The killer had to be found.

A Break

As often happens in matters of great consequence, the thing that resulted in the capture of Son of Sam was something utterly pedestrian: a traffic ticket. It was fortunate timing, because as Berkowitz was to report later, he was getting bored with these types of homicides and he wanted to do something a little more dramatic and climactic—a mass murder.

In fact, he almost did it.

On Saturday, August 6, Berkowitz decided that he would murder a group of people on a campground in Southampton, Long Island, a camp he knew because he had camped there the year before. The campground was at the peak of its season, loaded with young people. Berkowitz showered, dressed in fresh clothes, and loaded his Bulldog and a .45-caliber semiautomatic rifle.

It took him two and a half hours to reach Southampton, but the weather, which had started out fine, changed as he went. Great thunderheads dominated the gray sky, and before long, a few raindrops soon turned into a torrent. The sky shredded with lightning.

It got so bad that Berkowitz pulled off to the side of the road to wait out the storm and await word from his demons. The demons decided that the storm had cleared away too many potential victims. The demons instructed Berkowitz to go home, so home he went. A summer shower had prevented a bloodbath.

Then the demons turned on him. In his apartment, which was at 35 Pine Street in Yonkers, a community just north of the Bronx, they ripped at him for not being able to fulfill his mission. They didn't accept rain as an excuse—even though it was they who had ordered him not to complete the mission. Berkowitz's punishment was simple: he had to die. Meanwhile, forces were combining that would result in his capture.

The night he killed Stacy Moskowitz and wounded Robert Violante, Berkowitz parked at 290 Bay 17th. It was a location that was only a block and a half from the scene of the crime. During the investigation into the deaths of the young couple, a woman who had been walking her dog said that she spotted a policeman writing a ticket for a cream-colored parked car. But none of the cops could remember it, and the ticket seemed to have vanished.

Then, about two weeks later, someone found the ticket squirreled away with some others in the backroom of the precinct where it had been issued. The car belonged to David Berkowitz, 35 Pine Street, Yonkers, New York. Some detectives went up there and found his car parked in the street. Looking in it, they also spotted something that electrified them. Sticking out from under a gunnysack was the butt of a machine gun. They also saw two letters—and the handwriting resembled the handwriting Son of Sam used in the terrifying letters he had been writing to Daily News columnist Jimmy Breslin.

Soon there were three hundred cops surrounding Berkowitz's building, and the district attorney had gone on a frantic quest for a search warrant. They waited and waited and waited: no Berkowitz, and no search warrant. Finally Berkowitz appeared and the cops weren't sure what to do. Then, perhaps with the idea that Berkowitz would kill again, they acted when Berkowitz got into his car: guns drawn, they tapped on the car window and shouted at Berkowitz to freeze. Berkowitz looked at one of the detectives, Bill Gardella. "He had that stupid smile on his face," the detective was to say later, "like it was all a kid's game." But that could hardly describe what Berkowitz had done. He was put under arrest and the killing finally stopped.

A Gruesome Letter from a Madman

One day in late spring, 1928, a harmless-looking old man with watery blue eyes, wearing a dark blue suit and weighing not more than 135 pounds, showed up at the apartment of Grace and Albert Budd, allegedly to take their son Edward to work on a farm for him. The man said his name was Howard, but it was in fact a name that would come to live in infamy: Albert Fish. Howard had given the impression that he was wealthy, but that was as fake as the name he gave. In reality, Howard/Fish was a homicidal pedophile—perhaps the sickest of the twentieth century. While he was at the Budd home, Fish succeeded in conning them into letting him take their daughter, Grace, to a party in the city. That was the last they ever saw of their daughter. Six years later he sent them a gruesome, terrible letter, detailing little Grace's final hours.

On Sunday June 3 1928 I called on you at 406 W. 15th St. . . .
Grace sat in my lap and kissed me. I made up my mind to eat her: On the pretense of taking her to a party. You said Yes she could go. I took her to an empty house in Westchester I had already picked out. When we got there, I told her to remain outside. She picked wild flowers. I went upstairs and stripped all my clothes off. I knew if I did not I would get blood on them. When all was ready I went to the window and called her. Then I hid in the closet until she was in the room. When she saw me all naked she began to cry and tried to run downstairs. I grabbed her and she said she would tell her mamma. First I stripped her naked. How she did kick-bite and scratch. I choked her to death, then cut her in small pieces so I could take my meat to my rooms, Cook and eat it. How sweet and tender her little ass was roasted in the oven. It took me nine days to eat her entire body. I did not fuck her tho I could of had I wished. She died a virgin.

Front of envelope Albert Fish used to send horrific letter to the parents of a little girl he cannibalized. (Author's Collection)

Fish elaborated on the story told in a confession letter for the detectives. He said that after he killed Grace, he positioned her neck on a one-gallon paint pail and cut her head off, letting her blood drip into the pail. He said he then tried to drink the warm blood, but he vomited.

Albert Fish's Obsessions

In his book *Deranged*, author Harold Schecter lists the obsessions of Albert Fish. There are fifteen of them, including undinism, which means sexual preoccupation with one's own urine. The only missing one, seemingly, was bestiality.

Then he said he used a knife and a cleaver to cut her in half at the navel, and proceeded to cut her up. He said he planned on eating all of her except her head, guts, and skeleton. And it was all true.

Later, at his trial, it was determined that as he ate Grace over the nine-day period he was in a continual state of sexual excitation, and the memory of eating her would make him masturbate daily.

Q&A

Q: What Happened at These Locations?
- 77 Gainsborough Street, Boston, Apartment 3F
- 1435 Commonwealth Avenue, Boston, Fourth Floor
- 1940 Commonwealth Avenue, Boston
- 73 Newhall Street, Lynn, Massachusetts, Apartment 9
- 435 Colombia Road, Third Floor
- 7 Grove Street, Boston, Fifth Floor
- 319 Park Avenue, Lawrence, Massachusetts
- 315 Huntington Avenue, Boston, Apartment 4C
- 515 Park Drive, Boston
- 4 University Road, Cambridge, Massachusetts
- 224 Lafayette Street, Salem, Massachusetts, First Floor
- 54 Essex Street, Lawrence, Massachusetts
- 44A Charles Street, Boston, Third Floor

A: Women were murdered by Albert DeSalvo, the Boston Strangler.

The Boston Strangler Tells All

The unraveling of the Boston Strangler case began with a prison snitch, a man named George Nassar. Nassar, who had been committed to Bridgewater State Hospital, notified his attorney, the famed F. Lee Bailey, that one of the inmates was hinting that he was the Boston Strangler and that he wanted to talk with Bailey, who was in the process of making a big name for himself—he had just won a Supreme Court appeal reversing the conviction of Dr. Sam Sheppard for killing his wife. (Sheppard's story was the basis for the movie and television show The Fugitive.)

The man was Albert DeSalvo, a dark-haired, dark-eyed, well-built man who had been the middleweight Army boxing champion. He was twenty-nine years old. DeSalvo was in the institution for observation for having tied up and sexually assaulted a woman, and he

Not Sure You Understand That Word

Boston Strangler Albert DeSalvo had sex with his wife six times a day, seven days a week. He described her as "frigid."

had admitted to many other sexual assaults. Bailey was doubtful—Bridgewater was for crazies—but he decided to talk with DeSalvo. The first talk led to a second, and this time Bailey, armed with questions about the crimes to which answers had not been published, talked to DeSalvo again.

When Bailey repeated DeSalvo's answers to the detective who gave Bailey the questions, the detective was impressed. It wasn't long before Bailey became convinced that DeSalvo was, in fact, the Boston Strangler.

Some of the doctors at the hospital weren't convinced. They thought Nassar had a better psychological profile, and this led to a sort of debate over which one was the Strangler—a debate that ended up with DeSalvo agreeing to talk with John Bottomly, a special assistant to the state attorney general, who had taken overall charge of the case. Despite their differences—Bottomly was a child of privilege, while DeSalvo was a product of Boston's mean streets—the two men got along well and DeSalvo felt comfortable enough to detail his crimes.

Transcripts

Anyone reading the transcripts of what DeSalvo said could hardly doubt that he was, in fact, the Boston Strangler. He described in gruesome detail how he would talk his way into an apartment, posing, for example, as a handyman or plumber, and once inside he would maneuver behind a woman and choke her with his arm. He finished the job with her stockings or some other article, and arranged the body so the legs were spread wide. The bow he tied in the ligature, he said, was just a way of tying—it had no special significance

He would usually rape the woman while she was dying or dead, and violently assault her with various objects, among which was a wine bottle and a broom handle.

When Bottomly started to talk with DeSalvo, he assumed there were eleven victims. But DeSalvo told him of two more that Bottomly didn't know about because the MO did not include evidence of strangling. One victim was Mary Brown, of 319 Park Avenue in Lawrence, Massachusetts. For some reason DeSalvo battered her to death with a pipe he found on the premises. Her death occurred on March 9, 1963.

The other murder seemed, for some reason, particularly savage and sad, even against all the other savagery DeSalvo had wrought. He talked his way into the apartment of eighty-five-year-old Mary Mullen of 1435 Commonwealth Avenue in Boston. DeSalvo described to Bottomly getting behind the elderly woman and grabbing her around the neck. The next thing he knew, she slumped in his arms and he knew she was dead. And she was, having expired of a heart attack. He put her on the couch and left, and no one suspected that it was a murder. In all his confessions, he never displayed remorse—except once, when he spoke of the old lady Mary Mullen, and how he had grabbed her and she had died in his arms. DeSalvo wept bitterly.

Background Probed

DeSalvo's background was probed, and it was predictably unsavory. He came from a family of three boys and two girls; the boys were in and out of prison, as was his father, a savage man who beat his wife and his kids and openly went with prostitutes. The family was always on home relief and the boys got into trouble very early. Albert DeSalvo had married a German immigrant named Irmgard, and they had two young children, a boy and a girl.

Who Am I?

1. I was a trim man about six feet tall with wavy brown hair, penetrating eyes, and even features. Handsome.

2. My mother bore me out of wedlock, but that wasn't the sticky part. The sticky part was the strong suspicion that my maternal grandfather was my biological father.

3. I was shipped out West and raised as the son of my mother's sister. But I eventually found out who my real mother was, and the truth hurt me greatly.

4. In my twenties, I became active in politics and community events in the Northwest and was a volunteer at the Crisis Center in Seattle, where I became friendly with crime writer Ann Rule, who later was to write a book about me called The Stranger Beside Me.

Ted Bundy
(Author's Collection)

5. Also in my twenties I started murdering attractive young women who had long dark hair. I was so charming and devious that in one summer day in Lake Sammamish State Park in Washington, I was able to lure two women into my clutches—one in the morning and one in the afternoon—and murder them both. In all, I killed more than forty women.

6. Unconsciously I wanted to die, so in 1976, after escaping from a jail in Aspen, Colorado, I headed for the state of Florida—one of only two states at the time that still had the death penalty—where I kidnapped and killed a twelve-year-old girl and I was subsequently captured, tried, convicted, and executed in Old Sparky in the death house in the prison at Stark, Florida.

A: **My name was Ted Bundy.**

An Ordinary Person

Below is a questionnaire filled out by serial murderer John Wayne Gacy, who, as mentioned earlier, murdered at least thirty young boys. When he filled it out, he was in prison, awaiting execution for his crimes. His answers make him seem like a very ordinary person. Misspellings and other errors have been left as is (certain answers were partly illegible).

Full name: John Wayne Michael Gacy
Date of Birth: March 17th, 1942
Age, Ht. Wt: 50, 5 ? 9?, 208
Home: Menard Deathrow, Chester, Ill.
Marital Status: Twice Divorced
Family: 2 sisters, 5 children
Most treasured honor: 3 times son of the year Jaycees 3 different cities
Perfect woman or man: woman, independent thinker, self starter, mind of her own. Man: Bright, bold, honest dependable says what he is thinking
Childhood hero: J.F. Kennedy, R.J. Daley. Current Hero: M Cuomo, Donald Trump
Favorite TV shows: Unsolved Mysteries, National geographic Specials
Favorite movies: Once Upon A Time in America, Good fellas, Ten Commandments
Favorite song: Send in the clowns, amazing grace
Favorite singers: Judy Collins. Bob Dylan, Neil Diamond, Roy Orbison, Shan a na
Favorite Musicians: REO Speedwagon, Elton John, Zamfir
Hobbies: Correspondence, oil painting, study of human interests
Favorite meals: Fried Chicken , deboned lake perch drawn in butter, salad. Tea
Why you wrote JW Gacy: I don't just answer for him.
Recommended Reading: Texas Connection, Question of Doubt
Last book read: naked Lunch and wild boys William S Burroughs
Ideal evening: Dinner and concert or live show, drinks and a quiet walk by lake
Every Jan Ist: resolve: Correct things that I go year before
Nobody knows: "I'm a character who love to tease and joke around
My biggest regret: being so trusting and gullible. Taken advantage of.
If I were President I'd: make sure the of this country had jobs and a place to live before worrying about countries,
My advice to children: Be yourself, think positive respect parents

What I don't like about People: Phonies, people who don't keep their word.

My biggest fear: Dying before I have a chance to clear my name with truth

Pet Peeves: People who say things they have no intention in doing.

Superstitions: none its for negative people

Friends like me because: I am outspoken and honest, fun loving dependable

Behind my back they say: The bastard got it made and he grandiose

People in History I'd like to have met: Michelangelo, Leonardo DaVinci

If I were an animal: I'd be a Bear or and Eagle

Personal goals in life: To see to it that my children are provided for.

Personal interests: Reading, Writing meeting people, classic movies and music

Favotite color: Red

Favorite number: nine

I view myself as: a positive thinker, self starter, open minded, non judgmental.

What I think of this country: Great, if people would work for it instead of against it, pointing fingers at others, the problem takes all races to [illegible]

Political views: semi-liberal Democrat, that one party doesn't have all winners.

Thoughts of Crime: Too much political corruption, and allowed drugs by governed has set off the balance of the judicial reform and punishment.

Thoughts on Drugs: Make some legal to avoid crime [illegible]

I consider myself to be: Conservative_____ Moderate_____
Liberal with values [Gacy wrote in "Liberal with values" here]

What I expect from friendships: lighthearted, fun loving, dependable [illegible]

Religious thinking: My faith is in God. Churches need to work on the family unit.

What you're thinking now: why the hell did I fill this out and who cares what I have to say.

Your artistic interests: To please myself first and hope that expression is enjoyable to others. Art as in life is a journey not a destination. If you don't like it move on. Just like music to the ear, food to the smell and taste.

In His Own Words

Serial killer Robert Hansen admitted to killing seventeen women and burying their remains in the wilds outside Anchorage, Alaska. In his confession, Hansen went to great pains to rationalize his behavior. He said he would never kill "good women," but that prostitutes were something else. He could kill them with impunity.

He explained that he had had problems with women since he was a teenager in Pocahontas, Iowa, and that women wouldn't go out with him because of his acne and his stutter. He said he had always loved women, but he made a distinction—a very sharp one—between good girls and bad girls. Bad girls were expendable.

In the following portion of his confession, Hansen is being questioned by District Attorney Victor Krumm. The final question is by Glenn Flothe, a state police investigator—and the simple answer from Hansen is quite chilling when one realizes its homicidal implications.

Krumm: Why did you drive out the road instead of just going to a hotel or motel in town?

Hansen: You know if you go to a motel or something with it, it ah, it's more or less like a prostitution deal. I'm going and, or I'm—I guess I'm trying to even convince myself maybe I wasn't really, ah, buying sex, it was being given to me, in the aspect that I was good enough that it was being given to me. Maybe I can explain that a little bit better, gentlemen. Going back in my life, way back to my high school days and so forth, I was, I guess what you might call very frustrated—upset all the time. I would see my friends and so forth going out on dates and so forth and had a tremendous desire to do the same thing. From the scars and so forth on my face you can probably see, I could see why girls wouldn't want to get close to me, and when I'm nervous and upset like this here. I'll try to demonstrate if I can think about exactly what I'm going to say and if I talk slow I can keep myself from stuttering. But at the time during my junior high or high school days, I could not control my speech at all. I was always so embarrassed and upset with it from people making fun of me that I hated the word school. I guess this is why I burned down the bus barn way back in Iowa.

I can remember going up and talking to someone, man or woman, classmate or whatever, and started to say something and I'd start to stutter so badly that especially in the younger years I would run away crying, run off someplace and hide for a day or so. The worst there was that I was the butt of all the girls around the school and so forth. The jokes. I know now if I could have faced it and laughed along with them, it would have stopped, but I couldn't at the time and it just, it got so it controlled me, I didn't control it. I didn't start to hate all women; as a matter of fact, I would venture to say I started to fall in love with every one of them. Every one of them become so precious to me 'cause I wanted their, I wanted their friendship. I wanted them to like me so much. On top of things that have happened, I don't want to, I'm not saying that I hate all women, I don't. Quite to the contrary, if, I guess in my own mind what I'm classifying is a good woman, not a prostitute. I'd do everything in my power, any way, shape, or form to do anything for her and to see that no harm ever came to her, but I guess prostitutes are women I'm putting down as lower than myself. I don't know if I'm making sense or not. And you know, when this started to happen I wanted—you know—it happened the first time there you know and I went home and I was literally sick to my stomach . . .

Over the years I've gone in many, many, uh, topless and bottomless bars in town and so forth and never, never touched one of the girls in there in any way, shape, or form until they touched me first. It's like—it's like it was a game; they had to pitch the ball before I could bat. They had to approach me first—saying about I get off at a certain time, we could go out and have a good time, or something like this here. If they don't say that, we weren't playing the game right. They had to approach me. I've talked to, I suppose I made it a point to try to talk to every girl in there. Sometimes if I thought there was a possibility that she didn't say it the first time but she might come back and say it again, now I've invited two or three table dancers with her and comment to her how nice she looked and everything else and try to keep it in a joking tone, "Gosh you know, you sure would be something, you know, for later on," but that's as far as it would go until she, then she had to make, I guess play out my I fantasy. She had to come out and say, ah, we could do it but it's going to cost you some money. Then she no longer—I guess what you might call a decent girl. I didn't look down at the girls dancing, what the hell, they're just trying to make a buck.

Flothe: But when they propositioned you, then it made things different?

Hansen: Then, yes.

Like life—or death.

Snapshot:
The Childhood of John Wayne Gacy

Serial murderer John Wayne Gacy had what on the surface might seem an ordinary childhood. He was born in 1942 in Edgewater Hospital in Chicago, the only boy between two sisters. There was not an obvious rupturing of the family—such as a father who abandons the family or beats or molests them—nor did he have a background of insanity. Gacy's family stayed intact and lived a middle-class existence in a middle-class section of Chicago.

Nonetheless, while Gacy grew up, something terrible was happening between Gacy and his father. His father seemed almost obsessed with punishing "Little John," criticizing him, never thinking he could do anything right. For years they were at odds, and it was a lifelong regret of Gacy that he could never please his father. Indeed, Gacy's father died while Gacy, under arrest for murder, was in jail; he couldn't even get permission to attend the funeral.

Drawn to His Mother

Gacy's relationship with his mother was another story. She was apparently a warm woman who loved her son, and he was drawn to her. Gacy was an average student in grade school and high school, and he never got in a lot of trouble—at least, there's nothing on the record to indicate that he did. His personality, however, did develop a couple of noticeable quirks. He was a glad-handing person with an aggressive style that turned some people off, but his biggest problem was that he was a liar—he was always lying about his accomplishments, as if what he really did do was not good enough. To make himself feel good, Gacy had to exaggerate. He never seemed to notice that many people knew he was lying. Indeed, his stories were often so tall that it would have been impossible for him to have crowded into his life all the things he said he did.

Don't Work With Juan Corona!

Juan Corona, of Yuba City, California, was convicted of robbing and killing over thirty farm workers, many of whom were rootless and were not missed because they had no family.

Juan Corona, who murdered at least 30 people.
(Photofest)

Snapshot:
The Childhood of Henry Lee Lucas

The childhood of Henry Lee Lucas is one of the worst on record. Lucas was raised, as writer Ron Rosenbaum reported in *Vanity Fair* in 1990, "in a fairly primitive log cabin-like dwelling on a small farm in an isolated backwoods county in western Virginia, the kind of hillbilly milieu that produced the predators of *Deliverance*." Appropriately, the name of the town was Blacksburg.

But it wasn't the milieu that did Henry Lee Lucas in. It was mainly his mother.

"I was brought up like a dog," Lucas told Rosenbaum in a Death Row interview. "No human being should have to be put through what I was."

His stepfather, who was nicknamed "No Legs" by townspeople, was an alcoholic who had lost his legs to a slow-moving freight train. For whatever reason—perhaps lack of money—he did not buy prostheses, so he used to slide around the bare dirt floor of the shack, propelling himself on his stumps. Said Lucas of his father, as stated in *Serial Killers* by Joel Norris, "He hopped around on his ass all his life."

Henry Lee Lucas Memorial Highway

Henry Lee Lucas used to dump his victims' bodies on the stretch of highway between Odessa, Texas, and Gainesville, Florida. Cops nicknamed it the Henry Lee Lucas Memorial Highway.

Lucas's mother was part Cherokee Indian and all monster. She was a part-time prostitute who used to service men in the cabin and liked to force "No Legs" to watch. The legless man would watch as long as he could, then get sick. On the final occasion he watched, a winter day in 1950, he was so overwhelmed by what he was seeing that he dragged himself out in the cold, snow-covered landscape and lay there all night. Within a week he was dead of pneumonia.

Viola Lucas had a back-up observer. From the ripe old age of eight until he was fourteen, Henry Lee was forced to watch her practice her profession. To garnish the event, she liked to dress him as a girl. She also dressed him as a girl when he went to school, taking pains to curl his long blond hair.

When he wasn't dressed as a little girl, he went to school dirty, malodorous, and in ragged clothes. One teacher remembered that he was particularly pathetic among a group of students who came from dirt-poor families. He was constantly taunted by other children, particularly for his glass eye, the result of an accident.

The Glass One Was the Warm One

Writer Ron Rosenbaum of Vanity Fair said of serial murderer Henry Lee Lucas's glass eye, "That was the warm one."

Verbally, Viola constantly ripped him apart, detailing what a worthless person he was, what a burden. Physically, she was a

Far right, Henry Lee Lucas at body "dump" site with Texas investigators.
(Author's Collection)

savage. She beat him constantly with anything that was handy—including two-by-fours. Years later, the damage of her beatings would show up in CAT scans taken of Lucas's brain. His diet was minimal. He suffered from malnutrition. And later, as Joel Norris reports, there were excessive amounts of cadmium and lead found in his body—small wonder that Henry Lee would supplement what he was fed at home by foraging through garbage cans.

Viola's cruelty was not only constant, but inspired. For example, Henry Lee came to love a mule on the farm, and one day Viola asked if he liked it. He told her he did, very much. That was enough for Viola. She went into the shed, came out with a shotgun, and killed the mule as Henry Lee watched. And then she beat him for burdening her with having to pay for the animal's removal.

Years later Lucas had a reunion with his mother, who was then in her early seventies, and he murdered her, cutting her throat.

The MVP Award

Henry Lee Lucas is probably the most prolific serial murderer ever in the U.S.—he might have killed as many as three hundred people. Though there is some doubt about the actual number, most experts agree that he had at least one hundred victims, which still qualifies him as the most prolific.

An Amateur Photographer, Too

Serial murderer Jerry Brudos, who stalked Salem, Oregon, and the surrounding area in the late 1960s, kept a gruesome photographic record of his victims. And he did all this while ostensibly carrying on a normal life (except for one bizarre detail: in their house, he and his wife and kids walked around in the nude). His wife, Darcie, was to later say that she had no idea what was going on.

Brudos was also one of the physically strongest serial murderers. He was a six-foot, freckle-faced man with a moonish face and eyes that angled down at the corners. He weighed 190 pounds, but it was said that he could lift a three-hundred-pound freezer by himself.

Brudos's first victim was a woman who was selling encyclopedias, and hers was a case of monumental bad luck. In interviews with the police, he gradually admitted to and described her murder. When she knocked on the door, he opened it and lured her down into the basement, where he battered her to death with a two-by-four, cut off her feet, and made paperweights of them.

He continued to lure women into his house, and he used a horrific method to kill them. He took each victim to his garage, trussed her up, tied a noose around her neck, and, with the rope looped over an overhead beam, pulled her up and off the floor, strangling her. He also liked to photograph each victim as she died. Indeed, when police examined the picture of a woman, Jan Whitney, being hung, in a corner of the picture they saw a face reflected in a mirror in the photo—the face of the photographer, Jerry Brudos.

Brudos was convicted of the killings and sentenced to consecutive life terms.

The investigation into Brudos' background provided some interesting information. His criminal career started when he began stealing women's underwear and shoes, and he escalated to invading their apartments to steal the items. He finally reached the point where he stole their breasts, their feet, and their lives.

Meet Harvey Glatman

Harvey Glatman looked like a character often seen in B movies: a harmless nerd, a baggy-faced, bespectacled individual. He even looked slow-witted. But beneath the benign exterior he was sharp—his IQ, measured while he was in San Quentin, was 130, near genius. But he was also someone who harbored homicidal fantasies.

Glatman's problems showed up early. At the age of twelve, for example, his mother noticed red welts on his neck one day. When she asked what caused them, he said that he had tied a rope around his neck and was hanging from it—that torturing himself like this gave him pleasure.

Q&A

Q: What Happened at These Locations?
- 2900 East Chevy Chase Drive, Glendale, California
- 6510 Forest Lawn Drive, Glendale, California
- 2833 Alta Terrace, La Crescenta, California
- 4100 Block of Ramons Way, Highland Park, California
- 1500 Block of Landa Street, Elysian Park, California
- Los Feliz off ramp from southbound Golden Gate Freeway, California
- 1217 Cliff Drive, Glassell, California
- 2006 North Alvarado, Echo Lake, California

- Angeles Crest Highway, California Bellingham, Washington
- 703 Colorado Drive, Glendale, California

A: Locations where the Hillside Strangler dumped bodies. It later turned out that the Hillside Strangler was actually a team of killers: Angelo Bueno and Kenneth Bianchi.

Q&A

Q: What Happened At These Locations?
- 3123 Center Street, Salem, Oregon
- 47th and Hawthorne, Portland, Oregon
- Parking garage, Meier and Frank's Dept. Store, Salem, Oregon
- Rest area on road leading to Santiam Pass, just north of Albany, Oregon and slightly east of I-5

A: Places where serial murderer Jerry Brudos abducted and/or murdered victims.

Who Am I?

1. In a book penned by Jack Olsen, my nickname was "The Man with the Candy."

2. I met a young man named Wayne Henley, and I gave him money, food, a place to stay, marijuana, and plenty of other drugs. All Henley had to do was troll the streets of Houston for young boys and reel them in for me.

3. Henley and another boy, David Owen Brooks, would cruise the streets, and when they found a likely candidate for "partying" they would invite him to get in the car. Then they would proceed to my home, introduce the boy to me, and start to party. I would encourage the boy to drink, smoke marijuana, and sniff acrylic paint—paint that I stole from my job as a relay tester at the Houston Power Company.

4. Eventually the boy would pass out, and more than occasionally he awoke to find that I had pinned him to a sheet of plywood spread-eagled, his hands and feet constrained by nylon cord and handcuffs.

5. In preparation for what I was going to do to the boy, I would always place a sheet of plastic under the plywood to catch the excreta, blood, and vomit that would invariably be discharged while I had my fun.

6. I would use knives and other implements to work the boys over, sometimes castrating them.

7. Since the kids would naturally scream in agony, I would crank up the radio full blast so their screams could not be heard.

8. I varied how I tortured them; it might have lasted ten minutes to half a day, depending on my mood and spare time. To conclude, I shot or strangled the boy, alone or with help from Henley and/or Brooks.

A: My name is Dean Coryll.

The Real Psycho

When Robert Bloch wrote his classic novel Psycho, there is no question that his model for the Anthony Perkins character was Ed Gein (pronounced Geen). Thomas Harris also used parts (appropriately enough) of Gein to create his killer in The Silence of the Lambs.

Gein lived in a farmhouse about five miles from the northern town of Plainfield, Wisconsin. He was unmarried and had lived alone with his mother until she passed away in 1945 (a brother had died in 1944). He was a small, milky-eyed man whom townspeople regarded as a little weird, but the full depth of his weirdness came to light with the disappearance in November 1957 of a woman named Beatrice Worden, who ran a hardware store in town. The investigation led to Gein, and investigators went out to the farmhouse to check him out.

> **Sleep Tight**
>
> At any given time, it is estimated that there are seventy-five to one hundred serial murderers prowling America (FBI).

The investigators knocked, then pounded, on the door. No answer. Finally they entered the house, and one of the investi-

83

gators, Specks Marty, lit a match. The place was littered with papers and junk, and in fear of starting a fire, they extinguished the light and left. But both men had noticed a peculiar odor that neither could place.

Circus of Fear

Back in town, the lawmen watched a circus of fear building— and Gein was at the center of it. The investigators found a pool of blood in the hardware store, and the assumption was Gein had killed the beloved Beatrice. The townsfolk, if they found Gein, were going to kill him.

There was no evidence to substantiate this suspicion of murder except for one detail: some townsfolk remembered seeing Gein in Worden's truck earlier in the day. Another of the detectives, this one named Chase, knew that Gein sometimes hung around the house of a friend named Hill, and Chase went to Hill's house. Gein was there visiting. The cops quickly arrested him and put him in their car, instructing him to lie down across the back seat so townsfolk couldn't see him.

With Gein in custody, a second group of detectives was dispatched to the house. And this time, the men recognized the all-suffusing smell of decomposing flesh. Using flames to light their way, they went through the house and saw some bowls— but not ordinary bowls. These bowls were made of human skulls, severed just below the eyebrows.

It was, the investigators sensed, the tip of the iceberg. More cops with better lighting were summoned. The cops were right. The skulls were only preliminary items in what was a stomach-wrenching chamber of horror.

Chamber of Horror

On the walls the cops found death masks, made from the flesh of real people; there was a lamp made of human skin, a belt made of female nipples, vests made of skin with the breasts still attached, and, in the saucepan, a fresh human heart. It was all too much, and the men had to repeatedly exit and hit the November night to gulp down air and try to retain what was in their stomachs. It was horrific. What more could there be?

Eventually, someone yelled from a back shed to show the others what had been discovered. A body was there, but no one could be sure if it was Betty Worden—it had no head. It was hanging from a beam by the feet, cut from genitals to chest, and it had been disemboweled and washed; the breasts were intact.

The body had been prepared just like a dead deer.

Then came confirmation that it was Betty Worden: they found her head under a mattress on one of the beds.

The mind-boggling finds did not stop with Betty Worden. Gein had made chair seats with leg bones and dried fat. On his bedposts were human skulls preserved with salt. In a shoebox were nine vulvas.

Suddenly, the sleepy little town of Plainfield—where doors were never locked and neighbors trusted neighbors—was illuminated in a worldwide spotlight that generated fear and

Mommy Dearest

The great hang-up of Gein's life appeared to be his mother. He was devastated by her death and it appears that any way he could keep her alive was okay—even assuming a female persona.

Many Gein jokes have circulated. Some samples:

Q: What did Gein say to the lawmen who arrested him?

A: Have a heart.

Q: What did they find in Gein's cookie jar?

A: Ladyfingers.

anger that some people hold on to to this day. How could they be violated by one of their own?

Unfortunately, based on his appearance, Gein hardly seemed like a monster. He was a short, slight, bland-looking man who looked like he could harm no one.

He was quickly given a hearing and then sent to Central State Hospital at Waupun, Wisconsin, so doctors could discover what manner of creature could do this and to get details on what and why, and determine whether he was qualified to stand trial—in a word, whether he was legally insane. Gein said that he would regularly rob graves and don the body parts he recovered. He explained matter-of-factly that on more than one occasion he had donned a female scalp and secured female breasts to his body.

Edmund Kemper: In His Own Words

Serial murderer Edmund Kemper, who operated in the Santa Cruz, California, area, made the following statements to police concerning the day he picked up two girls, used a gun and knife to control them, and murdered both.

"At this time, I had full intentions of killing both of them. I would have loved to have raped them. But not having any experience at all in this area, with very limited exposure to the opposite sex and I guess the learning point—fifteen to twenty-one—I was locked up with all men [for murdering his grandparents], and there wasn't any opportunity to be with women or girls, and this is one of the big problems I had, and one of the biggest things that caused me to be so uptight.

"So even trying to communicate [with girls] before this happened, just casually, I felt like a big bumblebutt, and I think it's just like an over-aged teenager trying to fit in. They were both eighteen at the time, I think, and I was twenty-three, which isn't that much of a gap, but it was just like a million years.

"Anyway, I decided that Anita was more gullible and would be easier to control, so I told her that she was gonna go into the trunk. And she stepped right out of the car, and I had a pair of handcuffs I had purchased. I took the cuffs out and I reached for one of Mary Ann's arms and she grabbed it back. I picked the gun up like I was gonna hit her with it and told her not to do that again. I said, you know, I'm running the show here, or some such cliché. So she allowed me to put my handcuffs on her arm, and I put the other one around the seat belt, behind the lock so it wouldn't come up, and left her back there.

"I took the other girl to the trunk. Just before she got in, she reiterated something Mary Ann said—'Please don't do this,' or something like that. I said, 'What, are you gonna start in too?'"

Back in the car, Kemper found that Mary Ann was trying to get free: "I almost stuck the gun up her nose to impress her that that was a real gun and that she kept getting me more uptight than I was. And then my lips started quivering, rather than her friend's, and I started losing control, and I told her that if she kept this up, that they were all gonna be in a whole lot of trouble. At this point, she cooperated. I handcuffed her behind her back and turned her over, and I tried to put a plastic bag over her head. I had this nifty idea about suffocating her. I was going to be really smart, and the windows were rolled up, and just normal conversation wouldn't carry—it was a fairly populated area. It was up on the hill. You couldn't hear voices or anything way off in the distance. So I didn't want anything carrying that would be conspicuous. . . . She was complaining that she couldn't breathe. I said I'd tear a hole in the bag, not intending to really, and I had a terrycloth bathrobe with a long rope tie. I put a loop in it and started pulling it down over what I thought was her neck. I pulled it tight. That's about where I blew it."

What he meant was that he broke the rope, which had caught in her mouth, and she bit a hole in the plastic bag. Kemper, infuriated, pulled a blade. "I poised the blade over her back, trying to decide where her heart was, and struck and hit her in the middle of the back, and it stuck a little bit; and she said something like 'ow' or 'oh' . . . and I did it again and did the same damn thing, and I was getting mad now and I told her to shut up after the second time, and she said, 'I can't', and was moaning. She was struggling but she couldn't move too much. . . . Then I started thrusting hard and I was hitting, but apparently I wasn't hitting or the blade wasn't long enough, which it wasn't conceivable to me because she wasn't that large a girl, rather small in fact, about five feet two inches and maybe one hundred five pounds. I struck in several places in both sides of the back and noticed as I went further down the back that she was a little louder and more painful in her cries, but none got really loud. That always bothered me. I couldn't figure out why. It was almost like she didn't want to blow up and start screaming or something. She was maintaining control. But when I started doing this, then it got to be too much for her; she twisted around, and I hit her once in the side with the knife.

"She turned completely over to see what the hell I was doing, I guess, or to get her back away from me, and I stabbed her once in the stomach in the lower intestine. It didn't have any effect. There wasn't any blood or anything. There was absolutely no contact with improper areas. In fact, I think once I accidentally—this bothers me, too, personally—I brushed, I think with the back of my hand when I was handcuffing her, against one of her breasts, and it embarrassed me. I even said, whoops, I'm sorry, or something like that. She was pretty cognizant of what was going on, and it was getting pretty messy there in the backseat.

She turned back over on her stomach, and I continued stabbing. I don't know how many times I stabbed her. I'm trying to think. I usually checked something like that—you might say, almost comparing notes—and in this case I didn't. I did with Anita, 'cause that really amazed me. With Mary Ann, I was really quite struck by her personality and her looks, and there was just almost a reverence there. I didn't even touch her, really too much, after that. That is, other than to get rid of physical evidence, such as clothing, and later the body.

"Anyway, she was across the back of the seat with her head down towards the door, towards the space between the front seat and back seat, and I don't think the bag was on. She had shaken it off. She was crying out a little louder, and I kept trying to shut her up, covering her mouth up, and she kept pulling away, and one time, she didn't, and like it was a cry, and I could have sworn it came out of her back. There were several holes in the lung area and bubbles and things coming out, and the sounds shook me up, and I backed off; at that point, she turned her head to the back of the seat and she called her friend's name, her first name. It was slow and it was not loud. That was the last thing that she said. She wasn't passing out at that point. I don't think at that point that the full impact of what had happened had really hit her. I think she was pretty well in shock or something.

"I felt I was getting nowhere, not that I wasn't getting any kicks out of stabbing her, but hoped that one would do it. When it got quite messy like that, I reached around and grabbed her by the chin and pulled her head back and slashed her throat. I made a very definite effort at it, and it was extremely deep on both sides. She lost consciousness immediately, and there were no more vocal sounds anyway."

At that point, Kemper said he got up in a daze or shock and headed to the back of the car. "I knew I had to do it to the other girl right then, because she had heard all the struggle and she must have known something very serious was going on.

He hid his bloodied hands as he raised the trunk lid.

Anita said, "What's happening with Mary Ann?" Kemper said, "Well, she was getting smart with me."

"And I pulled my hands down kind of unconsciously, and she noticed how bloody they were and she panicked. Her lip was really quivering, and she was really scared. I was scared."

He lied and said he had broken Mary Ann's nose and that Anita should help her. Anita started to get out. While Kemper was talking to her, he picked up another knife from the trunk, with a very large blade. "It was called the Original Buffalo Skinner or something," and it had been "very expensive, about eight or nine dollars."

He turned to Anita with this knife and started to stab her.

Snapshot: Bobby Joe Long's Childhood

Bobby Joe Long, who would grow up to be a serial murderer, was an only child and was essentially raised by his mother, an attractive woman who was a waitress and who for years lived on the edge of poverty after having divorced her husband. Until he was twelve, Long and his mother shared the same bed in a series of single rooms she had rented. But she had a

Slightly Excessive

Bobby Joe Long, a Florida serial murderer, had sex with his wife two to three times a day and masturbated an additional five or six times a day.

reason for it. As reported in *Serial Killers: The Growing Menace* by Joel Norris, she said, "We just didn't have the money for two bedrooms." But she also said she never undressed in front of him or in any other way acted improperly.

For his part, Long apparently raged over his mother's lack of concern for him. When she got finished with her waitressing jobs, she would go out on dates rather than stay home with her son, whom she had neighbors watch. Her work and dating schedule also angered him because of the times she would come home: she would be getting home from work at five or six in the morning and Long would be getting ready for school. Their time together was almost nonexistent.

When Long was twelve, he stopped sleeping with his mother. But the damage had already been done. Perhaps sleeping with a grown woman diminished such a young boy. Indeed, in studies of serial murderers, psychiatrists have said that the most savage are those who feel sexually diminished by women. Feelings of guilt also might have been a factor: there is bound to be sexual contact when two people share a bed, however accidental it is. The boy or the woman rolls over during sleep, and contact is made. As mentioned earlier, Louella Long denied that anything improper went on—and she may well be telling the truth. But what the boy perceived may have been very different from what his mother thought was happening.

Control Is the Key

Ultimately, psychiatrists say, serial murderers such as Bobby Joe Long display a need to show women that they are in control. Time after time one sees evidence of this control, from capturing a woman, to binding her, to the ultimate control—taking her life. It is a way of saying, "I don't need you. To prove it, I'm going to make you go away."

Long demonstrated that control many times. Police figured he raped at least fifty women and murdered nine. Usually, he would strangle them, but he battered to death one woman, Kim Sann, in North Tampa. He was tried on multiple murder charges, sentenced to die in "Old Sparky," and eventually he was electrocuted.

A Psychiatrist on Albert Fish

When Albert Fish was tried in the 1930s for the murder of ten-year-old Grace Budd, Dr. Frederic Wertham, an esteemed psychiatrist of the time, testified in Fish's defense, in the process revealing the astonishing perversions of the man. Here's Wertham's words from that trial.

"I can tell you that to the best of my medial knowledge that every sexual abnormality that I have heard of this man has practiced. Not only has he thought about it, not only has he dreamed about it, but he has practiced them. The outstanding one of those on the medical examination is what we speak of as sadism, which is nothing else but the infliction of pain on somebody for a sexual motive. He has shown the most, I might say, incredible cruelty that one can think of. He has actually; all his mind was bent on the one idea of eliciting the response of pain in somebody else. He told me in many different words— he has told me that pain was uppermost in his mind, or words to that effect. That is one of the abnormalities. The other abnormality was he was homosexual, as we say, a man who prefers men to women. . . .

"As I say, he was homosexual and preferred men and boys— and all through his life women were just a substitute. I mean, that was an entirely secondary choice and entirely secondary pleasure, if I may say so. The third outstanding one is his love for children. This man's prime sexual interest has only been children from the age of about five to fourteen or sixteen.

"He started his sexual career, so to say, at the age of seventeen. I told you at the same time he became a painter. Now, that profession of painter this man has used as a convenience, primarily to satisfy his sexual abnormalities. He has done the following: he worked in very many different institutions. He shows that by design. He worked in YMCAs, he worked in Homes for Tuberculosis, he worked in any kind of a home where there were children, where he thought he would get children. In all these places he made his headquarters the basement or the cellar, and he had the habit of putting a painter's overalls over his nude body, which gave him two advantages: first of all he was nude in a second, and secondly he would be seen by his victims only in his painter's clothes, and if they later on met him on the street in his other clothes, they wouldn't recognize him. The painter's trade also had the advantage from his point of view that he could change from place to place. It wasn't a job where you would have to be for a long time. It was a job where once you got fired, which he has been frequently, when once you got finished you would go to another place, to another city, or you can go to another state.

"Now, this man has roamed around in basements and in cellars for fifty years. He has been in no less than twenty-three different states, from New York down to Montana, and in every state he has something to do with children. I questioned him—there are so many innumerable instances I can't begin to tell you how many there are, but I believe, to the best of my knowledge, that he has at least raped one hundred children, at least; and found when such an episode had happened would immediately change from one part of the city to the other part of the city, to a totally different neighborhood, or when it was particularly bad he would go from one city to the other city, or when it was very bad he would go from one state to the other state. Frequently he had to leave a place and leave all his belongings there and disappear."

Chapter 5
Mass Murder

The Difference Between Serial and Mass Murder

Many people confuse mass murder and serial murder. In mass murder, a group of people is killed all at once, whereas serial murder describes the act of killing many people one at a time over a relatively long period of time. An example of mass murder is the murders in Hamilton, Ohio, on March 30, 1975, when James Ruppert shot to death eleven members of his family. In contrast, serial murderer John Wayne Gacy killed over thirty young boys in a period of a few years.

Also, mass murderers usually operate alone. Anger, resentment, and malice build up in them until they explode in solitary savagery. The same is not true of serial murderers. There are more than a few serial murders that were committed by a duo; for example, Dean Coryll and Wayne Henley.

The Real Amityville Horror

On December 18, 1975, George Lee Lutz, his wife, Kathleen, and their three young children moved into their new home at 112 Ocean Avenue in the village of Amityville, a small community (the population was then around eleven thousand) in the town of Babylon in Suffolk County, on the south shore of Long Island.

George and Kathleen had been looking at homes for quite a while—they had looked at over fifty houses in all—and considered the house a steal. It was a large, two-and-a-half-story, dark-shingled, white-trimmed Dutch Colonial in fine condition and featured six bedrooms, three and a half baths, a pool and, on the east side of the property, access to Amityville Creek, which feeds into the Great South Bay. The house was selling for only $80,000 in an old, upscale neighborhood where the other homes were twice that price. Of course, there was a reason for that, and the real estate agent was up-front. She said that barely a year earlier something terrible had occurred in the house: an entire family, the DeFeos, had been murdered.

That didn't bother the Lutzes. The house was just what they were looking for. Lutz could relocate his surveying business office from Syosset to the house's finished basement, thereby saving rent; the kids would have their own rooms; and the family could get in plenty of boating.

Twenty-eight days after they moved in, the Lutzes fled the house in terror, leaving behind furniture and furnishings, taking with them only a change of clothes.

The Lutzes said they got out because they were not alone in the house. There was an evil force there: they spoke of such things as pigs with glowing red eyes looking through windows, being levitated, discovering a small room not on the house plans that was filled with an overpowering stench of human excrement.

The local media came at the Lutzes in waves. The story quickly spread across the country and they were besieged for interviews and information about their experience. Then, a few months after they left the house, the Lutzes suddenly stopped talking to the media, saying that the reportage was distorted and exaggerated. Shortly thereafter, they sat down with writer

Jay Anson to get it right. A year later, the book The Amityville Horror emerged. Or perhaps exploded would be more precise: it broke the bank, going through thirty-seven printings and selling 6.5 million hardcover copies at $7.95 a copy. It was a national bestseller for forty-two weeks.

The book spawned the first of several movies on the topic, which were even more lucrative, and it also released hordes of curious visitors who came both day and night—some traveling from foreign countries—to see the house where such horrific things had occurred. The book also spawned lawsuits: a writer sued, claiming he had a deal with the Lutzes before Anson. A family named Cromarty, who had moved into the house after the Lutzes, sued them, claiming that the book was fiction and had violated their privacy and made it more difficult to sell the house. Now, years later, with all the legal dust settled, it is clear that the book was less than accurate. As Federal Court Judge Jack Weinstein said during the writer's suit, "It appears to me that to a large extent the book is a work of fiction."

But there was never any doubt that in the wee hours of the morning of November 13, 1974, a real horror had occurred at 112 Ocean Avenue and had, in fact, made everything that followed possible and plausible. And perhaps the most horrible part of this horror was that the murderer turned out to be the sole surviving member of the family, Ronald DeFeo, Jr.

At the time of the killings, Ronald ("Butch") DeFeo, Jr. was twenty-three, a husky,

Ronald DeFeo, whose murder of his family triggered a spate of *"Amityville Horror"* movies.
(Author's Collection)

five-eight, dark-haired man who wore a beard and was given to open shirts to display chest hair; overall, he had a macho style that belied the emptiness inside. He was a sporadic drinker but heavy user of heroin, had used speed heavily for years, and occasionally used acid. He had a history of legal and psychological problems. The eldest of five children, he lived at 112 Ocean Avenue with his parents and two younger sisters and two younger brothers.

It was DeFeo who sounded the alarm that something might be wrong at the house. On the afternoon of November 13, he went over to the home of his friend Bobby Kelske, who lived in the neighborhood, and said that something strange was going on at his house. He said the family cars, a green Buick station wagon and a red Buick Electra, were in the driveway, but no one answered the doorbell when he rang it. He didn't have his house key, so he couldn't get in. He had also called twice; no one had answered.

Kelske said that someone had to be there, but the subject was dropped. Kelske and DeFeo, or "Butch," as Ronald was known to family and friends, arranged to meet that evening at Henry's, a bar about a half mile from the DeFeo house at the corner of Ocean Avenue and Merrick Road. Butch was already at Henry's when Kelske arrived at about 6:00 p.m. He was wondering out loud to some drinking buddies why he couldn't get into the house. What was wrong?

Finally, DeFeo said he couldn't stand it anymore. He told the group that he was going to have to break a window to get in and left. A short while later, Henry's patrons heard the squealing of tires, and moments later, Butch DeFeo, very agitated, was standing in the doorway.

"Bobby!" he cried to Kelske. "You got to help me!"

"What's the matter?"

"Someone shot my mother and father."

"Are you sure?"

"I saw them up there."

DeFeo asked the others to help as well, and a few seconds later four of the men, plus Kelske and DeFeo, were out of the bar and in DeFeo's blue Buick, speeding to the house.

It was Kelske who called the Suffolk County Police. The call was logged in at 6:35 p.m. It was, as often happens when people are under stress, very garbled in dialogue, but the message finally got through. Kelske and companions had discovered four bodies in the DeFeo house. The cop on the line told him to wait at the house and that he would contact the local Amityville police.

Amityville cops were on the scene in a couple of minutes and were followed by an army of Suffolk County cops, including Suffolk homicide detectives. They found that Kelske had made a mistake—there were not four, but six bodies: Ronald DeFeo Sr., forty-three; his wife, Louise, forty-two; their sons Mark, eleven, and John, nine; and their daughters Dawn, eighteen, and Allison, thirteen.

Jack Sturiano, a physician's assistant with the Suffolk County medical examiner's office who has pronounced death at thousands of scenes, examined the DeFeo crime scene photos and said there were a couple of unusual things about it. One was that it was neat. "Normally in scenes like this where people die so violently, you'll see blood splattered everywhere. Here, the blood was mostly confined to the beds the victims were on," Sturiano said. "Also, all the bodies were found in the same position, lying facedown. That's very unusual." Five of the bodies were found on the second floor. Autopsies would determine that they were killed between two and four in the morning, and that the murder weapon was a high-powered rifle.

Ronald DeFeo, Sr., and his wife were found lying side by side in two single beds that had been pushed together in the master bedroom. The elder DeFeo, a squat, dark-haired, heavyset man, had been shot twice in the back, through the right kidney and the base of the spine. Forensics evidence would indicate that he was trying to raise himself up when he was shot.

Louise DeFeo also had been shot twice in the back, one bullet entering through her right buttock and the other through her upper back on the right side. She also was trying to get up. Forensics would show that all four shots had been fired from the bedroom doorway.

The two boys, Mark and John, slept together in a room diagonally across from the master bedroom. Here the shots were taken up close: the killer had stood between the boys' two single beds and shot each once in the back from a distance of less than two feet.

The room of thirteen-year-old Allison was adjacent to her younger brothers. Here, investigators theorized that she had awakened, been shot in the face from a distance of less than two feet, and had flopped back belly-down on the bed.

The sixth body, of eighteen-year-old Dawn DeFeo, was the last to be discovered—and she was discovered by accident. The house was swarming with police, and one of them noticed stairs leading from the second-floor landing to what he assumed was an attic. He climbed them and found Dawn in one of the two bedrooms up there, the other bedroom being that of Butch DeFeo.

Gerard Sullivan, the Suffolk assistant district attorney who was to prosecute DeFeo, said of the victims that Dawn was "the most horrible to look at." She had been shot once, and the bullet had entered below her left ear, smashing into her temple and "collapsing the left side of her face."

DeFeo was to testify later that after the shooting, a smell came from her head that was "sickening." However, there is no medical reason for this; it was likely DeFeo smelled nothing except the aroma, as it were, of the madness inside himself, or excrement that Dawn had discharged at death.

Butch DeFeo was very cooperative with homicide detectives and understandably distraught over the loss of his family. And he had a theory as to who might have done it: an old but dangerous man named Louis Falini, who reportedly had been a mob contract killer and was a former friend of his father. Butch had had an argument with Falini a couple of years earlier and Falini had, Butch told the cops, vowed to whack out Butch and the rest of the DeFeos.

At first the detectives believed Butch and took pains to keep him safe, as they transported him to homicide headquarters in Hauppauge, to protect him from a possible hit attempt. It was later, by accident, that DeFeo was considered a suspect. The house had been thoroughly searched, but Jack Shirvell, one of the homicide squad detectives, was making a last sweep through when he noticed two boxes—both of which turned out to be empty—leaning against a wall by a radiator in Butch DeFeo's room. It was the printing on the boxes that caught Shirvell's attention. One had held a .22-caliber Marlin, the other a .35-caliber Marlin carbine. Just to be on the safe side, Shirvell brought them, along with other materials, to homicide headquarters. A few hours later, Shirvell learned more from a ballistics report on the bullets recovered at the scene: the bullets had been fired from a .35-caliber rifle.

Shirvell and the other detectives conferred and decided that before confronting DeFeo with the information, they would talk to his friends, so the detectives later could go into any confrontation with DeFeo armed with as much knowledge as possible. Meanwhile, DeFeo remained at homicide headquarters in protective custody.

Police talked to DeFeo's friend, Bobby Kelske, and he had some revealing information. Apparently DeFeo owned quite a few guns, including rifles, and just a couple of weeks earlier had been looking to buy a silencer.

The detectives returned to headquarters and read DeFeo his rights, confronting him with the fact that ballistics showed the bullets that had killed his family had come from a .35-caliber rifle, and that he owned one. DeFeo steadfastly maintained his innocence. "I'm trying to help you guys," he said at one point. Detectives continued to question him into the night but got nowhere. DeFeo went to sleep on a cot in one of the rooms.

The next day, November 14, the interrogation continued, but this time it was conducted by Dennis Rafferty, a homicide detective with a reputation as being the best interrogator in the department. Sympathetically, but persistently, Rafferty kept pointing out inconsistencies in DeFeo's repeated recounting of his story. First it was Falini alone who killed the family, then Falini had help, then Falini forced DeFeo to join in the bloodbath. The recitation was punctuated with tears.

Finally, at the end of six and a half hours, at around four in the afternoon, DeFeo rested his head on one of Rafferty's shoulders. DeFeo had already admitted that Falini was never in the house. Only he had been.

"Butch," Rafferty said softly, "tell me what happened."

"It all started so fast," DeFeo said. "Once I started, I just couldn't stop. It went so fast."

DeFeo said that he had been watching a war movie called Castle Keep (which was to play a role in his defense later) in the den and fell asleep. He awakened at two or three in the morning and went immediately to his room, where he loaded the Marlin.

Then he went to his father and mother's room and shot them, into Allison's room and shot her, then into the boys' room and killed them. Then he reloaded—the rifle only held seven shots—and started to climb the stairs. Later he would recall that the rifle's barrel was hot. Dawn had awakened and come out of the room.

"Is that you, Butch?" she had said.

"Yeah," he had said, "everything's all right."

His sister went back in her bedroom. DeFeo then followed her in and shot her.

Throughout it all, he said, the family pet, a sheep dog named Shaggy who was tied outside to a garbage shed, was barking. DeFeo, who had no love for the dog, remembered it later at the trial. "The fucking dog was screaming while this was going on. The dog was screaming." It was a remembrance that was to be extremely significant.

Following the shootings he went from room to room, picking up the spent cartridges he could find, at one point getting blood on his hand and wiping it on his pants. He put the cartridges and clothes he was wearing in a pillow case and the rifle in another. Then he trimmed his beard, showered, put on fresh clothes, and left the house, driving to Brooklyn to his job as a mechanic at Brigante-Karl Buick on Coney Island Avenue. Butch DeFeo's maternal grandfather, Michael Brigante, owned the shop, and Butch's father was the service manager. On the way, Butch threw the rifle into Amityville Creek and dropped the bloodied clothing and cartridges into a sewer on Rockaway Boulevard in Brooklyn.

And how did he feel during all this, the detectives asked? "Good," he said. "Very good."

Investigators and Assistant District Attorney Gerard Sullivan developed a logical reason as to why Ronald DeFeo, Jr., murdered his family: money. His father had regularly hidden jewels and cash in a box stored in a recess beneath the closet saddle of the master bedroom. After the murders, police found it empty, and Butch DeFeo had a history of stealing. At the time, Butch was on probation for being in possession of a stolen outboard motor and had on at least two occasions stolen from his relatives. He had once helped implement a burglary scam at Brigante-Karl, and just two weeks earlier he and another employee said they were robbed on the way to the bank with a deposit of $20,000—$1,800 in cash and the rest in checks—a story that no one believed.

But overwhelming evidence suggests that the real reason for the murders lay within the psyche of Ronald DeFeo. The emotional environment in which he lived and his psychological history easily could have contributed to his propensity to commit the murders.

By all accounts, DeFeo lived in what could be fairly characterized as a madhouse. Arguing, unrest, and physical violence were a way of life. Louise and Ronald DeFeo Sr. had been fighting since Butch was a baby, and the fights often ended up with Louise bloodied and black-eyed. The violent incidents sometimes defied belief. Frank Davidge, a friend of Butch's, remembered one such incident. Davidge had stopped at the house to get a car part. Butch and his father were at the table having dinner. Downstairs in the basement, the younger kids were acting up, and Mrs. DeFeo was screaming at them to shut up. Ronald Sr., in turn, yelled at her to shut up a number of times. She didn't, and she was still carrying on as she climbed the basement stairs, a laundry basket in hand. The elder DeFeo was there to meet her when she reached the top step. He punched her in the face and slammed the door. Davidge could hear her cascading down the stairs. The elder DeFeo had returned to the table. "Now we can eat in peace," he said.

Ronnie also warred with his mother and gave a clear indication of his relationship with her when talking to detectives less than twenty-four hours after he had killed her. They had asked him why he hadn't eaten with the family the night before the killings. "My mother," he said, "was a lousy cook. She cooked up some brown shit in a bowl. It looked like shit and it smelled like shit . . . if you had to eat it, it would taste like shit."

His relationship with his siblings was equally stormy.

He said—again, less than twenty-four hours after killing them—"My brothers is a couple of fucking pigs. I often used the same bathroom they used on the second floor. And I go in there and sometimes there is toilet paper hanging out of the bowl. Sometimes there is shit in the bowl and no toilet paper. The fucking pigs don't even wipe their asses. A couple of times there were even shit on the back of the seat."

Of his sister Dawn, after he had killed her, he said, "That fat fuck Dawn. Dawn is nigger music, fucking nigger music, nigger music. All fucking day and night. And I can't even tell her to turn it down, because if I tell her to turn it down I get my ass kicked."

"By who?" detectives asked.

"My father."

By far, the most malignant relationship in the house was between Butch and his father. Butch was battered by the elder DeFeo, and it started when he was very young. Butch's cousin, Michael Brigante, remembered an event that occurred when Butch was only two years old. Brigante said that during this incident, a lot of relatives were in the basement of the house where the DeFeos had lived in Brooklyn before moving to Amityville. Butch had done something wrong—Brigante doesn't remember what—and his father responded by grabbing him and pushing him against a wall so hard his head struck it.

When he was twelve (and grossly overweight, at 250 pounds), and after years of disciplinary problems, Butch was expelled from St. Jerome's, a Catholic school he was attending in Brooklyn. When he told his father, the elder DeFeo exploded, screaming at him that he wasn't really his son, he had only married his mother because she was pregnant with Butch, and that he was worthless. Louise DeFeo responded by going after her husband with a knife, and Ronald Sr. retaliated by throwing a chair—which hit Butch in the mouth and knocked out all his front teeth.

Later, as Butch got older, the elder DeFeo would not be above punching his eldest son in the mouth for some infraction. But there was a paradox in the way Ronald Sr. treated his oldest son. For whatever reason, his son could have virtually anything he wanted. When Butch was fourteen, his father bought him a $4,000 speedboat. When he was seventeen, his father bought him a car.

And he gave him money—lots of it. After Butch quit Amityville High when he was sixteen, he held a series of dead-end jobs from which he was repeatedly fired for absenteeism. At eighteen he went to work for his father at the car dealership, and though he only made around $80 a week as a mechanic, his father regularly gave him $500 a week in cash. It was not unusual for Butch to have thousands of dollars in his pocket.

It was around that time that he started taking speed, occasionally taking acid, and making the rounds of the South Shore bars. With plenty of cash, he played big man, regularly buying drinks for other people. A bar bill for one night could reach $100, a substantial amount in the late sixties and early seventies.

Butch had long shown an inclination toward violence, just like his father. His school record was dotted with altercations

106

of one kind or another, and his trek through the bar scene was studded with fights. He went out with a number of girls, and here, too, his relationships would ultimately be marred by violence; sometimes he was physical, and sometimes he would just threaten them.

His violence was coupled with and perhaps partly created by a liking for guns. Indeed, on a number of occasions, he had threatened both bar adversaries and girlfriends with shooting, and a couple of times he had to be restrained by friends from shooting somebody. Sometimes DeFeo would threaten friends with guns in an almost playful way, but his friends didn't like it. Bobby Kelske tells of the time DeFeo leveled a rifle at him and, though he didn't fire, Kelske was scared to death because he saw something "like fire" in DeFeo's eyes.

On another occasion, DeFeo actually did fire at a friend—Frank Davidge, the friend who had earlier witnessed DeFeo's father's brutality. DeFeo and Davidge were hunting in some woods, DeFeo leading. Davidge asked DeFeo to slow down. DeFeo responded by turning and firing his rifle, if not directly at Davidge, then close to him, as Davidge took shelter behind a tree. On that day, Davidge became an ex-friend of DeFeo's.

In retrospect, there was ample warning that DeFeo would one day turn his violence toward his family and kill them. For instance, a year before the murders there was a chilling incident.

One evening, the elder DeFeo was beating up his wife in the master bedroom. She was screaming, the kids were screaming, Dawn was trying to intercede. Finally the boys ran up to Butch's room and told him to come quick to save their mother.

DeFeo had a single-shot shotgun on his wall. He chambered a shell and went downstairs into the master bedroom.

His father was standing over his mother, who was on her back on the floor.

"Leave the woman alone, you fat prick," Butch said, "or I'll kill you."

Then he leveled the gun at his father.

He squeezed the trigger once.

Click.

Twice.

Click.

The shotgun wouldn't work. He left the room, leaving behind a white-faced father—and a reborn one. The elder DeFeo took the fact that the gun did not go off as a sign from God, a miracle. Thereafter, the elder DeFeo started to hang pictures of Christ all around the house. Butch, who made the miracle possible, helped install religious statues out front.

His parents also tricked him into seeing a psychiatrist over the incident. (Butch had been to psychologists on a number of occasions when he was young.) One morning Butch's parents drove to the city and insisted Butch go with them. Next thing he knew, he was sitting in a psychiatrist's office. Halfway through his discussion with the psychiatrist, the doctor suggested that DeFeo should be hospitalized, that he didn't belong on the street. Butch reacted by storming out of the office.

The psychiatrist bluntly told his parents that DeFeo would one day kill them all, that he must be hospitalized. The elder DeFeo responded with laughter, saying the psychiatrist didn't know what he was talking about. But Louise DeFeo had a different reaction. She cried.

DeFeo himself told his family that one day he would kill them. In fact, a couple of months before he killed them, he moved out of the house and into a girlfriend's house because he was afraid he might do it. (He had always been afraid of his potential violence and once gave that as a reason why he switched from speed, which agitated him, to heroin, which made him mellow.) But for some reason, the elder DeFeo bullied and cajoled Butch to move back into the house with tactics such as disabling Butch's car and cutting off his salary. So Butch moved back in. The die was cast.

On Thursday, November 12, the day before the murders, Butch did not go to work, complaining of an upset stomach, and his father left work early to go home and, he told people at the dealership, "have it out" with Butch over the phony robbery.

Before he left, he also made a cryptic, chilling, prophetic statement to his nephew Michael Brigante: that he felt that today was the day Butch was going to kill them all. Someone asked Brigante if he tried to stop him or do something, and Brigante responded that if you knew the elder DeFeo, you'd know no one could tell him anything.

At DeFeo's trial, the key issue was whether he was legally insane—whether he knew right from wrong—at the time of the murders. There was no real debate as to whether or not he was the murderer. On the side of the prosecution was Dr. Harold Zolan, who examined DeFeo twice and declared that he was an "antisocial personality . . . people who have a code of their own. People who are grossly selfish and callous, who are extremely egotistical, who have no capacity to experience or to feel guilt . . . their main purpose in life is self-gratification . . . and [they are] both passive and aggressive." Zolan's testimony indicated DeFeo had developed into a very aggressive individual. Killing his father and family was a way of proving just how "big" and aggressive he was. And Zolan saw no psychosis: DeFeo was responsible for his acts.

Defense psychiatrist Dr. Daniel Schwartz saw it differently: he believed that DeFeo did not know right from wrong when the murders were committed. Schwartz, in the first place, saw DeFeo as being terrified of his father. "As wild as he could be with others," the doctor said, "he could not respond in kind to his father. But the anger had to go somewhere. . . . His came out, among other ways, at most of his teachers and school authorities, who for many children quite naturally starred as parent figures."

DeFeo had both hatred and love for his father, and he was torn by them—so much so that he retreated into a world of paranoid delusions to "turn his anger away from his father. But it swung back." And DeFeo came to believe that on the night of the murders his family was going to kill him, said Dr. Schwartz. To him, it was an act of self-defense: he killed them before they killed him.

And the war movie he had watched, Castle Keep, had played a role, Schwartz continued. This was about a group of American soldiers who defend a castle filled with precious art, but in the end are all killed. Dr. Schwartz said that DeFeo told him he was moved by the violence in the film, but that the movie had other meanings to him. "There is a significant theme in the picture," the doctor said, "of some soldiers who have renounced violence and who walk through this town in Europe preaching religious nonviolence, but it's to no avail. Religion, peacefulness, has no effect in this movie. The violence will win out . . . and I think the message to the defendant [was that] nothing was going to prevent this final showdown."

Charles Manson's Teacher

While in federal prison on McNeil Island in Washington in 1960, Charles Manson was a cellmate of the notorious 1930s bank robber Alvin "Creepy" Karpis, who taught Manson how to read music and play the guitar.

One of the puzzling things in the trial was DeFeo's statement that he didn't hear the sound of the rifle firing. Schwartz cleared this up by saying it was the result of the process of "dissociation," where senses are shut down during intense experiences, a phenomenon Schwartz said was quite common. But DeFeo had admitted that he heard Shaggy, the dog, "screaming," and in rendering its verdict, the jury apparently counted this heavily as evidence that DeFeo was, as Zolan had suggested, a skilled liar, a "malingerer." Why could he hear one sound and not the other?

A curious matter that was never cleared up was how no one in the neighborhood heard the shots booming from the house in the dead of night—the neighboring homes were only fifteen to twenty yards away. One explanation was that the large house muffled the sounds. Another explanation might be that people heard it and were too terrified to act, a la the Kitty Genovese case. Or maybe DeFeo had found the silencer he sought to buy a couple of weeks earlier but the police never recovered it.

Finally, why didn't family members respond or defend themselves in any way—or at least scream?

Dr. Howard Adelman, the medical examiner, said there was a possibility the family was drugged, but he couldn't confirm it. Or possibly it all happened so fast that no one could respond, or for those few moments they were frozen in terror. And maybe Dawn, who did speak to DeFeo, had shut down her mind against what she was hearing. We probably will never know for sure.

On the first ballot, the jury voted 10–2 to convict. On the second, 11–1. The holdout gave in after being read the testimony that confirmed that DeFeo could hear the barking dog. The judge sentenced Ronald DeFeo Jr. to six life sentences, one for each murder (murder in the second degree), to be served concurrently. DeFeo did not react to the sentence. If there was shock or fear, he didn't show it. Then again, he had said that he never had any feelings about anything. "My feelings went away a long time ago," he once said. Some of them. Rage was surely still around.

As insane as life was within the house and as utterly contradictory as it may seem, there is little question that the DeFeos loved one another on some level. Human interactions, though, are very subtle and complicated; we may think that the love we have

The infamous *"Amityville Horror"* house after redesigning. (Author's Collection)

inside is being perfectly perceived by the person we intend it for, but a lot of times love isn't what's perceived. Another message gets delivered.

Sometimes, too, we are afraid to express ourselves, and particularly fear openly giving our love. It makes us vulnerable to rejection, so we try to express it another way. We buy a $4,000 speedboat for a fourteen-year-old boy when what he really wants is our arms around him, or a word of encouragement, or a wink. But the speedboat is all we can manage. Maybe somewhere in our past someone never hugged us, either; and like a curse, our fears pass from one generation to the next. . . .

On the day after the murders, my wife and I went to 112 Ocean Avenue to drive past. What I remember, mainly, are the religious statues outside the house, but also a sign that hung by the house number: HIGH HOPES. In light of what happened, in my mind it will always be savagely ironic, and very, very sad.

Who Am I?

1. When I was a soldier in World War II, other GIs regarded me as unusual in several respects. I was extremely quiet, unsociable, and I read the Bible constantly. In fact, I was a Bible student before entering the army.

2. In 1945, I was discharged from military service and returned to my native Camden, New Jersey, a town across the river from Philadelphia, to live with my parents.

3. I drifted a little and enrolled in Bible classes in Temple University, but I quit after a relatively short time.

4. Then I drifted some more. I held a series of meaningless jobs and showed the same basic personality I had shown in the army and even before that. I was a quiet loner. You never knew what I was thinking or feeling, except for anger. I seemed to people to be brooding, cooking inside.

5. I did not relate well to women. I was a tall, soft-spoken man, not unattractive, but extremely shy. One woman who had gone out with me said I was so shy I would never even kiss her good-night after a date. She pushed me into doing it, and that bothered me.

6. I never went out with women again. I continued to drift along, things cooking inside me. I was known in the neighborhood as a quiet man, and I lived in a second floor apartment on River Road with my mother, Freda.

7. One family angered me. They were the Cohens, a family who lived next to me and whose gate I had to use to get to my own apartment, or else go around another way which involved crossing a lot. The Cohens didn't mind me using the gate, but they wanted me to close it softly. That bothered me, and each time I used the gate, I slammed it.

8. I had a shooting gallery in my basement. I owned revolvers (including a Luger) and knives, and I practiced regularly with them.

9. The days before I went what people would describe as berserk, I went to the movies to see I Cheated the Law and The Lady Gambles. Years later, people would speculate if I saw a message in them like killer Ronald DeFeo did in Castle Keep: he perceived the message that all attempts at negotiation and peacemaking will fail, that the only solution to life's problems is violence.

10. September 6, 1946, began in a normal way. I left a note on the kitchen table for my mother which said, "Wake me up at eight o'clock." My mother did, and when I got up and dressed—dark suit, white shirt, bow tie—it looked like I was going to work or out on a date. But I had a Luger in my pocket.

11. I bolted down a quick break-fast, then left the kitchen and went down into the basement. I was there fif-teen or twenty minutes, then came back upstairs and went into the living room. I turned the dial on the radio until I found an announcer giving the weather for the Camden area.

Howard Unruh who killed 13 people in a matter of minutes. (Photofest)

A: I am Howard Unruh. On September 6, 1946, while walking through the streets of Camden, New Jersey, I randomly shot to death anyone who was around—including my neighbors, the Cohens.

The First Modern Mass Murder

After his shooting spree, Howard Unruh ended up in his home in a firefight with police. Unruh fired at cops from a second-story window, and the cops fired back.

Then something bizarre occurred, which was a tremendous coup for a newsman. As reported in *Spree Killers* by David Redstone, Philip R. Buxton, city editor for the Camden Evening Courier, figured out where Unruh was and dialed the number. Unruh answered. Following is their verbatim conversation:

"Is this Howard?"

"Yes, this is Howard. What's the last name of the party you want?"

"Unruh."

"What do you want?"

"I'm a friend. I want to know what they're doing to you."

"They haven't done anything to me yet. But I'm doing plenty to them."

"How many have you killed?"

"I don't know. I haven't counted. Looks like a pretty good score, though."

"Why are you killing people?"

"I don't know. I can't answer that yet; I'll have to speak to you later. I'm too busy right now."

Moments later, tear gas containers were tossed into the room, and after the gas had time to do its work, the cops entered the house. Unruh pleaded with them not to shoot him. They grabbed him and put him under arrest.

It was a wonder Unruh had not been killed. His only wound was from having been shot in the leg by Fred Engel, one of Unruh's potential victims and who had happened to be carrying a gun.

Howard Unruh was questioned extensively by the Camden prosecutor's office. But the prosecutor could come up with nothing more for Unruh's motive for the killing spree than "people were picking on me," citing the dispute with the Cohen family over the gate. Quite obviously, the motive did not cover all his actions of the day, such as shooting a six-year-old boy who was getting a haircut.

In the end, Howard Unruh was diagnosed by a panel of psychiatrists as being a schizophrenic with marked violent and paranoid tendencies. After it was learned that he had done the shooting with a souvenir Luger from the war, officials and the media were up in arms to try to make it mandatory for anyone owning such weapons to register them, and to also keep undesirable individuals from owning them to prevent such senseless deaths.

Two Lucky Bastards

After they had slaughtered the Clutter family, Perry Smith and Dick Hickock, the killers featured in Truman Capote's In Cold Blood, traveled all over the South and Northwest, including Mexico and Florida. While hitchhiking through Colorado, the pair—apparently nonchalant about killing—had decided to kill the next person who picked them up and steal his car. They waited and waited and no one stopped, but finally someone did and they trotted towards the car. However, the person in the vehicle must have been examining Perry and Hickock in the rearview mirror and

Charles Manson's Real Name

Charles Manson was born to a fourteen-year-old prostitute named Kathleen Maddox. The name on his birth certificate is "No Name Maddox." She later married a man named William Manson, who gave Charles the surname that was to shock the world.

made an excellent snap judgment, because just as they reached the car, the driver changed their mind and sped away.

Hickock yelled at the receding car, "You lucky bastard!"

The next person was also in great luck. He was described in In Cold Blood as a salesman and father of five. Capote called him "Mr. Bell." He picked up Smith and Hickock. They had devised a signal that would trigger his murder. Smith was in the back, Hickock the front. As soon as Hickock went to light a cigarette, Smith was to hook a belt over the man's head and strangle him while Hickock grabbed the wheel.

They were in the middle of nowhere, seconds from doing it, when what Capote described as a miracle occurred. They came over the crest of a hill and standing at the bottom of it was Mr. Bell's salvation: a hitchhiking black soldier. The goodhearted Mr. Bell stopped and picked him up, forcing Smith and Hickock to abort their murderous plan.

Q&A

Q: What happened on July 21, 1984, at a McDonald's near the Mexican border on Interstate Highway 5, San Ysidro, California?

A: James Oliver Huberty walked into the restaurant which, like the playground attached to it, was crowded. He was dressed in camouflage clothing and armed with an Uzi, shotgun, and pistol, the weapons in plain sight. He started to fire, as one observer put it, "at anything that moved"—men, women, children, it didn't matter. Soon the walls were spattered with blood, the floor awash with it. The carnage stopped over an hour later when a SWAT team member picked off Huberty with a shot from a sniper rifle. The final toll was twenty-one dead, including Huberty, and thirty adults and children injured.

The Unthinkable Crime

The neighborhood where one of the worst mass murders of the twentieth century occurred was in an unlikely setting for the event. Known as Jeffrey Manor, it is located on Chicago's southeast side in a typical white, middle-class area with clean streets, private homes, and garden apartments, and which has as its centerpiece South Side Community Hospital.

The house at 2319 East 100th Street, where the atrocity occurred, is in the heart of the neighborhood, just down the block from the hospital. It was an apartment house, one of six two-story town houses with pale green wood siding and yellowish bricks. The hospital had rented three of the town houses for its nurses, and 2319 had eight nurses in it the night of July 14, 1966.

Screaming Heard

The horror of what happened started to unravel around six o'clock in the morning. Mrs. Freda Windmiller, who lived in one of the town houses on the block, heard yelling coming from down the street. She and her husband discussed it, and he dismissed it as kids. Freda did not think so. She thought somebody was screaming. She got dressed and went out to investigate.

Meanwhile, someone else had heard the screams. His name was Robert Hall, and he was a supervisor at a steel mill. He was walking his dog when he heard the sounds coming from a short distance away. To Hall, it was clear: someone was screaming.

When Windmiller and Hall got to the site, they were greeted by a chilling scene. Crouched like a terrified animal on a ledge that went along the town house on the second floor was a pretty, dark-haired, dark-eyed girl with cocoa-colored skin. She was yelling, but the sounds were half in broken English, half in some foreign language. In fact, she seemed to be hallucinating, half of her consciousness back in her native Philippine Islands.

"Help me. Help me. Everybody is dead. I am the only one alive in the sampan. My friends are all dead, all dead, all dead. I'm the only one alive, oh God, the only one. My friends are all dead!" The girl was so terrified she looked like she was going to jump from the ledge to the ground, which was a good ten feet, but Hall and Windmiller exhorted her to go back through the open window—she had knocked out the screen earlier—and come down the stairs. Terrified, the girl agreed.

The first officer on the scene, a patrolman named Daniel Kelly, tried the locked front door to the townhouse. He went around to the back and tried the door. It was open. He went inside, into the kitchen. All was quiet and quite normal, down to a sink full of unwashed dishes.

He passed through the kitchen into the small living room. To his right were the front door and a small TV room. Then a shock: lying facedown on a pale orange couch was the nude body of a young woman.

Kelly went over to get a closer look, and when he saw the face he recoiled in horror. He knew her. It was Gloria Davy, a beautiful twenty-two-year-old whose sister, Charlene, he had once dated. Pulse racing, something occurred to Kelly. Maybe the killer was still in the building. He pulled his service revolver, then went to one of the windows that fronted the street and yelled to another officer, Leonard Ponne, to get inside, that the killer might still be on the premises. Ponne drew his gun and Kelly opened the living room door and let him in. Together they went up stairs that led from the living room to the second floor.

They went through the rooms and were stunned. The rooms and floors were littered with bodies. Kelly and his partner had only paused for one moment to speak with the woman who had been screaming on the ledge, who had by now come inside. Though she was almost in shock, she was able to articulate, at least in outline, what had happened.

What Happened?

The survivor's name was Corazon Amurao. She told Kelly that sometime during the night, a man had come into the house. He had killed everyone except her. She had hidden from him under the bed.

Could she identify him?

Amurao thought she could.

The conversation was brief, then Amurao was rushed to the hospital, where she was treated and sedated.

The crime made worldwide headlines, and though the details of the killings typically were not released, some reports did say that the women had been stabbed and strangled, and a number had been sexually assaulted. All eight women were student nurses at the nearby hospital. All were in their early twenties. Their lives had been brutally cut short.

They were:

Pamela Wilkening. She was twenty years old and from Lansing, Illinois, and was to celebrate her twenty-first birthday in less than a month. She had wanted to be a nurse since she was a little girl. She had been stabbed in the left breast, but the cause of death was asphyxiation; she was strangled with a strip of bed sheet.

Mary Ann Jordan. She was twenty. She had been stabbed three times, each thrust three to four inches deep, in the neck, breast, and eye.

Suzanne Farris. She was twenty-one. As it turned out, Suzanne had fought the killer, who stabbed her eighteen times in the back, neck, and chin in a frenzy. She was also strangled and showed signs of sexual assault.

Nina Schmale. Nina was twenty-four and a native of Chicago, where her father was a cement mason. Before becoming a nurse, she had taught Sunday school for four years and worked at DuPage Convalescent Home. She was stabbed in the back of the neck and strangled.

Valentina Pasion. She was twenty-three, a Philippine citizen and graduate of a nursing school in the Philippines. She was in the United States as part of an exchange program and had just started working at the hospital on June 5, along with a hundred other nurses from the Philippines Republic who were working in various U.S. hospitals. She had been stabbed in the neck.

Merlita Gargullo. She was twenty-two, from Santa Cruz in the Philippines, and was stabbed and strangled. Her body was found draped over that of Valentina Pasion.

Patricia Matusek. At twenty, she was the youngest of the nurses. She was a swimming champion, and after graduation from nursing school, intended to work at Chicago's Children's Memorial Hospital.

Gloria Davy. She was twenty-three, a very pretty girl, and it would be learned later that the killer had paid special attention to her—and likely for a reason that went beyond her beauty.

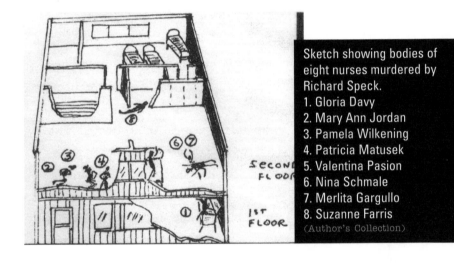

Sketch showing bodies of eight nurses murdered by Richard Speck.
1. Gloria Davy
2. Mary Ann Jordan
3. Pamela Wilkening
4. Patricia Matusek
5. Valentina Pasion
6. Nina Schmale
7. Merlita Gargullo
8. Suzanne Farris
(Author's Collection)

The crime was a stunning, horrific outrage, and the media, police, and politicians reacted strongly. It was not just that eight people had been murdered. It was that they were nurses. Caregivers. People who loved their fellow man enough to do a job that sometimes could be upsetting in the extreme.

The area was flooded with detectives, canvassing the area, dusting the house for prints, and setting up a huge perimeter for miles around the townhouse and questioning everyone within it to try to get a lead on who the killer might be. They talked to the only living witness and got a description of the killer, who Ms. Amurao described as being a lanky Caucasian with dishwater-blond hair, heavy lips, blue eyes, and bad skin. He talked with a southern drawl and spoke softly in a non-threatening way.

Ms. Amurao sat down with the police artist Otis Rathel and detailed what the man looked like, as far as she could remember. The next day, the likeness was published not only on the front page of the Chicago papers, but on the front pages of many other U.S. papers as well. As it turned out, Rathel's sketch bore a striking resemblance to the man who was the killer.

Police had many questions to ask Ms. Amurao, not the least of which was how a lone killer managed to kill eight young nurses. Admittedly, they were female and could not be expected to overpower a man on a one-to-one basis, but together they could have easily done it.

Amurao explained that the killer had been cunning. Ms. Amurao and two other nurses, Valentina Pasion and Merlita Gargullo, had answered a knock at the door. The man standing in the doorway was holding a knife in one hand and a gun in the other. He reeked of alcohol. He spoke in a soothing voice and told the women that he would not harm them, that he was just interested in their money. The nurses let him in.

He told them that he needed to tie them up, that he needed their money because he was going to New Orleans. He herded the three women ahead of him at gunpoint. They went upstairs to a back bedroom, where there were three more nurses. Keeping up his soothing chatter, he ordered them to lie on the floor. He took a sheet off of one of the beds and cut it into strips. In turn, he tied each of the women until they were all immobilized. Later, in examining the knots on the hands, police noted that they were good square knots, and the person doing them knew enough to have the palms facing out: it would be almost impossible for the victims to untie themselves because the fingers were facing away from the knots. He kept talking to them.

At around 11:30, Gloria Davy returned from a date. Speck marched her up to a back bedroom. At around midnight two more nurses, Suzanne Farris and Mary Ann Jordan, who was just a visitor, returned to the townhouse. He bound them, too.

Now, with nine girls bound, the carnage began—though the girls didn't know it. The killer untied the feet of Pamela Wilkening and led her from the room. Shortly thereafter, Corazon Amurao heard a deep "ahh," and then nothing. The killer had stabbed Pamela in the breasts then strangled her.

Over the next few hours, the killer repeated the procedure over and over, at one point taking two of the girls out at the same time and killing them almost immediately. No one knows for sure why the girls didn't attempt to free themselves, but it is likely that they rationalized their situation. Nothing was going to happen. After all, the killer kept reassuring them.

But one girl didn't believe the man's assurances and was terrified—Corazon Amurao. She felt she was in grave danger, that he was going to kill the girls, and she did what she could. She argued that they should try to do something, free themselves and resist, but she lost the argument and then did the only thing she could do: she rolled over and buried herself deep under one of the beds, hoping against hope that the killer wouldn't remember how many girls there were.

Sometime around three in the morning, only one girl was left visible in the room: Gloria Davy, the pretty brunette. From her vantage point under the bed, Corazon Amurao could see the killer with Gloria. "I saw," she was to say later in court, "that he, was removing Miss Davy's jeans . . . then I . . . saw that he was already on top of Miss Davy [Amurao paused, crying hard]

. . . I saw [he] was on top of Miss Davy. I put my face down. And then I heard the bedsprings moving. . . . After a few minutes he asked, 'Will you please put your legs around my back?' . . . I heard it [the movement of springs] for twenty, twenty-five minutes . . . about five minutes after the bedsprings stopped I looked up and saw [them gone]." Either before or after he killed Davy downstairs, the killer mutilated her anus with an object of some sort.

At any moment, Corazon Amurao thought that the killer was going to come into the room, look under the bed, and find her. She waited and waited, rigid with fear, for him to come back. At five o'clock the alarm went off and she expected him to turn it off. But he didn't. The alarm ran on and on until it finally ran down. Amurao still waited. She waited another hour, terrified that he might still be on the premises.

Shaking, she finally got out from under the bed and went outside the room—and tried to avert her eyes from the slaughter around her, her friends everywhere bathed in blood, the smell palpable from bowels that had relaxed. Finally, she made her way into the bedroom, knocked the screen out of the window, climbed out on the ledge, and started to scream.

Over a hundred detectives started to work on the case, as well as ten forensics technicians, who scoured the townhouse for evidence. They canvassed within the perimeter, visiting bars, gas stations, hotels, showing the sketch of the killer. They had good luck fast. An attendant in a gas station remembered a man who looked like the person in the sketch, who had a southern drawl, and who told the attendant he was a seaman looking for work at the National Maritime Union, which was just a few blocks from 2319 East 100th Street.

The cops sped to the union and had more luck. The man apparently was looking for work to earn enough money to get to New Orleans, the same place the killer had told the nurses he was going. And there was something else: his application for work had been discarded in a wastebasket at the union. Fortunately, the wastebasket had not been emptied yet, and the police ferreted through the trash and came up with the crumpled application. On it was a name that was to become infamous: Richard Franklin Speck.

The cops took the prints off the application and sent them to the FBI, along with thirty-one prints from the townhouse that did not belong to the nurses. Word came back quickly: the prints from inside the house belonged, indeed, to Richard Speck, a Dallas-bred small-time criminal who had been arrested twenty-seven times and had previously done time in Huntsville Prison for burglary. Richard Franklin Speck was no longer small-time.

After the killings, Speck wandered down to the skid row section of Chicago and went on a round of boozing, pill popping, and consorting with prostitutes. The stories of the nurses' killings were all over the papers, and at one point Speck heard two men in a bar talking about the killings and said, "I hope they catch the son of a bitch." Apparently he did not know that he had killed them, but he found out. Within two days of the killings, his picture—and his identity—were on the front page of most of the nation's newspapers.

Continuing to booze and pop pills, on the night of July 16 he finally ended up in a flophouse called the Starr Hotel at 524 West Madison Street in a fifth-floor room, where he slashed his right wrist and his left arm. He staggered out of his room and people saw that he was bleeding. An ambulance was called, and he was taken to Cook County Hospital at around 12:30 a.m.

The doctor who treated him there, Leroy Smith, asked his name.

"Richard Speck," he replied.

Within minutes, the police were on their way.

At the trial, the most dramatic testimony of all was that of Corazon Amurao, who pointed him out as the killer. The jury took all of forty-three minutes to convict him, and he was sentenced to death. In probing who Speck was and why he killed the nurses, prison psychiatrist Marvin Ziporyn interviewed Speck at length. He learned that Speck had been born in Kirkwood, Illinois, in 1941. His father, whom he had adored, died young, and his mother remarried and moved to Dallas. There was no love lost between the stepfather and Speck, and Speck once hit his stepfather. He loved his mother in an almost saintlike way, but simultaneously harbored deep anger against her for marrying the stepfather. Ziporyn called it the "Madonna/prostitute" complex.

It was an anger that was to ferment for years, never emerging. In fact, Speck was one of those people whose rage never emerged until he had sufficient booze and pills, and then the floodgates of his rage would open and he would become cunning and extremely violent. Often, he would awaken after having assaulted someone and not even remember it.

Speck's feelings of being deserted by his mother may have been made worse by his marriage to a woman named Shirley Maloney when he was twenty. They had a little girl, but then his wife left him, taking the little girl with her, and he often said that one day he would kill her. Probably no one will ever know for sure, but this hatred for his wife and mother may have been taken out that night on Gloria Davy.

At one point in his research into the case, Ziporyn visited one of Speck's sisters (Speck had five sisters and three brothers) and asked her if she could think of any reason why Richard would have killed the nurses. "Well, we've discussed this thing in the family over and over [and noticed] something," she replied. "We were looking at the pictures of the nurses and . . . one of them, Gloria Davy, looked just like Richard's wife, Shirley."

It was Ziporyn's theory that perhaps Speck only came to the townhouse to rob the nurses, but that the appearance of Gloria Davy, symbol of Speck's hated mother and his equally hated wife, triggered the homicides.

The Man on the Tower

On Monday, August 1, 1966, one can only surmise what Charles Whitman, twenty-five, a nice-looking, towheaded man, was thinking when he went up to the observation deck at the University of Texas and started shooting people. Even Whitman didn't know—a note he left behind made this clear. Still, it seems safe to say that in his mind he was engaged in some sort of death struggle. He was under threat, and he answered the threat the best way he could. That it was an imagined threat is irrelevant. It was real enough to him for him to shoot innocent people.

Unfortunately for many people strolling along at the University of Texas campus that summer day, Charles Whitman had the means to make a ferocious and deadly stand. He was an ex-Marine familiar with military tactics and hardware, and he knew that the high ground was the best defensive spot for a soldier to be. It was a place that could be protected, defended. While in the Marines, he had qualified as a sharpshooter, one grade below expert. If his imagined enemies were going to take him out, they were going to know he was there first.

Just how much he prepared for this battle, and how long is uncertain. Later, police pieced together some of Whitman's preparations. In a letter that Whitman wrote and which was read after the murderous assault occurred, he stated that he had assembled his weaponry during the night: a knife, a .35-caliber Remington pump rifle, a 30.06 rifle, a .30-caliber reconditioned army carbine, a 9mm Luger, a 6mm Remington with a four-power scope, a .357-magnum, a twelve-gauge sawed-off shotgun, and a large bowie knife. He might have assembled all the weaponry the night before, but certainly he had not come into ownership of these weapons all in one night.

Indeed, at around 9:30 a.m. the morning of the assault, Whitman had bought the carbine, hundreds of rounds of ammunition, and the twelve-gauge shotgun at a Sears Roebuck store on credit. Later, police found three other rifles and two derringers at his home.

The weaponry he had assembled was impressive, everything from automatic weapons that could take out a bunch of charging cops to others that were powerful enough to knock down a charging bull elephant. He also planned to be there some time. He packed the weapons in a marines trunk, along with canned goods, a Thermos of coffee, and toilet paper. He also carried nylon rope, binoculars, an extension cord, a Stilson wrench, adhesive tape, a clock, matches, a three-gallon can of gas, a three-gallon jug of water, and a flashlight with extra batteries.

Charles Whitman, the Texas sniper.
(Author's Collection)

The Carnage Begins

Whatever was going on in Whitman's mind the day he went to the tower, he started "acting out," as psychiatrists say, sometime in the wee hours of that morning. His mother, Mrs. Margaret Whitman, a stocky forty-four-year-old woman, was the first victim. He stabbed her to death in her apartment, number 505 in Penthouse Apartments at 1211 Guadalupe Street, Austin. At the time, she was separated from Whitman's father, C. J. Whitman, who was a well-to-do plumbing contractor in Lake Worth, Florida.

No one knows for sure what happened. His twenty-one-year-old wife, Kathy, who lived with him in Austin at 1001 Shelly Avenue, Apartment A, was his second victim. She was a science teacher at Laneier High School in Austin, and the daughter of a Needville, Texas, rice farmer who was also in the real estate business. He used a knife and gun to end her life.

How his mother and wife fit into Whitman's fantasies is anyone's guess. As mentioned, Whitman didn't know. In fact, he stated this in a note addressed "To whom it may concern." He said that he loved them both and had no idea why he had killed them. The only thing he could think of, said a police official later, was "to save them the embarrassment of what he was going to do."

By midday on August 1, Whitman was ready to put the centerpiece of his plan into action. He was dressed in a white T-shirt and jeans, over which he wore a light gray nylon jumpsuit with many pockets. He loaded his marine's trunk in his 1966 Impala and drove to the university.

A Placid Campus

He got a pass to park in the loading zone of the administration tower parking lot at the northwest corner of the tower. He used a three-wheeled dolly he had rented to pull the footlocker into the building, then trundled it down the tower's main hall to the twin elevators.

Apparently, no one noticed Whitman as he went about his business. Why should they? It was a typical summer day on the campus, hot (ninety-eight degrees and sunny), and summer school was still in session. Whitman himself was an honor student in the architectural school, carrying fourteen credits (heavy for summer school) and maintaining a B average.

The campus buildings, mostly white cement topped by red terra-cotta roofs in the Spanish-style, were dominated by the tower, which was the campus's centerpiece and housed the library as well as administration offices and other facilities. It was the highest point not only on the campus, but in all of Austin. It rose over a hundred yards in the air, with the observation deck about ninety yards off the ground. Indeed, from the vantage point Whitman would take, he would see miles into Austin. And indeed, with the high-powered rifles he had, one police official said later that "a big hunk of Austin could have been a shooting gallery for him."

Whitman rode the elevator to the twenty-seventh floor and exited. He left the footlocker there, then he climbed the two floors to the observation deck. There was a small reception room on the observation deck level. Edna Townsley, fifty-one, was on duty. It was her job to greet and monitor anyone who wanted to go to the observation deck. She was also undoubtedly there to spot people who were of a mind to jump off the tower; it had occasionally served that purpose. Whitman used his gun butt to smash in Townsley's head, then, as she bled profusely, he dragged her behind a couch in the room.

Then a young couple, Don Walden, twenty-two, and his date, Cheryl Botts, eighteen, entered the room from the observation desk.

"Hello," Cheryl Botts said, smiling.

"Hi, how are you?" Whitman said, smiling.

Bizarrely, Whitman let the young couple leave, but he followed them down the stairs to the twenty-seventh floor.

They got on the elevator and were gone, and a moment later the other elevator doors opened. It was another woman, who was there to replace Edna Townsley. Whitman growled at her not to get off the elevator. She didn't. Then Whitman carried the footlocker up to the observation deck.

Some tourists got off at the twenty-seventh floor and two young men, Mark Gabour, nineteen, and his brother Mike, fifteen, bounded up the stairs. Their mother, Mary Frances, and her sister-in-law, Mrs. William Lamport, followed. Bringing up the rear were Mr. Gabour and Mr. Lamport. Mark opened the door to the reception room and a shotgun blasted him and his brother and roared twice more, hitting the women. They all fell backward. In an instant, Mark Gabour was dead and so was Mrs. Lamport. Mrs. Gabour was to survive.

Tower Whitman shot from.
(Author's Collection)

Mr. Gabour and Mr. Lamport fled to one of the rooms on the twenty-seventh floor and locked themselves in. Employees in other rooms also locked themselves in. Whitman barricaded the door to the reception area with some furniture and went to the deck. He opened up the footlocker.

The deck was, indeed, built for observation. It ran around all four sides of the thin column that projected from the top of the building. Each side of the tower had a clock face with white numbers. After every win by the Texas football team, this portion of the tower would be bathed in orange light, the school color.

Bullets from Above

It is hard to know exactly who got shot from the tower first, but it is known that just before the clock struck noon, Whitman used one of the high-powered rifles and started to fire, and people all over the campus started to drop. "He was a hell of a good shot," one cop said later.

A man named Denver Dolman, owner of a bookstore at the edge of the campus grounds a few hundred yards from the tower, was gazing idly out his window. He saw a black kid riding by on a bike toward a meeting and entertainment center in the Texas Union Building, when the bicycle seemed to wobble and the kid fell off.

Then Dolman heard shots and saw other people starting to fall. He saw one young boy run to the doorway of his bookstore and step into the doorway for shelter. A shot cracked and the boy fell dead.

A woman was shot in the head; a bullet crashed through the window of a bookstore, hitting a boy inside in the arm. Many people started to duck for cover, but many people, confused or panicked, did not know what to do. They were killed or wounded as Whitman, using all four sides of the observation deck, fired at will at men, women, and children—it didn't matter. Indeed, one of his victims was an eight-month-old fetus in its mother's womb.

Police Arrive

The police had been notified quickly by two unarmed security guards who had discovered the bodies of the tourists, and by people still trapped in the tower, some making frantic calls to police as the cannonade rang out above them.

The police, under the direction of Chief C. A. Miles, immediately cordoned off the campus area and desperately tried to clear the campus, which at the time had thousands of students going about their everyday business. Immediately the police knew they had a real problem. Whitman had chosen his high ground well. Not only was it high, but there was no way to approach the building under cover. The terrain on all four sides of the building was flat, lined with roads, paths, grass—no one could approach without great risk of being picked off.

And the shooter obviously did not shy away from killing the authorities. A law student, Leland Ammons, says that he was standing behind Billy Speed, an Austin policeman, and suddenly Speed went down, the bullet either going between pillars they were standing behind or ricocheting. The bullet killed Speed.

The only thing that could operate safely in the open was an armored vehicle, which was able to pick up some of the wounded, but the flat terrain meant that the police could not get close to the tower entrance without putting themselves in mortal peril, particularly with a sharpshooter like Whitman. Other victims, because of their position close to the tower, lay dead or dying with no one able to get close enough to help.

The cops were frantic and were willing to try anything. A very brave pilot and sharpshooter in a plane circled the tower and tried to take Whitman out, but his shots drove it off. Police, joined by masses of other city cops, fired at the tower, many trying to ricochet bullets off the drain behind where Whitman had his main position, and at Whitman directly, whose blond head would pop up when he was ready to fire. But the cops' shots would smash off the facade, ineffectually kicking up puffs of cement. And people were still getting shot. Police didn't know what to do. They were at a standstill.

A Man Cooking a Steak

The solution to the problem was to come from a man cooking a steak, twenty-nine-year-old Romero Martinez. Martinez was a patrolman with the Austin Police Department and heard about the sniper on the radio as he was making lunch. Though it was his day off, he rushed—against the entreaties of family members—to the scene after heeding a call from Chief Miles for all available police to come in.

The situation remained at a standstill, and the gunman— still unidentified—was firing more or less at will, though it would be later determined that he had done most of the damage in the first twenty minutes; after that, people had their wits about them and took cover, and he also had to be concerned with return fire from police.

Someone had to get inside the tower building, up on the deck with him. Someone had the idea that they could travel conduits that went underground and into the tower building. It was settled on, and Officer Martinez was selected to lead a group which included three other officers: Jerry Jay, Houston McCoy, and George Sheppard. They were accompanied by Allen Crum, a civilian who worked in the area; he knew the way in and was deputized on the spot.

In the Building

They got into the tower building without a problem, emerging at the floor where the elevators were located. They took the elevator to the twenty-sixth floor: they had to be ready for an unpleasant surprise when the doors opened. Martinez had a walkie-talkie linked to a small plane circling the tower, telling the men in the tower of the location of the shooter, who would occasionally switch positions. Who knew if he might suddenly decide to leave the deck and go down to the twenty-seventh or even the twenty-sixth floor?

But Whitman didn't leave the observation deck, and Martinez and the other cops and Crum were able to get off the elevator without Whitman knowing. Now the problem was taking Whitman by surprise. Keeping in touch with the walkie-talkies, the men inched their way up the stairs and past the dead victims, a savage reminder of what the man on the observation deck was capable of doing. The chopper told them Whitman was on the northwest corner of the deck. They knew there was absolutely no way they could completely take him by surprise.

They pushed in the door to the reception room, gently easing the furniture out of the way. They paused by the door, waited, and then they rushed out onto the deck, spreading out. Crum fired a shot that apparently got Whitman's attention. When he turned, Romero Martinez was face-to-face with Whitman. He and Whitman both exchanged fire, and then Martinez squeezed off all the shots from his service revolver and Whitman went down. McCoy rushed through the door and fired at Whitman with a shotgun, and then Martinez, a little crazed himself by the terrible confrontation, grabbed the shotgun and fired it again, a blast into Whitman's head.

The sniper was dead, and Martinez waved a green flag to alert other cops that it was over. A short time later, Whitman, bathed in blood, was carried from the tower building. He had been on the observation deck for an hour and twenty minutes, and when the grim final tally was in, he had killed sixteen people and wounded thirty-three. In his crazed mind, they were all the enemy.

Why?

People trying to find out why a twenty-five-year-old graduate student would turn into a mass murderer one sunny day in August found the usual array of raised eyebrows, outstretched hands, and clichés, including one theorist who opined that maybe it was because he was taking too many credits.

How could he do it? When he was very young, he had been an altar boy and an Eagle Scout. He had been a Marine—honorably discharged—and indeed was going to the U of T with the aid of a Marines scholarship. How could an ex-Marine do this? He had no disciplinary problems at school. He suffered only the normal angst, according to his graduate school counselor, Leonard Kriesle, of someone who was unsure of what he wanted to do. "He was vacillating," says Kriesle, "between artistic endeavors and engineering endeavors."

There was one black mark on his otherwise unbesmirched life. He was court-martialed in the Marines for lending money for profit and gambling, but still he received an honorable discharge. There was perhaps a hint of violence in Whitman—at one point, he served as a bouncer in a local bar. On the surface, however, there was nothing to indicate that he was a homicidal maniac. But the surface, as these stories repeatedly show, does not usually tell the real story.

Whitman versus His Father

The one person Whitman hated above all others was his father. In one of the notes he left behind, he said that he hated his father with a "mortal passion." His mother had recently separated from his father, and he was constantly calling Whitman to intercede, to help work something out so he could get back with his wife. Why his father should appeal to Charles is a mystery. The psychiatrist who spoke with Whitman just a week before he erupted said he described his father as "brutal, domineering, and extremely demanding of other members of the family."

The psychiatrist said Whitman loved his wife and mother very much, but Whitman admitted that he had on occasion assaulted his wife physically. In other words, he was like his father in some respects. Whitman's visit to the psychiatrist was precipitated by his parents' reaction. It upset him greatly and perhaps fed a personality that was characterized by the doctor as "oozing with hostility."

Whitman told the doctor that something was happening to him and he didn't know what it was and didn't seem to be himself.

In an ideal world (or, perhaps, in today's world), he would have been hospitalized immediately.

Slaughter on Hamilton Avenue

From the outside, on Easter Sunday, March 30, 1975, the house at 635 Minor Avenue in the small Ohio town of Hamilton seemed perfectly normal. However, on the inside was a different, much more gruesome story—the bodies of an entire family lay slaughtered, adults and children, eleven in all. The only surviving member was forty-one-year-old James Ruppert, the shooter.

Investigation revealed that Ruppert, an alcoholic and also completely paranoid, was constantly being picked on by his brother Leonard and mother, Charity, and continually taunted for his inadequacies. Fantasies had been building within him for a long time, and by now he was sure that everyone was against him and had to be dealt with. So on that Easter morning he came from his room upstairs, armed with a rifle and three handguns, and he started to shoot people at point-blank range. He fired a total of forty-four times. Then he simply waited for the police. Ruppert was tried and convicted, receiving two consecutive life sentences.

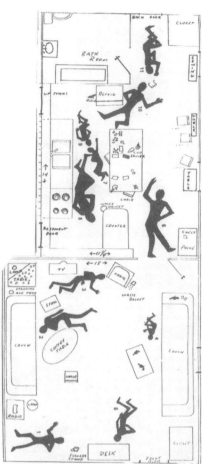

James Ruppert, *center*, mass murderer of his family in Hamilton, Ohio.
(Author's Collection)

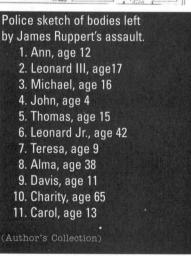

Police sketch of bodies left by James Ruppert's assault.
1. Ann, age 12
2. Leonard III, age17
3. Michael, age 16
4. John, age 4
5. Thomas, age 15
6. Leonard Jr., age 42
7. Teresa, age 9
8. Alma, age 38
9. Davis, age 11
10. Charity, age 65
11. Carol, age 13

(Author's Collection)

Chapter 6
Criminal
Investigation

Notable Quote

I always get a kick out of these shows that pinpoint time of death. That's impossible. There are just too many variables. The best way to tell when someone dies is to find the person who saw him last when he/she was alive.

—Eddie Meagher, NYPD Crime Scene Photographer

The Importance of a Roach

On November 11, 1934, Delia and Albert Budd of New York City received a letter that looked as though it might have something to do with their daughter Grace, who had been kidnapped by a kindly old man who said his name was Frank Howard. They turned the letter over to Will King, the dogged New York detective who had worked the case every day since the child had been taken six years earlier. He carefully opened the letter and read it. It was abominable. Howard recounted how, six years earlier, he got the Budds' permission to take their ten-year-old daughter Grace to a birthday party. But it wasn't a party. He had taken the little girl to an abandoned house in Greenburgh, New York, where he strangled her, cut her up, and brought her to his apartment in Manhattan, where he had cooked and eaten her over a nine-day period.

Will King was able to make out a crossed-out return address on the envelope that said NYPCBA, the abbreviation for The New York Private Chauffeurs Benevolent Association. King investigated and eventually discovered that one of the Association members had stolen a few envelopes and left some in a room in a flophouse on West 52nd street in Manhattan. They had been placed on a shelf high on the wall above the bed. King went there and described Mr. Howard to the landlady, who said the description matched that of a Mr. Albert Fish, who periodically rented a room. When King checked Fish's signature in the registration book, he was electrified: he didn't need to be a graphologist to know is was the same writing used by "Frank Howard" in his awful missive.

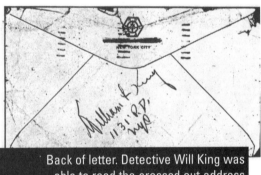

Back of letter. Detective Will King was able to read the crossed out address and track Fish down.
(Author's Collection)

Albert Fish, *left*, and his nemesis Will King
(Author's Collection)

Chain-smoking, subsisting on canned goods, Will King waited in a room in the flophouse for Fish to return, and one day Fish did—and King arrested Fish.

Later, Fish was to tell King that he didn't know there were envelopes on the shelf until he stood up on the bed to swat a roach on the wall and saw them. So, of course, he used one for the letter to the Budds. The roach, in effect, had helped solve one of the most notorious cases of the twentieth century.

Ultimately, in the winter, Fish led the police to the house in Westchester where the killing had occurred. He showed detectives where he had buried the parts he didn't want, and they used pickaxes and shovels to break through the frozen ground until they found Grace's head and various bones.

Investigative Jargon

1. **Busywork:** Routine, repetitive work involved in a criminal investigation.

   In criminal investigations, much checking of tiny details (such as merchandise receipts) and other repetitive work is required; it keeps police very busy, but usually it fails to reap concrete dividends. Sometimes, however, busywork pays big. For example, when the "Mad Bomber" terrorized New York City in the 1950s, checking utility records turned up the handwriting of an ex-employee that matched the writing on notes the bomber sent. It resulted in the apprehension, arrest, and conviction of George Metesky, ending the terror that had swept the city.

2. **Chain of evidence:** Evidence collected and catalogued in a homicide; also called chain of custody. It is important for investigators of homicides to keep everything in logical, consistent order when establishing their cases.

3. **Chalk the Site:** To outline a corpse on the ground with chalk. This is standard procedure in a homicide investigation. Police use chalk outlines not only to show where a body was located, but also to mark where small bits of evidence, such as bullet casings and blood, were found. But chalking must only be done after the crime scene photographs are taken; otherwise,

says Vernon J. Geberth in Practical Homicide Investigation, the defense attorneys can maintain that the crime scene was contaminated. Geberth uses another term that is not yet used universally but may well find its way into police lingo: "chalk fairy." One photo in his book is captioned: "Here you see the deceased lying in the position in which he was found. The crime scene photo may possibly be 'inadmissible.' While the first officers were securing the scene, a 'chalk fairy' suddenly had the irresistible impulse to draw chalk lines around the body."

Here, cups mark the spots where bullet casings were thrown. (Dave Green)

4. **Coroner:** The official in charge of determining the cause of suspicious deaths.

In some locales, the coroner is the same as the M.E., or medical examiner, and actually determines the cause of death. In other places, coroners are strictly political appointees who simply move the body to a funeral home. In those cases, the coroner is not personally qualified to determine the cause of death, but instead the coroner hires a qualified pathologist to do so.

5. **Corpus Delecti:** The body of a murder victim. Like a number of other law enforcement terms, this one is Latin and derives from Roman law. Originally, it meant the sum of the physical evidence that shows that a crime has been committed, but over time it came to refer to the body.

6. **Algor mortis:** The cooling of the body after death. How quickly a body cools depends on many factors, but it generally takes about forty hours for a corpse to cool to room temperature. Over the first few hours, body temperature drops 3 to 3.5 degrees per hour, then about one degree per hour until it stabilizes at the temperature outside the body.

   On television it always seems possible to determine exact time of death by scientific means, but this is rarely possible in the real world because of circumstantial variables. For example, the body temperature will change much more rapidly in warm weather than in cold, because destructive bacteria grow faster in warm weather.

7. **Bag the hands:** Encasing the hands of a homicide victim in bags. Bagging the hands of a homicide victim is standard procedure. This helps preserve any trace material, such as skin or hair that might be on the victim's hands or under their fingernails. When a victim is fighting for his or her life, a natural reaction is to defend with the hands, scratching or grabbing the perpetrator. Minute quantities of the attacker's DNA could be preserved, evidence which can be crucial in identifying the culprit or culprits.

   Movies or television often show the victim's hands bagged in some sort of plastic wrap or plastic bag, but real-life investigators prefer paper bags because plastic tends to speed up putrefaction, thus cutting into time for analysis. In addition, plastic does not allow the hands to "breathe," and the lack of air may alter the trace evidence.

8. **Grounder:** An easy case to prosecute or solve; also known as a ground ball. The term is used by both prosecutors and cops. For example, if an assault has occurred and the prosecutor

has the weapon involved, fingerprints on the weapon, and three eyewitnesses, that's a grounder. It will be easy to get a conviction. For homicide investigators, such cases also tend to include family disputes gone bad or a fight that escalates into a homicide; the witnesses and obvious motives make these cases easy to prove. Everyone knows each other, and there is usually a history of chaos before the homicide occurs. People around the family know who killed whom and why.

9. **Hit-and-run:** An automobile accident in which the responsible driver flees the scene. The first use of this phrase was recorded in 1924 by Scientific American, in an article that envisioned eliminating hit-and-run accidents if the bumper could somehow be mechanically linked to the vehicle's ability to move or not move. "With the bumper in circuit with the ignition, there would be no more 'hit and run' driving." The idea, it seems, was that if the car couldn't go forward after hitting a person or another vehicle, no one could really run away.

While most people think of a hit-and-run as a very serious crime, it is not viewed so by the law. In fact, it is only a Class 1 misdemeanor, which only carries a penalty of up to a year in prison: the only way a serious penalty can be administered is to upgrade the crime to "reckless homicide." For example, if you are driving recklessly in an area where it's clear that you shouldn't—say, a crowded street—you can receive up to five years.

Accident investigators say that they approach all fatal accidents as murders. "You'd be surprised," said one cop, "on how many people are killed deliberately [with cars]. These days we find that a lot of drug dealers take each other out this way."

10. **Complaint:** A formal allegation against a person or persons. The complaint is normally in writing, except in homicides, where it is implied: I've been murdered, and I want something done about it. Police slang for a complaint is *squeal*.

11. **Complainant:** The person who files a criminal complaint to the police. The term was first used by Shakespeare in the play Henry VII in 1498. "The same complainuyant not proving the mater of his seid bill to be true."

The Origins of the Ten Most Wanted List

The FBI's "ten most wanted" fugitive program was instituted in March of 1950 by J. Edgar Hoover as a result of the publicity generated by an article about the "toughest guys" sought by the FBI. The ten names are determined through information provided by the 56 FBI field offices. The fugitives remain on the list until they are captured or if charges against them are dropped. Only seven women have appeared on the ten most wanted list since its inception.

The most media attention involving the ten most wanted list was in the search for Andrew Cunanan, who, in roughly a three-month period, killed five men, among them fashion designer Gianni Versace. Cunanan ultimately committed suicide in Miami as the FBI was closing in.

Town without Witnesses

Ken Rex McElroy, who lived and died violently in Skidmore, Missouri, was the town bully. He was a hulking bear of a man, and he had a very bad and quick temper. He didn't care how old you were or who you were—if he thought you crossed him, things would get ugly. Things reached a melting point one day when a storekeeper accused McElroy's daughter of stealing a piece of candy. McElroy got his shotgun and shot the man in

Crime Can Be Funny

A Nasty Trick

I was with another NYPD rookie named Johnston, and we were left at the scene of a DOA to await the M.E. and the meat wagon. The DOA, who looked like he died of natural causes, was on the floor, between the bed and the wall. Johnston was a former worker at the morgue and knew most of the M.E.s. He recognized the responding M.E.'s name and decided he was going to play a joke on him. So Johnston took off his shirt, rubbed talcum powder on his face and upper body, got into the bed and pulled the covers over himself. A short while later the M.E. came in and asked where the body was, and I directed him to the bedroom. The M.E. started asking questions I couldn't answer about medications and so forth, then he pulled back the blanket on the bed, leaned over and started to inspect the body. Johnston reached up with both hands and grabbed the M.E.'s throat . . . and the M.E. fainted! I thought my career was toast. Amazingly, when the M.E. came to, he remembered nothing! "Must have been something you ate, doc," we told him.

the neck. The storekeeper survived, but McElroy was tried and convicted of assault. Then a judge relapsed McElroy on bail pending his appeal, and the town started to tremble again.

On July 10, 1981, McElroy came into town to appear in court on charges he had violated his bond agreement by carrying a loaded gun—a carbine with a bayonet—into a local bar. At the same time, about sixty townspeople were meeting with the county sheriff and mayor to determine what could be done to stop McElroy. Then, someone relayed the information that McElroy and his wife, Trena, were having a drink at the D & G, a local bar.

Favorite Song

One of murderer Gary Gilmore's favorite songs was "Don't Fear the Reaper" by the group Blue Oyster Cult.

When the couple came out of the bar and got in their pickup truck, the townspeople were there. The crowd clustered around. Suddenly, Trena shouted,

"They've got a gun!" But it was too late. Someone shot McElroy multiple times in the head with a high-powered rifle. He was killed instantly.

Trena promptly identified the shooter as Del Clement, owner of the D & G bar. And though there were dozens of witnesses, no one would come forward and corroborate what she said. Because no one ever did come forward, ultimately the coroner refused to issue an arrest warrant. His wife said McElroy knew that someone was going to shoot him, but he showed no fear. One of the townspeople said that he was surprised that Ken Rex lived as long as he did.

Lizzie Borden, Not Guilty

Lizzie Borden, the accused axe murderess who spawned the famous children's rhyme, "Lizzie Borden took an axe . . .," was actually found not guilty at her trial.

Q&A

Q: What country has the highest murder rate?

A: Brazil leads with almost 45,000 murders a year. Next in line are South Africa and Russia. (Source: UPI and Xinhua News Agency)

A Clever Way to Commit Murder

There are, of course, many different ways to murder someone, but one of the cleverest we've ever heard was perpetrated by a young Japanese boy in feudal times who killed a powerful warlord. As it happens, the father of the boy got into conflict with a warlord, whose word was law at the time. The warlord killed the man, and then took his boy as a sexual plaything.

This abuse went on for some time, but the boy brewed a plan for killing the warlord. One night, the boy stole off and paid a covert visit to an X-rated section of the local town. About a week later, he thought the time was right to try to kill the warlord. The warlord was asleep and his guards were at the lowest ebb of their alert. The boy, who had obtained a knife, snuck his way to the warlord's bed, ready to drive the knife into the warlord's heart. But the boy didn't count on the warlord having purposely loosened boards around his bed, and when one squeaked, the guards appeared instantly.

The warlord was not amused by attempts on his life—the kid was ultimately boiled to death. But before the boy died, he told the warlord that, though the warlord was about to kill him, he, the boy, had already killed the warlord. The warlord had no idea of what the boy was talking about.

A few months later, the warlord found out. A note was delivered, and it alerted the warlord that the kid had gone to a brothel in the town of Nora and had sexual interaction with one of the prostitutes who had what was known as the "Geisha Disease"—syphilis. And had he transmitted it to the warlord, first a sore would appear on his privates, then rashes and various eruptions would occur. The warlord would get weaker and weaker and finally be driven mad with pain by the growths inside his head. When he started to experience these things, the warlord killed himself.

In World War II, according to writer Guy deMaupaussant, French prostitutes infected with syphilis made it a point to have sex with as many German officers as they could—and many of the officers died.

Crime Can Be Funny

Alive Works Better

When I was in the NYPD Police Academy, they taught me that if there are severed body parts at a crime scene or an auto accident, pick up the part, pack it in ice, and get it to the hospital, because they may be able to reattach it.

So there was a car accident in town and a guy was decapitated, and the first cop on the scene packed the accident victim's head in ice. When I arrived, I saw this and I said to the cop, "What the hell are you going to do with that?"

"In the Academy they tell us to pack parts in ice to reattach them."

"Yeah, you jackass. But if they reattach this head, think the guy's coming back to life?"

Not As Good As It Seems

Many murderers who employ poison as their weapon of choice favor arsenic, but it's not that perfect a means to murder. For one, you can't put arsenic in a cold beverage without it being visible—the white powder will float on top. If the poisoner uses a hot beverage, the poison will dissolve very well, but when the beverage cools, it will float to the top as visible sediment. If the beverage has milk in it, such as hot tea, coffee, or cocoa, the arsenic will curdle the milk.

Arsenic is also unreliable as a killer. While there have been cases of some people dying after receiving an infinitesimal amount, such as two grams, one woman who attempted suicide took 230 grains and her only complaint was indigestion for three days.

If foul play is suspected when someone dies, it is a fairly easy procedure for the medical examiner to determine if someone has been poisoned with arsenic. Residue will linger indefinitely in fingernails, bones, and other part of the body. In terms of a victim detecting it when it is used on them as a murder weapon, arsenic is virtually tasteless and a very small dose can cause death. It is also possible to give arsenic to someone in small doses over a period of time—it will build up in the body and eventually cause death. The person will get sicker and sicker as the arsenic takes effect, and the symptoms appear to be any of a number of nonlethal, everyday maladies. Arsenic first came into existence in the eighth century, and for the next several centuries it was not able to be detected— imagine how many victims it may have claimed during this time that we'll never know about!

Movies Made About True Crimes

- *Murder in New Hampshire (1991).* Helen Hunt as Pamela Smart, who seduced a teenage boy named Billy Flynn, played by Chad Allen, and persuaded him to kill her husband.
- *Martha Inc. (2003).* Cybill Shepherd as Martha Stewart. *A Woman Scorned (1992).* Meredith Baxter as Betty Broderick, who murdered her ex-husband.
- *The Preppie Murder (1988).* The murder of Jennifer Levin, played by Lara Flynn Boyle, with William Baldwin as her murderer, Robert Chambers.
- *The Patty Hearst Story (1988).* Natasha Richardson as Patty Hearst.
- *Billionaire Boys Club (1987).* Judd Nelson as Joe Hunt, who committed two murders to finance the investments of his club.
- *The Positively True Adventures of the Alleged Texas Cheerleader Murdering Mom (1993).* Holly Hunter as Wanda Holloway, who wanted to eliminate competition for her cheerleader daughter.
- *Getting Away With Murder (2000).* The murder of JonBenet Ramsey, starring Julia Granstrom as JonBenet.
- *Honor Thy Father and Mother (1994).* Starring David Beron and Billy Warlock as the Menendez brothers, who were convicted of the shooting deaths of their mother and father.
- *The Perfect Husband (2004).* Dean Cain as Scott Petersen, Tracy Middendorf as Amber Frey.

Chapter 7
Rape

You're Not His Type

One day Dr. Ed Baker (name changed), a psychologist at the Avenal Diagnostic Treatment Center ("Diagnostic Treatment Center" being a euphemism for a sex-offender prison) in Avenal, New Jersey, was having dinner with his wife at a little Italian restaurant in the town where they live. Baker waved to a big man sitting at another table, then he stood up.

"I'll be back in a minute," he said.

Baker walked over to the other table, shook hands with the man, and then Baker pointed to his wife and the man smiled and waved. She waved back, and then Baker returned to the table.

"Who's that?" Baker's wife asked.

Baker told her the man's name.

"Where do you know him from?"

"The prison."

"What was he in for?"

"Rape."

Mrs. Baker almost dropped her linguini.

"But he saw me. He might go after me."

"No, he won't."

"Why not?"

"Because you're a small woman. He likes 'Big Units.' "

"What's that?"

"Big women. Most sex offenders like a specific type of person—other people don't need to be afraid."

Q&A

Q: Where does the word rape come from?

A: From the Latin *rapere*: to seize or take by force.

Q: How frequently are women sexually assaulted?

A: Every two and a half minutes, a woman in America is sexually assaulted.

Q: What is a rapist's true motive?

A: It is well known among law enforcement investigators that what drives a rapist is primarily a desire to dominate and humiliate his victim rather than achieve sexual gratification.

Q: How many American women have been rape victims?

A: One in six American women has been the victim of a completed or attempted rape.

Q: How many rapists know their victims?

A: Fifty percent. Rapists who know their victim either casually or intimately are far more common than is generally believed. The act is known as acquaintance, date, or convenience rape. One myth is that such rapes are less traumatic than when the victim does not know the assaulter. In fact, the sense of betrayal and shock is likely to be greater.

Q: Has rape always been seen as a crime?

A: For ages, rape was seen in most cultures less as a crime against a particular girl or woman than against the male figure she "belonged" to. Thus, the penalty for rape was often a fine payable to the father or the husband whose "goods" were damaged.

Q: How many rapists use weapons?

A: In 2004, 8 percent of all rapes/sexual assaults involved the use of a weapon.

Q: What are date rape drugs?

A: Drugs used to render victims unconscious. The drugs often have no color, smell, or taste and are easily added to flavored drinks without the victim's knowledge. There are at least three date rape drugs: GHB (gamma hydroxybutyric acid), Rohypnol (flunitrazepam), and Ketamine (ketamine hydrochloride). GHB has a few forms: a liquid with no odor or color, a white powder, and a pill. Rohypnol ("roofies") is a pill and dissolves in liquids. The pills are now made so that they turn blue when added to liquids, but the old ones, with no discernable color, are still available to those who look hard. Ketamine ("special K") is a white powder.

The drugs usually work quickly, but the length of time the effects last varies. It depends on how much of the drug is taken and if the drug is mixed with other substances, like alcohol. Alcohol can worsen the drug's effects and can cause more health problems. Also, one drug—GHB—can be made by people in their homes, so you don't know what's in it. These drugs all work essentially the same way, with the victim rendered unconscious and with no memory of the rape. Some of the drugs can cause death.

The drugs are legal in the U.S. but are designed to be used for other purposes, such as an anesthetic for humans and animals.

Other Types of Rape

1. **Marital Rape:** Forcible, unwanted sex in a marriage. Until 1973, there was no such thing as marital rape. When people got married, a woman was automatically considered to be the property of the man she married, and the state of being married gave a husband access to his wife for sex on a permanent basis. But in 1973, it became a crime for a husband to rape—have forcible sex—with his wife, first in North Dakota, followed by the other states.

2. **Statutory Rape:** Sex with a minor under the age of consent, even if the minor agrees (consents) to allow the act.

3. **Blitz rape:** An unexpected sexual assault committed by a stranger. It is one of the terms coined by Ann Burgess and Lynda Holmstrom in their studies in the early 1970s of rape victims at Beth Israel Hospital in Boston. When women think of rape, it is the unexpected assault that most often comes to mind and is most feared because of the level of violence with which it is associated. "Blitz" is a German word that means "lightning."

4. **Acquaintance rape:** As mentioned earlier, a rape committed by someone known to the victim.

5. **Incest:** The rape of a child by an elder relative. Psychologists estimate that 40 million adults in the U.S., 15 million of those being men, were sexually abused by parents, close relatives, or other elders—of both genders—on whom they were dependent. The victims of incest are often called "secret survivors" by psychologists, as often they are unable or unwilling to tell anyone about

these rapes due to implicit or explicit threats by the adult rapist, fear of abandonment by the rapist, and/or overwhelming shame. Since the signs of these insidious rapes are usually invisible except to trained professionals, these victims often suffer ongoing offenses in silence until attaining independence from the adult rapist. By that time, the statute of limitations is often long-expired, and the child-rapist is able to escape justice. In addition, people who rape their own children are considered less culpable, legally, than other rapists in most U.S. states. There has also been substantial controversy over the claim that childhood rape becomes repressed memories that can later come to the surface.

Can't Talk to Rapists

The Avenal Diagnostic Treatment Center has two kinds of sexual offenders: pedophiles and rapists. Dr. Baker says there's one main difference between the two: "Pedophiles will talk to you, have a conversation," Baker said, "but not rapists. They're just too angry all the time and are always looking for ways to vent."

6. **Group Rape (also known as gang or pack rape):** This occurs when a group of people participate in the rape of a single victim. It is far more physically damaging to the victim than a single-person rape, and in some jurisdictions is punished more severely. The term, "gang bang" was a synonym for gang rape during the times when sexual activity in general was considered taboo; however, with the advent of the pornography industry and relaxed sexual tensions, it is now often used as a slang term for consensual group sex. Also, the term group rape is now often preferred to gang rape, as the word gang can have racial connotations when used to describe the alleged acts of minority defendants.

According to sexual crime profiler Roy Hazelwood, gang rape "involves three or more offenders, and you always have a leader and a reluctant participant. Those are extremely violent, and what you find is that they're playing for each other's approval. It gets into a pack mentality and can be horrendous."

7. **Gray Rape:** There is often more difficulty in securing conviction against an assailant who is known by the victim due to the nature of the situation—the only evidence is basically the victim's word against the alleged assailant's. In what is colloquially described as a gray rape case, the victim is unable to demonstrate nonconsent, although he or she expresses displeasure at the encounter. Contributing factors to gray rape include poor communication by either party, misleading or (possibly deliberate) misreading of body language, or the feeling by one party of being unsure or unable to express what they want (which may be due to many reasons, including pressure from the assailant). The standard of proof required for nonconsensual sexual activity is often harder to meet (or easier to deny) than when two strangers meet, or where there has been violence.

Can a Woman Rape a Man?

While the universal perception of rape involves the sexually aggressive male violating the female, there exist numerous cases of women raping men. Criminologists feel a large majority of these incidents are never reported because victims fear not being believed and/or don't wish to endure the embarrassment of filing a police report or having to testify in an often unsympathetic courtroom. Most people think it would be impossible for a woman to rape a man due to the anatomical prerequisite of sexual arousal (i.e., an erection) to complete the act, but, in fact, males who are psychologically unwilling participants can find themselves becoming erect due to autonomic response (related to the part of the nervous system which governs involuntary actions). An aggressive female can achieve the desired result in her male victim through manual stimulation and other sexually provocative contact. Heightened emotional states (such as fear) also can produce an erection. At this point, forced penetration can occur (which is the legal definition of rape). Drugs and/or alcohol are often found to be contributing factors.

More Rape Facts at a Glance

1. Rape is supposed to be a power trip instead of a purely sexual assault, but a woman sixteen to nineteen years of age is eight times more likely to be raped than a woman over fifty.

2. The FBI has estimated that around 8 percent of rape accusations are false.

Cases have come to trial revealing situations where a female employer has coerced a male underling to have sex or face termination, but perhaps the most sensational and topical of all these female-on-male scenarios is when a sexually experienced school teacher seduces her teenaged student. Whether the student is willing or not, the law still regards it as statutory rape.

While females raping males accounts for only a small percentage of the total rapes committed, the male victim can be left every bit as traumatized as his female counterpart.

Know the Law

Under the law, there are a number of situations that constitute rape. To wit:

- Not stopping having sex when your partner is indicating that they want you to. Just because a partner has had sex with you in the past does not mean they have consented to having sex with you whenever you want it. Forcing the issue could result in a rape charge.

- Push sex when your partner doesn't want it, and you could be charged with rape.
- If you get a person drunk or high and then "pet" with them, you have committed a sexual assault. If sex follows, it's rape.
- If you do not get a person drunk or high, but you know they are and you still have sex with them, then you have committed rape.
- If you are unaware that a person is drunk or high and you have sex with them, you could be charged with rape.
- Even if you are also drunk or high when you have sex with a person who is drunk or high, you could be charged with rape. It is not a sufficient defense to say, "I was wasted, too!"

Rape of Males by Males

Although rape and sexual assault is usually known as a crime that men commit against a woman, men can also rape other men. According to the U.S. Bureau of Justice Statistics (BJS) in 2003, 9.9 percent of rape and sexual assault victims in the United States aged twelve and older were male; therefore, nearly seventeen out of every one hundred thousand males are victims. According to the data for 2006, this number has fallen to 2.95 percent; therefore, slightly more than five out of every one

Facts on Campus Rape

- Up to 85 percent of all women raped on campus know their attacker.
- Seventy-five percent of the time, either the offender or the victim has been drinking around the time of the rape.
- While 40 percent of all rapes are reported in the U.S., only 5 percent of all rapes on campus are reported.
- Embarrassment is the main reason why women don't report the rapes.

hundred thousand males are victims. Many of these male victims are likely children, and there may be many more male victims under age twelve that aren't included in BJS figures. In addition, according to the CDC, one in thirty-three men (3 percent) reported experiencing an attempted or completed rape at some time in their lives.

Rape in Prison

Research carried out by Cindy Struckman-Johnson and David Struckman-Johnson of the University of South Dakota found that 22–25 percent of male prisoners in the United States have been the victim of sexual assault, 10 percent of rape, and 6 percent of gang rape. The Human Rights Watch report "No Escape" says that prison rape is routine in U.S. prisons. Women prisoners are especially vulnerable to assault by guards and other staff members, and Amnesty International and Human Rights Watch have criticized the United States for not policing this policy better. Women prisoners also are vulnerable to other women prisoners.

Rape and Sexual Torture

In circumstances where torture is employed as a means of military or governmental policy, the rape of both female and male detainees is a common element of torture. It is often used as a means to "soften" the detainees for interrogation or to intimidate them into compliance. In societies with strong taboos on sexuality, sexual torture is commonly used to destroy the credibility and influence of political dissidents.

Do You Have Rape Fantasies?

Psychologists have determined that rape fantasies are relatively common across populations. Many people assume that people aroused by rape fantasies must be more likely than others to commit the actual act, or that women with rape fantasies actually want to become victims of violent sexual assault. This does not correspond with observed scientific evidence, however; while rapists usually fantasize about rape, so do normal, psychologically healthy people. Criminal psychologists would be more concerned about a person's tendencies if that person were only capable of achieving sexual gratification through the fantasy.

Rape as Punishment

Though modern societies claim to recognize the practice as barbaric, rape itself sometimes is still used as a form of punishment. The victim of the rape is commonly a female relative of the person targeted for retaliation. In June 2002, a Pakistani woman named Mukhtaran Bibi was sentenced to be gang raped by a vigilante mob after her brother was (falsely) accused of rape himself. The Pakistani government, along with local religious officials, condemned this action and sentenced the rapists to death. Many such events are reported in Pakistan and in other countries.

Chapter 8
Sexual Perversions

Supreme Thrill

When pedophile and serial murderer Albert Fish was convicted of murder in 1934 and sentenced to the electric chair, he looked forward to it as the supreme sexual thrill of his life because, among other things, he was a masochist—pain gave him pleasure. What could be better than multiple jolts of electricity?

Q&A

Q: What is pedophilia?

A: Recurrent, intense, sexually arousing fantasies, sexual urges or behaviors involving sexual activity with a prepubescent child. The word comes from the Greek paidophilia—paid ("child") and philia ("love, friendship").
—*American Psychiatric Association's*
Diagnostic and Statistical Manual

Q: Who dubbed it pedophilia?

A: The term was coined in 1896 by the Vienna psychiatrist Richard von Krafft-Ebing in his writing Psychopathia Sexualis. He gave it the following characteristics:
- the sexual interest is toward children, either prepubescent or at the beginning of puberty
- the sexual interest is the primary one; that is, they are exclusively or mainly attracted to children
- the sexual interest remains over time

Strictly speaking, this definition would include many adolescents and prepubescents for whom such an interest might be normal; thus, some experts add the criterion that the interest be toward children at least five years younger than the subject. However, according to some experts, there is evidence that a diagnosis of pedophilia can be appropriate for a post-pubescent adolescent.

Jargon

1. **Chicken hawk:** A male homosexual who frequents young male prostitutes (chickens). It's also prison slang for child molester.

   In prison there is a hierarchy of convicts based in part on the crime committed. Near the bottom of this pecking order is the child molester. Other prisoners loathe these inmates, perhaps because some prisoners have children themselves and can imagine their own children as prey. More likely, some psychologists say, prison is such an ego-debilitating place that prisoners often shore up their own self-image by tearing down other prisoners. The only convict in the prison hierarchy lower than the child molester is the snitch. Being a child molester can be precarious for one's health in prison, but being a snitch can be a death sentence.

2. **Shotaro complex:** This generally refers to the attraction toward adolescent or older underage males.

3. **Lolita syndrome or Lolita complex:** Terms sometimes used to refer to attraction to adolescent or older underage females.

4. **Grooming:** This is the technique that pedophiles use to prepare their victims, or intended targets, for their advances. They might take the intended target to the movies or dinner,

buy them things, just in general do things to make the target enjoy their company. But they also might do disturbing things, such as show them pornography, to break down what might be a resistance to sexual advances and desensitize them to it.

Q&A

Q: What percentage of pedophiles recover from their interest?

1. 1 out of 10
2. Half
3. 9 out of 10
4. None

A: None. It is generally believed that once a pedophile is afflicted, he will never change.

One psychiatrist knew a lawyer who was a pedophile; one day he met him in town and asked him what he was doing now that he had been discharged from prison.

"I'm getting my affairs in order. I'm going back in."

"Oh, they caught you re-offending?"

"Not yet. But I can't stop myself. And it's just a matter of time until I re-offend and get caught."

And later the psychiatrist heard that that was exactly what happened.

Crime Can Be Funny

Doin' The Dog

My partner and I were on patrol in Harlem one day and we got a call from a young guy about a domestic dispute. So we pulled up to the house and saw this seventeen- or eighteen-year-old kid sitting on the front steps. We got out and asked him, "What's the matter?" "My mother caught my father doing it again and she whacked him in the head with a frying pan."

"Doing what?"

"You know, doing it again. Doing the dog."

I thought it was an MTV dance or something; I didn't know what he meant.

"What do you mean 'doing the dog'?"

"You know, man. She caught him doing the dog, having sex with the dog!"

So we went upstairs and into the apartment, and there was this guy holding his head, which was bleeding. When the woman saw us she yelled, "I want him out of my house! Out of my house! He keeps doing my dog! This is the second time I caught him!"

I was thinking, *Second time you caught him? How many times does a man have sex with your dog before you call us?*

We arrested the man for bestiality, and when we got him back to the station and booked him, all the other cops started making jokes. I remember someone said to the DA, "So you know what's going to happen when you get the dog on the stand and ask her to describe what happened in her own words. She's going to say, 'Well you know the sex was ruff! Ruff!'"

Another cop asked what kind of a dog it was.

"A German Shepherd mix."

"Oh, then I can understand why it happened. That happens to be a very sexy breed."

And someone else said he knew what the defense attorney was going to say: "Can you blame my client? That dog was walking around with her tail in the air and her tongue out. What would you do?"

Pedophilia and the Church

1984: The Reverend Gilbert Gauthe of the Lafayette, Louisiana, diocese pleads guilty to molesting eleven boys and admits victimizing dozens more. In a widening scandal, nineteen other priests are accused of abuse, and the diocese negotiates costly out-of-court settlements with victims.

1985: The Reverend Thomas Doyle, a canon lawyer for the Vatican embassy in Washington, wrote a confidential memo for the nation's Catholic bishops citing thirty pedophile cases with one hundred victims, projecting a cost to the church of $1 billion over ten years. Also, the secular media is drawn to the problem of pedophilia in the church thanks to an article in the National Catholic Reporter that discusses the problem.

1989: Joseph Ferrario, a bishop in Hawaii, is accused of child molestation, but charges are not filed because the statute of limitations had run out. Ferrario retires in 1993.

1990: The Reverend Bruce Ritter, founder of Covenant House in New York City, is accused by one boy of molestation. Accusations from other boys follow. The archdiocese first approves a plan to send him to India, but public outrage makes them cancel it and Ritter retires.

1992: Jason Berry publishes a book called Lead Us Not Into Temptation, which outlines 400 cases of molestation that are costing the church an estimated $400 million.

1994: A man named Steven Cook takes back his claim that Chicago's Joseph Bernandin molested him. The Catholic diocese in Cincinnati does pay Cook a settlement based on a claim that a seminary teacher abused him.

1997: A Dallas jury hears charges from eleven victims of ex-priest Rudy Kos and returns a $120 million verdict. The award was later cut to about $30 million, but the diocese needs to take out mortgages and sell property to cover the judgment. Bishop J. Keith Symons of Palm Beach, Florida, becomes the first U.S. bishop to resign after admitting to being a molester. Later, Symons' successor, appointed to clean house, resigns for the same reason.

2000: The Reverend Andrew Greeley, an author and sociologist, writes an introduction for a new edition of Lead Us Not Into Temptation: Catholic Priests and the Sexual Abuse of Children by Jason Berry. The sex abuse situation, he contends, "may be the greatest scandal in the history of religion in America and perhaps the most serious crisis Catholicism has faced since the Reformation."

2000: Defrocked Boston priest John Geoghan, sixty-six, is convicted of indecent assault and battery as a priest sex scandal in the archdiocese widens. Geoghan has been accused of abusing 130 children over a thirty-year period while he was actively serving as a priest in the Archdiocese of Boston. He faces more criminal and civil suits and is convicted of abuse. He is sentenced to nine to ten years in prison, but he is not to serve it: he is strangled to death by January of 2000 by another inmate.

2002: Pope John Paul II summons America's cardinals to the Vatican to discuss the sex scandal and how to deal with it.

Minister suspected of child molestation.
(Dave Green)

Q&A

Q: How much has the problem of pedophilia cost the church?

A: Lots. First, and most costly, in terms of lost faith and broken lives, but of course the damage also has been financial. The nationwide financial toll of the wrongdoing is not known, since most settlements are confidential. Estimates of payouts to victims nationwide range from $300 million up to $1 billion.

Q: How many pedophiles are there?

A: A University of Ottawa psychiatrist named Dr. John Bradford estimated that about 4 percent of the population are pedophiles.

Q: How many sexual abusers are the parents of the victims?

A: Half; other relatives commit 18 percent of the offenses. And the truth is that preventing incest is nearly impossible. Fewer than one-third of perpetrators know their victims from outside the home.

Q: How can one spot pedophiles outside the family?

A: Beware of people who give uncommon attention to children. Abuse may be their real goal.

Crime Can Be Funny

Subway Peep Show

As a cop on the job, of course you meet all kinds of weirdos, including perverts. One guy who always stood out in my mind when I was a cop was a guy I spotted on the Lexington Avenue Subway station at 42nd Street. I was on plainclothes duty, and when I first saw this guy standing on the platform he didn't seem like anything special to me. Quite the contrary. He was a well-dressed, middle-aged guy with a tie and shirt and wearing a nice fedora and Camel-hair overcoat. He was standing a couple of feet from the edge of the platform, facing the tracks.

A train came into the station as I went about my business, but when the train left the station and I looked back, I was surprised to see the guy still there. So I made myself as invisible as I could and watched when the next train came in. When it pulled to a stop, I saw the man's head swiveling back and forth, like he was checking out who was getting on and off the train, but the doors finally closed and it left the station without him.

I didn't know what to think. I thought maybe we had an EDP (emotionally disturbed person).

Another train came into the station, and he did this head-swiveling thing again, and then I saw him take a few steps forward so that he was standing next to one of the windows. I also saw a pretty woman sitting by the window.

The doors closed, and a millisecond before the train started to pull out, I saw him open his coat and spread it apart—and the woman in the window looked his way and started freaking out. As the train passed me, I saw her looking back, her arms waving, screaming.

The train went into the tunnel and by then he had closed and rebuttoned his coat. But he stayed on the platform.

I sidled up to him, flashed my badge, and said, "Hey, pal, what you got under that coat?"

"Nothing," he said.

"Let me see."

He opened the coat and his answer was undeniably true: nothing. His pants, the top of which were overlapped by the bottom of the coat, only went to his mid-thigh and were attached to the bottom of his shirt with suspenders. From the waist to the pants he was totally naked. Cops who heard about it called it "The Subway Peep Show."

Q&A

Q: What is the most shocking thing that pedophiles will do?

A: This is a subjective question dependant on individual standards, but the most shocking thing to these authors is when a pedophile will marry a woman, impregnate her, and then raise the child or children until they are what doctors call the "target age." For example, their wives could have a boy, but his father—the pedophile—won't strike until the child is six or seven or whatever age he finds most appealing. It is amazing and horrifying to us that someone could raise and love a child for the sole purpose of hurting him.

Q: Do only pedophiles perpetrate criminal sexual acts on children?

A: No. Plenty of sexual abuse of kids is committed by ordinary people not generally attracted to children. That's one reason the incidence of child sexual abuse is so maddeningly high. A Department of Health and Human Services study estimates that victimizers sexually abused 93,000 U.S. children in 1999 (the latest year for which data are available). But there is some good news. Last year, the Department of Justice reported that the number of substantiated cases of child sexual abuse has been decreasing, from a peak of nearly 150,000 in 1992 to about 104,000 in 1998—a drop of almost one-third. The authors say vigorous incarceration of offenders over the past few years may be partly responsible for the decline in child sexual abuse cases.

Q: How many years, on average, do pedophiles serve in prison?

A: Eleven.

171

Q: Is there a way to lessen the risk of a pedophile striking?

A: Active pedophiles who find their way into the few treatment programs around the country turn out to be less of a risk than those who are locked up for a while and released.

Q: What is nepiophilia, also called infantophilia?

A: This is the attraction to toddlers and infants (usually ages zero to three). Some researchers have suggested a distinction between pedophilia and nepiophilia, as it is unusual for pedophiles to prefer toddlers.

Q: Do drugs that lower sex drive work with pedophiles?

A: Drugs and counseling are effective. Contrary to popular belief, a host of studies has shown that once in treatment, few pedophiles relapse. In 1991, the American Journal of Forensic Psychiatry published a study of 400 of one doctor's patients; only 1.2 percent of those who had complied with his two-and-a-half-year treatment were known to have molested kids again three years after finishing the course. Surprisingly, only 5.6 percent of those who were discharged for noncompliance offended in that period. Similarly, a 2002 study by St. Luke Institute, a psychiatric hospital outside Washington, followed 121 priests for one to five years and found that after treatment, only three had relapsed. But over the longer run of years, the percentages of relapse go higher.

Q: Do pedophiles like being pedophiles?

A: Not at all. According to the Reverend Stephen Rossetti, who runs St. Luke's, "People don't grow up and say, 'I want to be a pedophile,'" says Rossetti. "All the people I've ever talked to hate it."

Q: How widespread now is pedophilia among priests?

A: Between 5 and 10 percent are emotional pedophiles, but actual contact between priests and young children is very rare, perhaps only .3 percent. The most extensive study of priests and pedophilia considered 2,252 priests over a thirty-year period and found only one case of pedophilia, a priest who was also uncle to two six-year-old nieces. The number of pederasts or ephebophiles (priests involved, usually homosexually, with an adolescent minor, which is viewed by psychologists as a more consensual relationship) was much larger, but still less than two percent.

Q: In the 60s and 70s, how did schools, hospitals and other institutions react when they found children being molested by their staff members?

A: Like religious institutions: they shipped them to other places—not solving the problem, just giving them fresh victims.

Q: Have people always understood that pedophilia is incurable?

A: Not at all. During the 60s and 70s, there was no understanding—or maybe they were afraid to understand—that pedophilia is incurable. At the time, such prestigious institutions as Harvard said that it was against the child's interest to treat sexual abuse as a crime; they believed that police investigations and court procedures would be more traumatic than the pedophile's assault.

Q: How often does pedophilia occur?

A: The extent is not known. Some studies have concluded that at least a quarter of all adult men may have some feelings of sexual arousal in connection with children. A study by Kent State University, for example, found that 32.5 percent of their sample—eighty adult males—exhibited sexual arousal to pedophilic stimuli that equaled or exceeded their arousal to the adult stimuli. Further studies indicate that even men erotically fixated on adult females are generally prone to react sexually when exposed to nude female children. In 1989, Briere and Runtz conducted a study on 193 male undergraduate students concerning pedophilia. Of the sample, 21 percent acknowledged sexual attraction to some small children; 9 percent reported sexual fantasies involving children; 5 percent admitted masturbating to these fantasies; and 7 percent conceded some probability of actually having sex with a child if they could avoid detection and punishment.

Q: Why is sexual abuse of children so devastating?

A: Among other things, it is an unforgivable violation of trust. Children, despite their rampant egos, depend on adults to nurture and help them. When they are sexually abused, they develop the idea that their worth is tied up in their sexuality. This is devastating—what some psychiatrists and psychologists call "soul murder." Dr. David Finkelhor, a U.S. researcher, describes some of the consequences of childhood seduction: confusion about sexual identity and sexual norms, inability to differentiate sex from love, confusion between care-getting and care-giving, lowered respect for adult authority, guilt, shame, anxiety, lowered self-esteem, depression, vulnerability to drug and alcohol abuse, and an impaired ability to judge the trustworthiness of others. We also see an age-inappropriate sexual knowledge, and sex acts are sometimes compulsively reenacted with other children. Victims of sex abuse appear to be at higher risk for suicide. They may also repeat the sexual abuse in adulthood in order to gain a feeling of psychological mastery over the experience. Children who experience prolonged abuse are more likely to view the abuse as positive or neutral, suggesting that as the molestation continues, children eventually identify with the molester—a dangerous identification that could lead to an abused child perpetuating the abuse as an adult. If the abuse was homosexual, the boy is likely to question his sexual orientation; if the abuser was a male and the child a girl, she may defensively turn to lesbianism.

Q: What is pedophile activism?

A: This is referred to by some supporters as the child/love movement. It is a social movement that encompasses a wide variety of views, but generally advocates one or more of the following: social acceptance of adults' romantic or sexual attraction to children; social acceptance of adults' sexual activity with children; and changes in institutions of concern to pedophiles, such as changing age-of-consent laws and mental illness classifications. The movement, of course, is extremely controversial.

Q: Any examples of famous people who were pedophile victims?

A: In his life story, Breaking the Surface, Olympic diver Greg Louganis tells the poignant tale of his own experience with adult-child sex. He was an unusually sensitive boy, with an intense closeness with his mother and a distant, fearful relationship with his father. Lonely and starving for male affection, he was molested by an older man he encountered on the beach. In his childish neediness, Louganis—like many victims of man-boy molestation—perceived the relationship as loving.

Q: Who is likely to be an abuser?

A: Child molesters are typically immature men who want to "give love" to a boy, love that they did not receive in childhood. A child molester makes a narcissistic identification with the child, seeing him as an idealized version of himself, and perceives himself as giving the love he wishes he had received from his own father. Thus, the pedophile cannot understand that he is inflicting emotional damage.

Q: Do pedophiles believe they are born that way?

A: Many of them do—and believe they cannot change.

Q: Do some pedophiles think that being a pedophile is a good thing?

A: Many do, and they also believe that sleeping with children can help them.

A Very Controversial Call

Mark Hullet, a thirty-four-year-old man from Williston, Vermont, was found guilty of repeatedly raping a six-year-old girl for four years. From the ages of six through ten, this girl was raped over and over and over again. The prosecutor was seeking twenty years imprisonment. However, Judge Edward Cashman said the damage was already done to the victim, and Hullett had a mental disease and jail wasn't going to change him. He sentenced him to a shocking sixty days in jail. The ruling threw the nation—not just Vermont—into an uproar, and Judge Cashman changed his tune and sentenced Hullett to three to ten years.

Chapter 9
Terrorism

People tend to think of terrorism as an act that is parochial, that applies only to their country, but this is hardly true. A look at most countries, including Ireland, Spain, Africa, Germany, the Philippines, and India, reveals some sort of terrorism, in short, it would be difficult to name a country where terrorist acts have not been perpetrated.

The more important question is why terrorism occurs. There are many theories, but on one level, terrorism is certainly a copycat crime carried out by psychotics. Years ago, one of the authors approached the airline industry with an idea for a story. He told the public relations person who answered the phone that psychotics engage in copycat behavior: When someone puts a bomb in a plane, you can be sure that someone else will copy that action. The PR person's response was: You're right, and please don't write the story—it might give psychos ideas.

World Trade Center, September 11, 2001
(Gary Thomas/Photofest)

This copycat action can be seen in many areas. For example, whenever a school shooting occurs, the authors just wait for it to happen one or two more times. Psychotics observe and say: Hey, looks good to me!

Of course, this theory does not explain why someone becomes a terrorist or a mass murderer, which is really the same thing. The authors believe it is simply the way psychotics solve their own personal problems. Terrorists are very sick people who project their own internal problems onto the world, and then they believe the acting out will solve their problems. We believe this theory even when there seems to be a logic for terrorist acts, such as Palestinian terrorists becoming suicide bombers against Israel, whom the Palestinians have hated for a long time. The psychotic's action, in some way, solves his or her problem. For example, if a seventeen-year-old Pakastani kid has no self-esteem and unconsciously loathes himself, a solution to the problem is to imagine that his problems are problems in the world, someone else's fault. By solving those problems, he solves his own—and he becomes somebody at the same time. So the bottom line is this: terrorists become terrorists because of personal problems which they project into the world. As Caesar said to Brutus in Shakespeare's play Julius Caesar, "The fault is not in the stars, dear Brutus, it's in ourselves."

WTC

As the saying goes, you don't know what you've got 'til it's gone. And so it is with the toppled World Trade Center. It was designed to reenergize the seedy area in which it was built. David Rockefeller, chairman of the Chase Manhattan Bank and founder of the development association, and his brother, New York governor Nelson Rockefeller, spearheaded the project. The architect was Minoru Yamasaki and Associates of Michigan. His design involved two huge, controversial towers—one criticism was that they would mar the New York skyline—but the project was ultimately approved. Construction began in 1966.

To build it, five streets were closed off and over 160 buildings within the area were removed. Construction required the excavation of more than 1.2 million cubic yards of earth, which was used to create 23.5 acres of land along the Hudson River (now part of Battery Park City in lower Manhattan). During construction, up to 3,500 people worked on the site and over 10,000 on the towers themselves; 60 people were killed in accidents during construction of the towers. In December 1970, the north tower was opened; the south tower followed in January 1972. The towers were dedicated in April 1973, and until May of 1973, when the Sears Tower opened, the World Trade Center was the tallest building in the world. Around 50,000 people worked in the building, and 200,000 passed through the complex of stores beneath it every day.

Each WTC tower:

- was made up of 200,000 tons of steel; 425,000 cubic yards of concrete; 43,600 windows; and 12,000 miles of electric cables
- had its own zip code, 10047 or 10048
- had 110 floors
- was 208 feet by 208 feet at base
- weighed 500,000 tons
- was 1,368 feet high (north tower)
- was 1,362 ft high (south tower)
- contained 198 miles of heating ducts
- had 97 elevators for passengers, 6 for freight

In 1993, a bomb containing 1,100 pounds of explosives was secreted in a truck parked beneath the buildings by Islamic terrorists trying to take the buildings down. The attack was not successful, but the explosives that detonated left a crater 22 feet wide. Six people were killed and more than one thousand were injured.

Q&A

Q: When did the first skyjacking of a commercial airliner occur?

A: May 1, 1962. The plane was a National Airlines twin-engine plane flying from Miami to Key West, Florida. The plane lifted off with eight passengers at 3:23 p.m. In flight, a passenger named Antillo Ortiz announced himself and threatened crew and passengers with a pistol and knife, forcing the crew to fly him to Havana, Cuba. They dropped him off and the plane flew back to Key West, arriving at 8:35 p.m. with no one hurt in the incident.

Timothy McVeigh

On April 19, 1995, the name of twenty-seven-year-old Timothy McVeigh was to become inextricably interwoven with the concept of terrorism in the minds of all U.S. citizens.

Around 9:00 a.m., McVeigh drove a Ryder Rental truck carefully through the streets of downtown Oklahoma City. The vehicle pulled into a parking lot outside the Alfred P. Murrah Federal Building. McVeigh parked and walked away. At 9:02 a.m., the truck's 5,000-pound cargo of explosives went off, blasting the government building with enough force to blow one-third of the seven-story structure into oblivion and kill and wound scores of innocent adults and children. But McVeigh wasn't contrite. He pictured himself as a warrior hero defending the Constitution.

Inside the broken building, a person's survival depended entirely on where they were when the bomb detonated. Some of the lucky ones had left their usual posts to get a coffee, deliver documents, or simply visit nearby offices; as they did, their offices and fellow workers were blown away. In the children's day-care center directly above the mobile bomb, the devastation was horrific. Upper floors collapsed on those beneath them, setting up a chain reaction that crushed everything and everyone below.

Rescue workers rushed to the scene almost immediately. Professionals and volunteers alike clawed through the rubble to help dig out the wounded and remove the dead. Temporary silences were observed so listening devices sensitive enough to detect human heartbeats were employed to locate anyone still living. In one dramatic instance, sounding devices finally located a buried woman, Dana Bradley, as she cried for help. The twenty-year-old lay bleeding in a foot of water. For five hours, her leg had been pinned under a pile of cement. The massive pile of rubble that pinioned her could not be shifted, so the rescue team's only hope of getting her out alive was to amputate her crushed limb. To complicate things, Dr. Gary Massad knew that if he administered anesthetic it could trigger a fatal coma, so he had to do the amputation with Dana awake. Once the operation was complete, she was pulled from the ruins and hospitalized. But Dana lost more than just a part of her leg—her mother and two young children were killed in the blast.

The final toll was 168 people killed and more than five hundred wounded.

Terrorists and Their Acts, Past and Present

1. Aum Cult: Religious terrorist cult that attracted some of Japan's brightest young people and amassed a billion dollars in assets, much of which was used to fund development of anthrax and other weapons of mass destruction.

2. **Mohammed Bouyeri:** Murderer of Theo Van Gogh, the controversial Dutch filmmaker who made a film portraying Muslim women who were abused for their religious convictions. Bouyeri was sentenced to life in prison.

3. **Baader-Meinhof Gang:** German Marxist terrorists spoiled by prosperity and haunted by their Nazi past who carried on terrorist activities in Western Europe.

4. **Birmingham Church Bombing:** The 1963, KKK bombing of the Sixteenth Street Baptist Church during Sunday service resulted in the deaths of four teenage girls. It altered the course of history by stirring the conscience of a nation.

5. **Carlos the Jackal:** The premier terrorist of the 1970s and 1980s. Now in jail serving a life sentence for the killing of two French secret service agents, the Jackal married his French-born lawyer, Isabelle Coutant-Peyre, in August 2001. Coutant-Peyre, who shares the Jackal's love of cigars and Marxism, says "He is a very warm man." The Jackal's activities resulted in eighty-three murders as well as many bombings and kidnappings.

6. **Hambali:** Chief conspirator behind the horrific terrorist attack a few years ago in Bali that resulted in the deaths of numerous Australians. He was captured in Thailand while planning more mayhem.

7. **Patty Hearst:** Member of the wealthy Hearst Family, Patty Hearst was kidnapped by the Symbionese Liberation Army and served as an accomplice in a bank robbery. It was said that Hearst suffered from Stockholm syndrome, which caused her to identify with her kidnappers. Hearst later stood trial for her part in the SLA's crimes, and she was convicted of bank robbery on March 20, 1976. Her seven-year prison term was eventually commuted by President Jimmy Carter, and Hearst was released from prison on February 1, 1979, having served only twenty-two months. She was granted a full pardon by President Bill Clinton on January 20, 2001, the final day of his presidency.

8. **Ted Kaczynski:** Also known as the "Unabomber," Kaczynski was a brilliant professor turned bomber. Kaczynski was a bomber for years without killing people, but that changed in a parking lot behind the Rentech Computer Store in Sacramento, California. Owner Hugh Scrutton noticed a block of wood lying in the lot with nails protruding from it. He figured it could damage tires, so went to remove it. An enormous blast went through the strip mall. Its force was so great it blew off most of Scrutton's hand and blasted metal fragments into his organs and heart, killing him instantly. Later Kaczynski used mail bombs, the first of which was sent to a professor at Northwestern University in 1978. Kaczynski's younger brother David recognized Ted's writing style from a published manifesto Ted had sent to the press and David notified authorities. After a team of forensic linguists compared text samples provided by Kaczynski's brother and mother with the Unabomber's writings and determined they had been written by the same person, officers were sent to arrest Kaczynski on April 3, 1996, at his

remote cabin outside Lincoln, Montana. Kaczynski was convicted and is serving a life sentence without the possibility of parole in ADX Florence, the Federal ADX Supermax prison in Florence, Colorado.

9. **Dr. Larry C. Ford:** Brilliant and outwardly respectable doctor is believed to be involved in South African bioterrorism, the attempted murder of his colleague, and the poisoning of his mistresses with mysterious toxins.

10. **The Weather Underground and Black Liberation Army:** Two 1980s homegrown American terrorist groups, one white and one black, joined forces to fund anti-American causes. They robbed a Brink's truck and murdered New York police officers in cold blood. A number of the terrorists from these groups were brought to justice.

11. **Palestinian homicide bombers:** Teenagers and women are now being recruited to murder Israelis.

12. **Eric Rudolph:** Rudolph bombed an abortion clinic, a gay bar and, most famously, Olympic Park in Atlanta in 1996. He was finally apprehended.

13. **Osama bin Laden:** The most wanted terrorist in the world, mastermind of the 9/11 attacks and other atrocities worldwide.

14. **The Shankill Butchers:** Hiding under the veil of Northern Ireland's "troubles," a vicious gang of thugs carried on a reign of terror from which no one was safe.

15. **Zebra Killers:** An elite corps of young Black Muslims that set out to exterminate the white people of San Francisco, so called "blue-eyed devils," to earn themselves a special place in heaven.

16. **Tylenol Murderer(s):** This was one of the first terrorist cases in the U.S. In 1982, seven people in the Chicago area died after taking Tylenol that had been laced with cyanide. The authorities never apprehended the culprit(s).

17. **El-Sayid Nosair:** His assassination of Rabbi Meir Kahane, the founder of the Jewish Defense League, was one of the opening shots in the Islamic war of terrorism against the U.S.

The Original Terrorist: New York City's Mad Bomber

In New York City in the 1950s, the mysterious "Mad Bomber" terrified the city with the bombs he had been planting all over town for the past sixteen years. The bomber was clever and made tracing the devices nearly impossible. The detectives working the case were at their wits end and ready to try anything, their frustration enhanced by the increasingly powerful bombs the bomber planted and his incessant, arrogant letters to the police.

In one of the earliest examples of criminal profiling, a Manhattan criminal psychiatrist named Dr. James Brussel examined the bomber's letters and other forensic material and came up with what turned out to be an astonishing, Sherlock Holmes-like description of the criminal. However, it was a handwriting sample and an exhaustive search through records from Consolidated Edison, the electric company where he had worked, that finally identified the Mad Bomber as George Metesky.

Chapter 10
Auto Theft

Q&A

Q: How many airbags are stolen every year?

A: Nationally, more than seventy five thousand. Thefts of the very expensive xenon headlights are also a growing problem.

Q: Is carjacking getting more common?

A: Carjacking—when someone steals a car while the driver of the car is present—is on the rise, in part because so many cars now have good anti-theft devices—car thieves have discovered that it's much easier to steal a car when you can make the driver give up the keys.

Q: How can I keep from being carjacked?

A: Be aware of the possibility that it might happen. Look around you when you approach your car in a parking lot or on the street to see if anyone is close by. Always check the back seat to make sure no one is hiding there before you get into your car. Have your keys in your hand so that you can get into your car very quickly, and lock the car immediately once you're in. Keep the car doors locked and windows rolled up when driving in a dangerous area. Whenever you stop, be sure that you can see the road between your car and the car in front of you; that will provide enough space to maneuver if you have to suddenly pull out to one side or the other.

Q: What should I do if I am carjacked?

A: It depends on what's involved. If someone who is armed approaches you while you are getting into your car, it may be best just to let them take the car. One way to foil their plan is simply to throw your keys as far away as possible. The one thing you should try to avoid at all costs is letting the carjacker take both you and the car. If, despite everything you can do, you find yourself in the car with the carjacker (who is now a kidnapper), you might try making the car crash by grabbing the steering wheel or attacking the kidnapper's eyes. If you are put in the trunk, use your cell phone to call for help or try to kick out a tail light and wave your hand through the opening.

Auto Theft Facts at a Glance

- Every 26 seconds, a motor vehicle is stolen in the United States (2004 data). The odds of a vehicle being stolen are 1 in 190 (2003 data). The odds are highest in urban areas.
- U.S. motor vehicle thefts fell 1.9 percent in 2004 from 2003, according to the FBI's Uniform Crime Reports. In 2004, 1,237,114 motor vehicles were reported stolen.
- Nationwide, the 2004 motor vehicle theft rate per 100,000 people was 421.3, down 2.9 percent from 433.7 in 2003. The highest rate was reported in the West, 664.5, up 1.7 percent, the only region registering an increase. The rate of motor vehicles stolen was 397.8 in the South, down 4.2 percent from 2003; 341.6 in the Midwest, down 4.8 percent; and 262.5 in the Northeast, down 9.9 percent.

- In 2004, only 13 percent of car thefts resulted in arrests.
- Carjackings account for only 3 percent of all motor vehicle thefts.

Car Theft by City

According to a National Insurance Crime Bureau (NICB) study released in August 2005, California leads the country for vehicle theft, as shown below:

1. Modesto, CA
2. Las Vegas/Paradise, NV
3. Stockton, CA
4. Phoenix/Mesa/Scottsdale, AZ
5. Visalia/Porterville, CA
6. Seattle/Tacoma/Bellevue, WA
7. Sacramento/Arden-Arcade/Roseville, CA
8. San Diego/Carlsbad/San Marcos, CA
9. Fresno, CA
10. Yakima, WA

Q&A

Q: How many stolen cars are recovered?

A: While 90 percent of stolen cars are recovered, most have suffered physical damage or have parts missing from them.

Top Ten Car Makes and Models Stolen in 2004

1. 1995 Honda Civic
2. 1989 Toyota Camry
3. 1991 Honda Accord
4. 1994 Dodge Caravan
5. 1994 Chevrolet Full Size C/K 1500 Pickup
6. 1997 Ford F150 Series
7. 2003 Dodge Ram Pickup
8. 1990 Acura Integra
9. 1988 Toyota Pickup
10. 1991 Nissan Sentra

Chapter 11
Death Row

Death Row Jargon

1. Big Jab. Lethal injection. Also, "stainless steel ride," "doctorate in applied chemistry," or "the needle."

2. Ride the Lightning. Be executed in the electric chair.

Angry Last Words of the Condemned

1. "I'd like to thank my family for loving me and taking care of me. And the rest of the world can kiss my ass."—Johnny Frank Garrett, executed February 11, 1992

2. "I just want everyone to know that the prosecutor and Bill Scott are some sorry sons of bitches."—Edward Ellis, executed March 3, 1992

3. "I'm an African warrior born to breathe and born to die."—Carl Kelly, executed June 29, 1993

4. "There is not going to be an execution. This is premeditated murder by the appointed district attorney and the State of Texas. I am not guilty of this crime."—Jesse DeWayne Jacobs, executed January 5, 1995

5. "Hurry up, you Hoosier bastard. I could hang a dozen men while you're screwing around."—Serial murderer Carl Panzram, executed by hanging, September 5, 1930

Humorous Last Words of the Condemned

1. "Capital Punishment—them without the capital get the punishment."—John Spenkelink, executed May 25, 1979

2. "I guess nobody is going to call."—Earl Johnson, executed May 20, 1987

3. "Yeah, I think I'd rather be fishing."—Jimmy Glass, executed June 12, 1987

4. "Well, gentlemen, you are about to see a baked Appel."—George Appel, executed by electric chair on April 1, 1928

5. "How about this for a headline for tomorrow's paper? 'French Fries.'"—James French, executed by electric chair, June 30, 1966

6. "You can be a king or a street sweeper, but everyone dances with the Grim Reaper."—Robert Alton Harris, executed on April 21, 1992

Would You Like Fries with That?

French fries are the most requested last meal, followed by (in order of popularity) hamburgers, steak, ice cream, and fried chicken.

Gary Gilmore's Ad Idea

Before he was executed for murder, Gary Gilmore had an advertising idea: Gilmore proposed that after his own execution by firing squad, John Cameron Swayze, the famous spokesperson for Timex, should hold a stethoscope to Gilmore's chest and say, "This one is not ticking, folks . . ." and then the camera would pan down to the Timex on Gilmore's wrist and Swayze would put the stethoscope on it and say, "But this one is!" The ad might not have worked: despite being shot in the heart with four .30 caliber bullets, Gilmore lived—along with his ticking heart—for two minutes.

Someone's Shooting Blanks

Although there are five sharpshooters in a firing squad, only four bullets enter the condemned because one bullet is a blank. Hence, each shooter can rationalize he was not the one to deliver the fatal shot.

Nicknames for the Electric Chair

The Electric Chair has had many nicknames over the years:

"The Chair"
"Sizzlin' Sally"
"Old Smokey"
"Old Sparky"
"Yellow Mama"
"Gruesome Gert"

Ol' Sparky

Of the thirty-eight states that have a death penalty, only Nebraska uses the electric chair as its primary method of execution. All others use lethal injection, but some states do offer the prisoner an alternate choice (e.g., gas chamber, firing squad).

Electrocution Painless?

Death experts say that electrocution is painless for the person being executed. The theory is that the electrical current hits the brain before the nerves can relay the message that the sensation hurts. Hence, when the person is seen thrashing around in spasms, it isn't a response to pain, it's just the body's natural and involuntary reaction to the electrical current.

Wrong Last Meal!

Thomas Grasso, who was executed in an Oklahoma prison in 1995, ordered Spaghetti-O's as his last meal but was mistakenly given spaghetti. He complained bitterly to the press about it and even mentioned it in his final words.
(Author's Collection)

Unusual Print

On April 25, 1935, one of the most unusual fingerprints ever lifted was taken from a hand that was found in the belly of a recently captured 14-foot tiger shark. While in an aquarium in Coogee Beach, Australia, the shark vomited a tattooed arm. Upon examination, investigators said that the arm had been cut from the body, thereby indicating foul play. The shark had not digested the arm, apparently because, said the local shark expert, the shark was not engaging in its normal feeding regimen because it was depressed since being captured and simply didn't feel like eating.

The arm was identified as belonging to a petty thief and forger named James Smith. And his murderer was long suspected to be one Patrick Brady, who denied killing Smith until his dying day twenty years later (most of which was spent in jail for other crimes).

The Execution of the *In Cold Blood* Killers

Perry Smith and Dick Hickock, the murderers at the center of the *In Cold Blood* case, were caught quickly, but the carrying out of their death sentence by hanging was by no means swift. Various appeals, all the way up to the Supreme Court, took almost five years, while Smith and Hickock waited on Death Row.

This appeals process was frustrating for author Truman Capote. He had gotten permission from their defense attorney to talk to Smith and Hickock and had conducted in-depth interviews with both of them, particularly Smith.

Consequently, he had written almost all his book, but he lacked an ending until the final verdict was handed down.

The "*In Cold Blood*" killers Perry Smith, top and Dick Hickock. (Author's Collection)

Finally, the word came: the convictions were affirmed. Smith and Hickock had exhausted all legal appeals and were to die on the night of April 14, 1965, five years and five months after they had killed the Clutter family.

First Hickock was hanged, then Smith. All the people involved in the pursuit of Smith and Hickock were at the execution, as was

Truman Capote, who had received the killers' personal invitation to attend the event, which was held in an old warehouse where scaffolding had been erected. Alvin Dewey, the Kansas Bureau of Investigation's lead detective on the Clutter family murder case, remembers thinking at the execution how hard it must have been on Smith to have to wait to die until after Hickock was hung. But he didn't worry about it for long. "I thought of the gentle Bonnie Clutter, who lay tied to her bed listening to first one and then another and then another shotgun blast before her turn came." No, he didn't agonize over it long at all.

Dead Man Really Walking

In the motion picture *Dead Man Walking*, the guard who started Sean Penn on his way to the execution chamber and dramatically uttered "Dead man walking" was a real-life prison guard and could have been talking about himself— he died shortly after the movie was completed.

Lethal Cocktail

Two or three drugs are administered during a lethal injection:

- Sodium Thiopental (Pentathal): a barbiturate that induces general anesthesia
- Pancuronium Bromide: a paralyzing agent that stops the breathing
- Potassium Chloride: a toxic agent that stops the heart

Death Wish?

"Where are most people likely to be executed now?" serial murderer Ted Bundy asked his lawyer. At the time, Bundy was in jail in Silver Springs, Colorado.

"I suppose it might be Georgia . . . no," Bundy's lawyer corrected himself, "it'd probably be Florida now."

"Florida?" repeated Bundy.

The lawyer explained that the constitutionality of Florida's death penalty had recently been upheld by the U.S. Supreme Court.

"Florida," murmured Bundy, "Florida. Hmmm."

Shortly after the conversation, Bundy, who had dieted to the point of emaciation, squeezed his way through a hole in the ceiling tiles and escaped—to travel all the way to Lakeland, Florida. Once there, Bundy abducted and brutally murdered the twelve-year-old daughter of a sheriff and then, with a broken taillight at night in a Volkswagen which contained handcuffs, rope, etc.—all the tools in a murderer's arsenal and easily enough evidence to pin the little girl's killing on him—drove around until he was spotted by a cop and collared after a pursuit.

> ### First to Ride the Lightning
>
> On August 6, 1890, Walter Kemmler, described as "a brute who chopped a woman to death with an axe," was the first person to die in the electric chair.

It makes you wonder why Ted Bundy would travel all the way across the country, from the state of Colorado to Florida, to kill somebody—and then get caught. Why not one of the other forty-nine states? Answer: guilt and the need to be punished. Florida obliged, and Bundy was put to death on January 24, 1989.

Close Call

On March 12, 2003, Delma Banks was in the Texas death house, strapped to a gurney and being readied to receive a lethal injection to carry out his death sentence. With just ten minutes to spare, the prison authorities were instructed by the Supreme Court to stop the execution. The court wanted to review his conviction for possible prosecutorial misconduct. On February 23, 2004, eleven months later, the court found that prosecutors had withheld crucial information and threw out the conviction.

Going Gently into the Good Night

The original concept of the gas chamber was to execute the prisoner in his cell while he slept. Authorities figured this would save him the anguish of waiting for the specific execution date. The idea had to be scrapped, however, because prison officials could not find a viable way to keep the gas from seeping into adjacent—and occupied—cells.

By the Skin of Their Teeth

The number of people freed from death row (as of 2005) stands at 118, and would be higher if DNA testing had come along earlier. One controversial case is that of a man named Roget Colman who was executed in Virginia in 1992. The state won't allow DNA testing of his remains, despite strong indications that he was innocent. One inmate, Frank Lee Smith, was cleared of the murder of an eight-year-old Florida girl, but he died of natural causes before he could be released.

And the MVP Goes to . . .

Robert G. Elliot was America's most prolific executioner: in his fourteen-year career, he executed 387 men and women in five states and kept a diary of each event.

Chapter 12
Prisons

Q&A

Q: What is the predominant race in prison?

A: At the end of 2003 (the most recent year it was fig-ured), in a demographic study of all inmates in state and federal prisons sentenced to one year or more, the prison population breakdown was as follows: 44 percent blacks, 35 percent whites, 19 percent Hispanics, and 2 percent other.

Q: Who has spent the most time in jail and is still behind bars?

A: Chicagoan William Heirens has served more time—going on 61 years—than any other prisoner in America. In 1946, he killed a little girl and two women in a case that shocked the world because of what he scrawled on a mirror in lipstick in one victim's home: "For Heaven's sake, catch me before I kill more. I cannot control myself."

Attica, whose stylish sandstone wall and fancy towers belie the toughness of the prison lurking behind that wall.
(Author's Collection).

Q: Who holds the record for having served the most time in an American prison?

A: Paul Geidel holds the record for having served the most time behind bars in the U.S. Convicted of murder when he was seventeen, Geidel served sixty-eight years and seven months behind bars before being released to a nursing home to live out the remainder of his life.

Prison Capitol of the World

Based on the number of prisons, Florence, Colorado, and surrounding Fremont County is the prison capital of America. There are fourteen prisons located there, ten state and four federal, including maximum security facility ADX—Colorado's only maximum security facility and home to such criminals as the Unabomber (Ted Kaczynski); Ramzi Yousef, the WTC bomber of 1993; and Charles Harrelson, actor Woody Harrelson's father, who killed a federal judge.

Q&A

Q: What's the difference between a prison and jail?

A: Jails house people who commit relatively minor offenses and spend a short time—a year or less—incarcerated. Prison is for longer terms and more serious crimes.

Capsule Guide to Sex Offenders

Offenders in General

On any given day in 1994, there were approximately 234,000 offenders convicted of rape or sexual assault under the care, custody, or control of corrections agencies; nearly 60 percent of these sex offenders live in communities under conditional supervision.

- The median age of the victims of imprisoned sexual assaulters was less than thirteen years old; the median age of rape victims was about twenty-two years.

- An estimated 24 percent of those serving time for rape and 19 percent of those serving time for sexual assault had been on probation or parole at the time of the offense for which they were in state prison (1991 data).

> **Room for Rent**
>
> One of the problems with U.S. prisons is a lack of space; in fact, Michigan and Vermont rent empty cells in Virginia and send their prisoners there.

- Of the 9,691 male sex offenders released from prisons in fifteen states in 1994, 5.3 percent were rearrested for a new sex crime within three years of release.

- Of released sex offenders who allegedly committed another sex crime, 40 percent perpetrated the new offense within a year of their prison discharge.

Child Molesters

- Approximately 4,300 child molesters were released from prisons in fifteen states in 1994. An estimated 3.3 percent of these 4,300 were rearrested for another sex crime against a child within three years of release from prison.

- Among child molesters released from prison in 1994, 60 percent had been in prison for molesting a child thirteen years old or younger.

- Offenders who had victimized a child were on average five years older than the violent offenders who had committed their crimes against adults. Nearly 25 percent of child victimizers were forty years old or older, but only about 10 percent of the inmates with adult victims fell in that age range.

- About one in four convicted violent offenders confined in local jails committed their crime against an intimate; about 7 percent of state prisoners serving time for violence had an intimate victim (i.e., a relative).

- About half of all offenders convicted of intimate violence and confined in a local jail or a state prison had been drinking at the time of the offense. Jail inmates who had been drinking prior to the intimate violence consumed on average an amount of alcohol equivalent to ten beers.

- About eight in ten inmates serving time in state prison for intimate violence injured or killed their victim.

Medical Problems in Prison

1. Nearly half of state inmates who served six or more years said they had been injured after admission. Fewer than 20 percent of those in prison less than two years reported an injury.

   Two point four percent of state inmates and 48 percent of federal inmates age forty-five or older said they had had a medical problem since admission to prison.

HIV in Prisons and Jails

1. Between 1998 and 2002, the number of HIV-positive prisoners decreased about 7 percent, while the overall prison population grew almost 11 percent.

2. At the end of 2002, 3 percent of all female state prison inmates were HIV-positive, compared to 1.9 percent of males.

3. In 2002, the overall rate of confirmed AIDS in the prison population (0.48 percent) was nearly three and a half times the rate in the U.S. general population (0.14 percent).

Characteristics of State Prison Inmates

(Note: Figures are from the government, which does not conduct surveys every year; some surveys are five or more years apart).

1. Women comprised 6.6 percent of the state prison inmates in 2001, up from 6 percent in 1995.

2. Sixty-four percent of prison inmates belonged to racial or ethnic minorities in 2001.

Not a Safe Job

Forty-one percent of the prosecutor's offices had a staff member who had been threatened or assaulted in 2005.

3. An estimated 57 percent of inmates were under age thirty-five in 2001.

4. About 4 percent of state prison inmates were not U.S. citizens by 2002.

5. About 6 percent of state prison inmates were held in private facilities at the end of 2001.

6. Altogether, an estimated 57 percent of inmates had a high school diploma or its equivalent.

7. Among the state prison inmates in 2000, nearly half were sentenced for a violent crime (49 percent), a fifth were sentenced for a property crime (20 percent), and about a fifth were sentenced for a drug crime (21 percent).

Comparing Federal and State Prison Inmates

1. In 1997, federal inmates were more likely than state inmates to be:

women (7 percent vs. 6 percent)
Hispanic (27 percent vs. 17 percent)
age forty-five or older (24 percent vs. 13 percent)
college educated (18 percent vs. 11 percent)
noncitizens (18 percent vs. 5 percent)

2. In 2000, an estimated 57 percent of federal inmates and 21 percent of state inmates were serving a sentence for a drug offense; about 10 percent of federal inmates and 49 percent of state inmates were in prison for a violent offense.

3. Violent offenders accounted for 53 percent of the growth in state prisons between 1990 to 2000, while drug offenders accounted for 59 percent of the growth in federal prisons.

Recidivism

1. Of the 272,111 persons released from prisons in fifteen states in 1994, an estimated 67.5 percent were rearrested for a felony or serious misdemeanor within three years, 46.9 percent were reconvicted, and 25.4 percent resentenced to prison for a new crime.

2. The 272,111 offenders discharged in 1994 accounted for nearly 4,877,000 arrest charges over their recorded careers.

3. Within three years of release, 2.5 percent of released rapists were rearrested for another rape, and 1.2 percent of those who had served time for homicide were arrested for a new homicide.

4. Sex offenders were less likely than non-sex offenders to be rearrested for any offense—43 percent of sex offenders versus 68 percent of non-sex offenders.

5. Sex offenders were about four times more likely than non-sex offenders to be arrested for another sex crime after their discharge from prison—5.3 percent of sex offenders versus 1.3 percent of non-sex offenders. Generally, sex offenders only commit that one type of crime, while other criminals commit many types of crimes.

Use of Alcohol by those Committing Crimes

1. Among the 5.3 million convicted offenders under the jurisdiction of corrections agencies in 1996, nearly 2 million, or

Prison Populations Worldwide

There are over 9 million jailed prisoners throughout the world. Many of these prisoners—25 percent, or 2.2 million people—are in U.S. prisons. China is next with 1.5 million people behind bars, and Russia has 860,000.

about 36 percent, were estimated to have been drinking at the time of the offense. The vast majority, about 1.5 million, of these alcohol-involved offenders were sentenced to supervision in the community: 1.3 million on probation and more than 200,000 on parole.

2. Alcohol use at the time of the offense was commonly found among those convicted of public-order (victimless) crimes, the offense most often seen among those on probation and in jail. Among violent offenders, 41 percent of probationers, 41 percent of those in local jails, 38 percent of those in state prisons, and 20 percent of those in federal prisons were estimated to have been drinking when they committed the crime.

Women Offenders

1. In 1998, there were an estimated 3.2 million arrests of women, accounting for 22 percent of all arrests that year.

2. Based on the reports from victims of violence, women account for 14 percent of violent offenders, an annual average of about 2.1 million violent female offenders.

3. Women accounted for about 16 percent of all felons convicted in state courts in 1996: 8 percent of convicted violent felons, 23 percent of property felons, and 17 percent of drug felons.

4. In 1998, more than 950,000 women were under correctional supervision, which is about 1 percent of the U.S. female population.

Parole

1. At least 95 percent of all state prisoners are released from prison at some point. Nearly 80 percent are released to parole supervision.

2. At the end of 2002, 1,440,655 prisoners were under the supervision of state or federal correction authorities.

3. In 2001, 592,000 state prisoners were released after serving time.

Criminal History

1. Fifty-three percent of jail inmates are on probation, parole, or pretrial release at the time of arrest.
2. Four in 10 jail inmates have a current or past sentence for a violent offense.
3. Thirty-nine percent of jail inmates in 2002 served three or more prior sentences before the current incarceration or probation, down from 44 percent in 1996.

4. 670,169 adults were under state parole supervision at the end of 2002.

What Are the Chances of You Going to State or Federal Prison?

1. If recent incarceration rates remain unchanged, an estimated 1 of every 15 persons (6.6 percent) will serve time in a prison during their lifetime.

2. Lifetime chances of a person going to prison are higher for: men (11.3 percent) than for women (1.8 percent) blacks (18.6 percent) and Hispanics (10 percent) than for whites (3.4 percent)

3. Based on current rates of first incarceration, an estimated 32 percent of black males will enter state or federal prison during their lifetime, compared to 17 percent of Hispanic males and 5.9 percent of white males.

Prison Jargon

4 piece: A full set of restraints (cuffs, leg irons, waist, and security cover).

10–10 Furlough: Death by unnatural causes, murder, as in "He wronged too many, and got his 10–10 furlough last night."

13 1/2: The sum of twelve jurors, one judge, and a fifty-fifty chance of acquittal, often seen in tattoos.

5–0: Correctional officer.

38: Masturbation.

AB: Aryan Brotherhood.

Ace Boon Coon: Best friend.

Alphabet: A sentence so long that it can't be described in numbers.

All Day: A life sentence, as in "He's doin' all day . . . ."

All Day and a Night: Life without parole.

Ass Betting: Gambling without being able to pay back.

Baby: A weak prisoner used for sex.

Back Gate Parole: Dying while in prison.

Bastille by the Bay: San Quentin Prison.

Bean Chute: Slot through which food trays are passed to prisoners in solitary confinement.

Beat Your Feet: Order by an officer to move out.

Bit: Term spent in prison.

Big Bitch: Life without parole.

Birds on the Line: Someone is listening to a private conversation.

Bitch Up: To give in.

Blade: A prison-made shank. To "blade up" is to cut someone up.

Blanket Party: Throwing a blanket over a prisoner so he or she can't identify their attacker.

Blickey: AIDS, as in "He or she has the blickey."

Blind: Area where correctional officers can't see prisoners.

Blazed: High.

Bonaroo: One's best clothing.

Bone: The dominant person in a gay relationship.

Bone Crusher: A large weapon.

Boneyard: Family (conjugal) visiting area.

Boof: Contraband in the rectum.

Booty Check: Rectal search.

Border Brothers: Mexican nationals.

Box: Disciplinary segregation.

Brick: A carton of cigarettes.

Bricks: The outside world.

Buck Rogers Time: A parole date so far into the next century the prisoner cannot imagine release.

Bug: A prisoner who is mentally disturbed.

Bulldog: A prisoner who uses fear and intimidation to get something.

Bullet: A one-year prison sentence.

Bumpin' Ya Gums: Talking too much.

Bunkies: People who share a double bunk bed.

Burn Rubber: Exclamation meaning "Leave me alone!"

Butched In: Performing oral sex to get something.

Catch a Square: Get ready to fight.

Catcher: Sexually passive person in a relationship.

Cat Nap: Short prison sentence.

Cell Gangster: Someone who talks tough only while in his cell.

Chasing the Dragon: Looking for heroin.

Cheese Eater: Snitch.

Cherry: New prisoner.

Chester: Child molester.

Chin Check: To hit someone in the jaw to see if they'll fight back.

Chip: When a homosexual prison inmate, pledged to one man, has an "adulterous" liaison with another. Chipping is viewed very severely by the cuckolded party and verbal or physical violence is virtually certain to occur.

Coffee and a Day: Out of prison in just over a day.

Commandos: Prisoners who seek sex from others after lights out.

Convict: A prisoner with traditional values.

Crime of Passion: prisoner serving time for a sex crime.

Cutting Up: Suicide.

Ding: A prison inmate who is mentally disturbed, or feigning so.

Daddy: Dominant homosexual.

Date: When a prisoner is to be released.

Dead Mouth: Told by a guard to keep quiet.

Debrief: Method of proving someone has left a gang by implicating ("snitching on") other gang members. Officials must then protect the person who has implicated the other gang members.

Deuce: A two-year sentence.

Diaper sniper: Child molester.

Diesel Therapy: Constant transfers to keep prisoner from associating with certain prison cliques.

Dime: A ten-year prison sentence.

Ding Wing: Where mentally ill prisoners are housed.

Dirt Nap: To die.

Dis: Disrespect.

Donkey Dick: Sliced cold cuts.

Down Letter: Rejection letter from the parole board.

Dragon's Tongue: Very tough sliced corned beef.

Dressed Out: To be assaulted by a prisoner with urine, feces, or any other liquid mixture.

Drug Charge: Child molestation, as in, "He's in on a drug charge—he drug them out of the sandbox."

Dump Truck: Attorney who does not fight hard for a client.

Ear Hustling: Eavesdropping.

Escape Dust: Fog.

Eyeball: To give a long , disparaging look to an officer.

Family Style: Sodomy in the "missionary" position.

Fence Parole: Escape.

Fifi: An artificial vagina used for masturbation.

Fish: New prisoner.

Floor Wet: Call to alert other prisoners that guards are coming.

Flop: Time between parole hearings.

Fluff: A feminine lesbian.

Fudge Packer: Homosexual.

Gashley: A woman.

Gas House: Public toilet in the cell block.

Gate Money: Money given to a freed prisoner.

Gated Out: Released from prison.

Gazer: Guard who watches the prisoners shower.

Goof: An insult; a fighting word; a complete idiot who has no pull in the prison; a child molester.

Goon Squad: Guard task force.

G.P.: General population.

Green Light: Marked for death.

Grey Bar Hotel: Prison.

Gunner: Prisoner who masturbates while looking at female guard.

Hack: Guard.

Heat Wave: Prisoner who invites scrutiny by guards.

Heart Check: A prisoner proving he's still with a gang by murdering someone.

High Class: Hepatitis C. As in, "She's high class!"

Hit in the Neck: Hopeless; from the almost always fatal target of a prison knife attack to the neck.

Hole: Solitary confinement.

Hooped: Hiding contraband, such as drugs, in one's rectum.

Hot Rail: Prisoners in a circle or group, hiding a prisoner and his girl having sex.

House: Cell.

Iron Pile: Weights.

Jack Mack: Canned mackerel. Occasionally used in a sock as a weapon.

Jackrabbit Parole: Escape.

Jail: A short-term prison facility (for terms that are less than a year).

Jolt: A long sentence.

Jones: Drug habit (or any other habit).

Jump the Broom: When prisoners marry.

Kill: To masturbate.

Laying the Track: Having sex.

Life on the Installment Plan: Life sentence served by stringing shorter sentences together.

Lifer: A prisoner serving a life sentence.

Limbo: Jail time before trial.

Line: The mainline, or general prison population, as in "on the line."

Lockdown: Locking prisoners in their cells.

L.W.O.P.: (pronounced "el-wop") Life Without Possibility of Parole.

Mafias: Dark sunglasses.

Mainline: The general prison population.

Make Paper: Make parole.

May Tag: Homosexual forced to do favors for another prisoner.

Max Out: To serve one's full sentence.

Moe: Married homosexual in prison.

Mud: Coffee.

Mule: Someone who carries contraband to a prisoner.

Nickel: A five-year prison sentence.

Nut up: Go crazy, become enraged.

Old Lady: Passive gay partner.

On Pipe: Homosexual. As in, "He's on pipe."

PC: Protective custody.

Pecker Palace: An area for conjugal visits.

Phone: The toilet is emptied and used to talk to other prisoners.

As in, "Hey Joe, get on the phone."

Pillow Biter: Someone who gets sodomized.

Pitcher: The dominant homosexual partner.

Pole Smoker: Gay person.

Policing: An officer who is doing his or her job. "That officer is policing hard."

Prize of the Poor: The death penalty.

Pruno: Alcoholic drink prisoners make.

Pull the Pin: Call for help.

Pumpkin Head: The appearance of someone's head after it is beaten with a weight inside a pillow case.

Punk City: Protective custody.

Rabbit: High escape risk.

Rag: A bandanna.

Reals: Name brand cigarettes.

Red Light Special: A hit ordered on a rival gang member.

Retired: Someone in prison for life.

Rev: Religious prisoner.

Ripper: Convicted rapist.

Safe: Using the vagina to hide contraband.

Sallyport: A secured area which leads in and out of the prison.

Scooper: Someone who eats with a spoon.

Short Eyes: Child molester.

Shower Hawk: A prisoner who preys upon others in the showers.

Siberia: Isolation unit.

Signed In: To enter protective custody.

Sister: A young prisoner who trades sex for protection.

Skating: Prisoners being someplace in the prison that is off limits.

Slam: Prisoner thrown to the ground by a guard.

Sleep: To knock someone out. "I sleeped him."

Smoke on the Horizon: Bad blood that may turn into violence.

Son: Punk or bitch.

Speeding Ticket: Violation in visitor's room, like touching or kissing.

Spider Monkey: Doing hard time, climbing the walls.

Spud Juice: Homemade alcohol.

Stand Your Gate: Order for prisoner to stand outside the door to his cell.

Stash: To hide something.

Stitched up: Resolved a problem, usually through a fight.

Sucker Stroking: Missing one's girlfriend so much that tears result.

Swag: Sandwich made by kitchen workers to pay off a debt.

Sweetie-Gold: Wrapped cakes that are used as money for gambling.

T-Jones: a prisoner's mother, usually black.

Tack: Tattoo.

Tack Head: Someone's woman.

Tally Ho: Rubber cement that is inhaled.

Teardrop: Ten-year sentence.

Tip: Prison gang.

Tailor-made: Packaged cigarettes, as opposed to those rolled on your own.

Tat: Tattoo.

The Go Slow: Disciplinary unit, as "They gave him seven days in the go-slow."

Three Knee Deep: Stabbed as a warning, but not deep enough to kill.

Tit: Drugs, heroin.

Toosh Hog: A hard ass.

Tossing Salad: Young, weak inmate being made to lick the anus of an older, stronger inmate.

To the Door: The length of a sentence, as in, "I got six to the door."

Trailer: A conjugal visit.

Trick: Person not in prison who provides money or favors.

Tuck: To hide contraband in one's anus.

Tune Up: A severe beating by an officer.

Turn Out: To turn a person into a "punk" by raping them.

Twist Your Cap: To kill someone.

Up The Road: Being transported from jail to prison.

The Walk: Yellow lines that lead to different areas of the prison. Prisoners must walk on one side of the line or the other.

Walkalone: Prisoners (such as those sentenced to death) who aren't allowed to exercise with other prisoners.

Walking Down Paper: Serving the part of a sentence that happens when one could have been out on parole.

Warehouse: An overcrowded prison with no facilities or programs.

Waterhead: A dumb inmate.

Wave Cap: Cloth worn on the head of a prisoner.

Weedy-Weedy: To snitch or provide information on someone.

White Shirts: High-ranking prison officers.

Wire: Information that comes over the phone.

Wobble Head: Mentally ill prisoners.

Wolf: Predatory prisoner.

Wreck: When a prisoner gets into some sort of trouble.

Yard: The exercise area.

Yo Yo: A person who is not sexually active with other prisoners.

General Rules of Prison Conduct

Do your own time: The fundamental prison maxim. Don't bother other prisoners or pry too deeply into their affairs.

It's mind over matter . . . they don't mind and you don't matter: An official action that lacks any logic and that basically denotes that officers do not care and a prisoner does not matter.

There are no secrets in the penitentiary: In prisons, rumor and gossip circulate fast.

Chapter 13
Stalking

Q&A

Q: Which gender more commonly stalks the other?

A: Men. Eight percent of men are stalkers while only one-quarter of that (two percent) are women. All told, experts estimate that there are 1.4 million stalkers in America.

Stalking at a Glance

1. A common technique of stalkers is to kidnap, injure, or kill the victim's pet, knowing that this will often devastate the victim emotionally.

2. Victims of stalking often say it would be better to be murdered than have to go through the horrendous mental anguish of being stalked.

3. Slashing the victim's tires or vandalism/destruction of the victim's home and property is standard behavior for stalkers.

4. Friends and family who support the victim are themselves in danger. The stalker views these people as obstacles to what he wants and will turn his wrath on them as well. Cases exist where relatives or a new boyfriend of the victim have had their home burned to the ground.

5. For someone being stalked, everyday things such as answering the phone or going out for a ride alone can no longer be done without constant fear.

6. Stalkers have been known to hire private detectives to help track down the victim when they've moved to another state.

7. Victims often are subjected to being followed, continual drive-bys of their homes and workplaces, and being inundated with unwanted phone calls, answering machine messages, letters, emails, notes left on doors and car windshields, and so forth. It is, for all intents and purposes, an act of terrorism.

8. Having police confront the stalker or getting a restraining order often will provoke or escalate the violence in the case.

9. While police in general do everything they can within the law, some stalking victims complain that their cries for help are looked upon as exaggerations, overreactions, or even lies.

10. The first stalking law was instituted in 1990 in California, and since then, all fifty states have enacted stalking laws.

11. Even after the stalker has been successfully arrested, prosecuted, and jailed, the victim still lives in fear of the day the stalker will be released.

12. Forensic psychologists divide stalkers into two general categories. About 25 percent of stalkers fall into the "love obsession" group. People who stalk celebrities fall into this category. They are also the people who become

fixated with a coworker, acquaintance, teacher, and so forth. They live in a delusional fantasy world complete with their own script of how this object of their fixation loves them and is already in a relationship with them. Those in this category suffer from a form of mental illness, like paranoia or schizophrenia. The other 75 percent or so of stalkers are in the "simple obsession" group. These people previously have been in some form of relationship with the victim, either romantic or personal. When the relationship ends, the stalker feels lost and powerless. He cannot bear the thought of the victim being out of his life, so the patterns of stalking behavior begin. Unfortunately, this category produces the majority of domestic violence, the worst of which ends in murder-suicide.

Cysberstalking Facts at a Glance

1. "Cyberstalking" is the term used to describe repeated threatening or harassing electronic communications (emails) sent through the Internet. What begins as an innocent correspondence with a stranger in a chat room can develop into an obsessional pursuit by the online stalker, who can be every bit as devious as his offline counterpart. They will wait for the victim to go online and then send constant instant messages (IMs), or the victim will find their inbox full of emails from this one person when they go online. Because of the anonymous nature of the Internet, the cyberstalker can be down the street or on the other side of the country.

2. During his tenure as vice president, Al Gore said of cyberstalking, "Make no mistake, this kind of harassment can be

as frightening and as real as being followed in your neighborhood or watched in your home."

3. If the cyberstalker has the victim's personal information (which was willingly given to the would-be stalker when they thought the stalker was just a "nice guy"), the stalker can go to chat rooms impersonating the victim and post enticing or inflammatory messages on the bulletin board (sometimes giving out the street address and phone number of the victim at the same time), which can bring third parties into the harassment.

4. One cyberstalking victim in California kept receiving the number 187 on her pager. 187 is the police code for a homicide.

Q&A

Q: How many women and how many men will be stalked in their lifetime?

A: Eight percent of American women and 2 percent of American men—1.4 million stalking victims every year. Most stalkers have been in relationships with the people they stalk, but many have never even met the victims or were just casual acquaintances.

Q: How many stalkers are violent?
1. 1 percent
2. 10 percent
3. 30 percent
4. 50 percent

A: Thirty percent, almost one third—a scary figure.

Q. If someone is being stalked, is it wise to get a restraining order, which will theoretically keep the stalker a certain distance away?
   1. Yes
   2. No
   3. Possibly

A. If you are being stalked, consult an expert to see if it will work in your case. Sometimes it does and sometimes it doesn't.

Who Am I?

1. At the time of the event, I was nineteen years old, an unemployed janitor, and resident of Tucson, Arizona.

2. One day I was watching a commercial for a TV show called My Sister Sam, and on it I saw a beautiful young woman with big brown eyes, dimples, and a beautiful smile. As I told the police later, "Her personality came out . . . an open personality . . . it interested me in her . . . I felt like I knew her . . . ."

3. I gathered all kinds of information on her, including pictures she sent me.

4. I became obsessed with her and vowed to meet her, so on July 18, 1989, I went to Los Angeles.

5. I waited outside her Hollywood apartment for a long time until a vehicle came along and she answered the door. I went up and asked if she could talk to me but she said she was "too busy at the moment."

6. That bothered me, so I went back to her door later and rang the bell. She answered.

Answer: My name is Robert John Bardo and I stalked and murdered promising actress Rebecca Schaeffer, shooting her once in the chest as she stood in her doorway.

A Horrific Stalking

Undoubtedly one of the most horrific and traumatic stalkings of the twentieth century was that propagated by Mark David Chapman, a psychotic who traveled all the way from Hawaii to the building opposite Central Park in New York City, where John Lennon lived. Chapman stalked Lennon until the night of December 8, 1980. Lennon had signed some autographs—including one for Chapman—and then turned and headed toward his apartment house. Chapman shot him in the back multiple times, and the world, for a lot of people, changed forever. Perhaps the best line describing this tragedy came from journalist and novelist Pete Hamill, who said that later, in the morgue, "two attendants were having fun and playing grabass . . . while there, behind them, in a refrigerated box, was the Sixties."

Top left photo—The death certificate of John Lennon.
(New York City Medical Examiner)

Mark David Chapman, *center*, the man who stalked John Lennon
(Photofest)

Chapter 14
Female Killers

Q&A

Q: What happened at these addresses?
924 Belmont Avenue, Lincoln, Nebraska
South 24th Street, Lincoln, Nebraska
Superior Street, North of Lincoln, Nebraska
August Meyer Farm, Lincoln, Nebraska
Highway 87, off Ayers Road, Wyoming

A: Charles Starkweather and his girlfriend Caril Fugate murdered a series of people in these locations starting in January 1958.

Q: Are female serial killers more efficient than male serial killers?

A: Most experts say yes. Females are quiet killers with low visibility. In 1998, Kelleher and Kelleher examined the careers of one hundred female serial killers and found that, in one hundred murders since 1900, it took eight years to catch a female serial killer—double that of a male.

She Puts Jack to Shame

Jack the Ripper may be more notorious, but while he was busy killing five prostitutes in the alleyways of Victorian London, another Victorian murderer, Jane Toppan (1880–1901), was apprehended on charges of having killed close to one hundred people in Connecticut as a live-in nurse. Her murder method was poisoning. She confessed to thirty-one counts of murder, and she was confined to an insane asylum, where she died. Toppan said in court, "That is my ambition, to have killed more people—more helpless people—than any man or woman who has ever lived."

Q&A

Q: For how much crime are females responsible?

A: Females usually account for about 15 percent of all violent crime and 28 percent of all property crime. However, there has been about a 140 percent increase in the number of crimes committed by women since 1970, and the upward trend is steady. Women have significant numbers in embezzlement (41 percent), fraud (39 percent), forgery (36 percent), and larceny-theft (33 percent). For homicide, one of the most frequently-cited facts is a Justice Department study in 1991 that states females who were imprisoned for murder were twice as likely as men to have killed an intimate (husband, boyfriend, or child).

Q: What percentage of serial killers are female?

A: Female serial killers account for only 8 percent of all American serial killers, but American females account for 76 percent of all female serial killers worldwide.

Most Horrific Murder?

While many murders are gruesome and mind-boggling, our candidate for most horrific is what Susan Smith of Union, South Carolina, did. Because her prospective boyfriend didn't like kids, she strapped her own two little baby sons in the back of her car and rolled the car into a lake, drowning them. She made up a story—giving everyone hope that the kids might still be alive—that a black man had carjacked the kids, but police became increasingly suspicious of her, and her lie detector test was inconclusive. She was finally confronted, arrested, and sentenced to life in prison.

Ladylike Murder Weapons

1. Poison (80 percent)
2. Shooting (20 percent)
3. Bludgeoning (16 percent)
4. Suffocation (16 percent)
5. Stabbing (11 percent)
6. Drowning (5 percent)

Female Murder Motives

1. Money (74 percent)
2. Control (13 percent)
3. Enjoyment (11 percent)
4. Sex (10 percent)
5. Drugs, cult involvement, cover up, or feelings of inadequacy (24 percent)

Uniquely Feminine Killers

There are two types of killers that are overwhelmingly female.
1. **Black Widow.** Someone who kills her spouse or other family member, usually for financial gain.
2. **Angel of Death.** Nurse or other medical worker who kills patients.

Black Widows

The name, of course, comes from the black widow spider, who kills her mate after mating. Human black widows do the same thing.

Black widows usually start killing after the age of twenty-five, beginning a decade or longer cycle of systematically killing spouses, partners, family members, and indeed, anyone with whom they develop a personal relationship. They usually claim six to eight victims over a period of ten to fifteen years, although in places where law enforcement is lax, the victim count could go as high as thirteen or fourteen. Poison that can't be detected easily is the preferred method of murder. Following are some infamous black widows and the years they were active.

1. **Belle Gunness (1896–1908)** lived on a farm outside Chicago and was known as "Lady Bluebeard." She was the first known twentieth-century black widow. She murdered forty-nine people, but was never prosecuted. She killed adults, children, ranch workers—anyone. Most of them were poisoned.

2. **Amy Gilligan (1901–1914)** ran a private nursing home in Windsor, Connecticut, and married and killed five older men and got herself named in the wills of nine elderly women before killing them. Eventually her crimes were discovered, and she died in prison.

3. **Lydia Trueblood (1915–1919)** operated in Pocatello, Idaho, and poisoned her only child as well as her brother-in-law—not to mention five husbands.

4. **Rhonda Bell Martin (1932–1956)** murdered her mother, two husbands, and five of her children in Birmingham, Alabama. She was caught and died in the electric chair.

5. **Waneta Hoyt (1965–1971)** suffocated five of her six children in Oswego, New York. She claimed sudden infant death syndrome (SIDS) was responsible for the deaths, but she was convicted of murder in 1995 and sentenced to life in prison.

6. **Margie Velma Barfield (1969–1978),** of Lumbetton, North Carolina, killed seven husbands, a handful of fiancés, and her mother. She burned some victims to death while they slept (made to look like smoking in bed), arranged prescription drug overdoses for others, and occasionally used arsenic made to look like gastroenteritis. She was finally caught for the murder of her boyfriend, Stuart Taylor, when an autopsy found traces of arsenic in his system. She was sentenced to and died by lethal injection in 1984, the first woman to be executed in the U.S. since 1976.

7. **Blanche Taylor Moore (1966–1989)** of Burlington, North Carolina, varied her M.O., doing away with lovers, husbands, her pastor, her father, and her mother-in-law. Men, it was said, were all symbols to her of her abusive father. She also died by lethal injection.

Angels of Death

These killers usually start killing in their early twenties and typically kill about eight people over a one- or two-year period. They tend to brag about their murderous achievements, which leads to their arrest.

1. **Genene Jones (1950–)** was a vocational nurse who loved to work with terminally ill children. She was convicted and sentenced to life imprisonment in San Antonio, Texas, for eleven child murders in 1984. She used heart medication to kill. After she was convicted, the hospitals and clinics where she worked destroyed her records so no one could examine them and discover more murders, which cops were convinced she had committed.

2. **Terri Rachals (1985–1986)** was an old intensive care nurse in Albany, Georgia, indicted on six counts of murder in 1986. However, she was only sentenced to seventeen years in prison for aggravated assault because of her mental state. She murdered by injecting patients with potassium chloride, stopping their hearts.

3. **Madame Popova (1879–1909)** ran a contract murder service in Russia that freed women from abusive husbands. She had at least three hundred victims and was known to kill by using poison, her own hands, a weapon, or assassins. She was caught and executed.

Female Serial Murderers

1. **Aileen Wuornos** is undoubtedly the most famous female serial killer. She was born in the Midwest and by the time she was fourteen, she was working as a prostitute. She had developed a profound hatred of men, and in 1992 in Florida, she started picking them up, leading them into the woods—ostensibly for sex—and then shooting them to death. She claimed that they tried to rape her, but this didn't hold water. All told, she murdered seven men and ultimately died in the electric chair. Ironically, it was not a man but a woman, her obese, gap-toothed lesbian lover, who set her up to be arrested by taping incriminating telephone conversations. Charlize Theron gave an Academy award-winning performance as Wuornos in the motion picture Monster.

2. **Lila Young (1927–1947)** was a twenty-eight-year-old midwife who operated a baby farm in Halifax, Nova Scotia. She and her husband, both devoted Seventh Day Adventists, catered to unwed mothers who wanted to give their babies up for adoption. When business got slow, they simply cut

back on the babies up for adoption, killing, sometimes by starvation, over one hundred infants. They were never brought to justice and died in the 1960s.

3. **Anna Marie Hahn (1932–1937)** was a twenty-six-year-old German immigrant who cared for elderly men, bilking them of their money and then killing them when the money ran out. She offered a "mercy killing" defense but the jury didn't buy it, and in 1938 she became the first woman to go to Ohio's electric chair.

4. **Dorothea Puente (1986–1990)** was a charming and attractive fifty-seven-year-old woman who got Social Services to refer clients to her for care. She killed at least twenty-five, but she kept their Social Security checks long after they were gone. She was finally caught when the stench of the seven bodies she buried in the backyard called the neighbors' attention to her. There was a protracted trial, and she came close to being sentenced to death, but at age sixty-four she was finally sentenced to life in prison.

Team Killers

Team killers can be any combination of people: male-male, male-female, female-female, or a cult, like Charlie Manson and his brood. They may kill up to fifteen people and favor guns or knives for their dirty work. The relationships usually last no more than two years. Following are some of the more famous team killers and the years they were active.

1. Maybe the most famous male-female killing team is Bonnie Parker and Clyde Barrow (1930–1934). She was only seventeen, he twenty-one. They stole cars, robbed

banks, and murdered people, cutting a wide swath of carnage across the Midwest. All told they killed sixteen, thirteen of them police officers. They enjoyed killings cops. Cops killed them in an ambush in Shreveport, Louisiana.

2. Martha Beck and Raymond Fernandez (1947–1949) aka, "the Lonely Hearts Killers," were a twenty-seven-year-old couple from Pensacola, Florida, who murdered twenty women throughout various cities in the U.S. They posed as brother and sister, placing personal ads in newspapers and various lonely heart magazines to attract female victims looking for companionship or matrimony. They robbed and then killed twenty women, and they were executed in Sing Sing's electric chair.

3. Charles Manson and his "family": Susan Atkins, Patricia Krenwinkel, Leslie Van Houten, Mary Brunner, Linda Kesabian, Charles Watson, et al. (1968–1969). They lived on an abandoned studio ranch in the California desert, and at its height the family numbered fifty people, led by thirty-four-year-old ex-con Charles Manson. Manson and his "family" were suspected of ritualistically killing at least twenty people, but in 1970, they were convicted of killing the pregnant actress Sharon Tate and her four friends. Manson and the others responsible were sentenced to death, but the death penalty was overturned and instead all were sentenced to life in prison.

4. Carolyn McCrary and Sherman McCrary, Ginger Taylor, Ray Taylor, and Daniel McCrary (1971–1972), aka "the McCrary Family." They started their careers as robbers in Athens, Texas, and eventually they expanded into murder,

raping and killing young female employees in stores from Florida to California. They would rape their victims repeatedly in the car, then shoot them and throw the bodies out the window. Their brutal spree came to an end during a shootout with police in Santa Barbara and their subsequent arrest after a car chase. Although the FBI linked them to twelve additional unsolved homicides, they were only convicted of ten, the ten being the ones to which they could be directly linked. Each member of the family received a sentence of imprisonment ranging from five years to life.

5. Charlene Gallego and Gerald Gallego (1978–1980), dubbed "the Sex Slave Murderers," were a twenty-two-year-old married couple from Sacramento, California who abducted, brutally raped, tortured, and buried alive ten young female victims between the ages of thirteen and sixteen. Gerald told his wife that raping and killing young females was the only cure for his impotence, and she helped him secure his prey. They murdered people in California, Oregon, and Nevada. But someone remembered a license plate and it led to Gerald getting the death sentence and his wife, for some strange reason, only sixteen years in prison.

6. Judith Neelley and Alvin Neelley (1980–1982), aka "the Night Rider and Lady Sundance." Alvin was twenty-nine and Judith nineteen. This married couple roamed Alabama, Georgia, and Tennessee, abducting fifteen young girls and torturing them for days until finally killing them by injecting them with drain cleaner. Judith taunted police with calls as to where to find the bodies, and it proved to be the couple's undoing. Cops were able

to analyze the background sounds when the calls were made, and it led them straight to the couple. Alvin got life and Judith was sentenced to death.

7. Carol Bundy and Doug Clark (1980), known as "the Sunset Slayer" or "Hollywood Slasher," were a thirty-eight-year-old Los Angeles couple whose specialty was decapitating people. They would abduct both males and females and then sexually torture and kill them: Doug particularly liked having oral sex performed on him, then shooting the victim in the head while the act was occurring. The couple would keep the heads. Carol, who would lie about being related to serial murderer Ted Bundy, slept around and bragged to boyfriends about the killings—which necessitated the victim being killed to be silenced. But one potential victim got away, and it resulted in Carol getting life in prison and Doug getting the death penalty.

8. Debra Brown and Alton Coleman (1984). Brown was an easily influenced high school dropout, and Coleman had an extensive criminal record; she was twenty-one years old and he was twenty-eight. Both were Waukegan, Illinois, residents. They were an unusual pair of team killers because they were black—in fact, black serial killers are rare in general. They went on a seven-week homicide binge, killing many people, at least eight of whom—ranging in age from seven to forty-one and all also black—were raped and murdered. Their bloody foray took them through Indiana, Michigan, and Ohio, and when finally caught, they were tried and convicted, and received death sentences.

9. Cynthia Coffman and James Marlow (1986) were a twenty-four-year-old and twenty-nine-year-old couple who, for five weeks, cut a bloody swath through the country from California to Kentucky. They specialized in robbing females who were withdrawing money from an ATM. They strangled four of the women. Marlow was a white supremacist (Coffman met him while visiting her boyfriend in prison) and his intelligence left something to be desired: while on the run, they registered in a California motel under their real last names, and the police showed up and arrested them.

10. Gwendolyn Graham and Catherine May Wood (1987) were a lesbian couple in their mid-twenties who got off sexually by smothering old women to death. They murdered at least five, but when Graham, the dominant partner, deserted Wood for a job in Texas, the 450-pound Wood emotionally collapsed and went to the authorities. She got twenty years in prison, and Wood got life.

Team Killers Supreme: Caril Fugate and the Tiny Terror

The first inkling of trouble came on a Saturday night, January 25, 1958. Lincoln, Nebraska, police got a complaint from Bob Von Busch, brother-in-law of the Bartletts, saying that he and his wife were being kept out of the house on 924 Belmont Avenue by the Bartletts' adopted daughter, fifteen-year-old Caril Ann Fugate. Caril Ann told the brother-in-law that the doctor didn't want anyone to come in because everyone had the Asian flu. But Von Busch and his wife were suspicious and concerned.

Police went over to check things out at around 10 p.m. They pounded on the door until Caril Ann answered. She was dressed in a kimono and acted as if she had been sleeping. Fugate, annoyed, told the police that everyone was down with the flu and "the doctor told me not to let anyone in. Besides, my aunt had her baby with her. I'd have to be crazy to let her in." The police left, thinking they were in the middle of some harmless family dispute.

However, Bob Von Busch was still suspicious. He could not see any reason why he and his wife could not at least talk through the door with the Bartletts. He went back to the police station on Monday morning and convinced the cops to come back. When the police knocked, no one answered. The front and rear doors were locked, but the police were able to enter the house through a basement window.

There was no sign of anyone. The house looked like it had been lived in; it was very messy. There was also a small dog there, and it seemed to be okay, so they left. But Bob Von Busch was determined. He returned to the house yet a third time and tried to figure out where the Bartletts might have gone. He found no sign of them, but then remembered their chicken coop, a low-slung shed about twenty yards from the back of the house. Marion Bartlett sometimes liked to go out there. Thinking that it was probably absurd to think anyone was there now—it was very cold out and the coop was unheated— he decided to check it out anyway.

He opened the door and was shocked: the body of Marion Bartlett was lying in the shed. He looked like he had been shot in the head, perhaps stabbed. The brother-in-law called the police again. They arrived and immediately checked out the rest of the property. There were two more bodies in the out- house: Velda Bartlett was stuffed partly into the toilet seat hole. They found the baby, Betty Jean, in a corrugated cardboard box, her head smashed, her throat cut ear to ear.

APB Issued

Cops started to look for Fugate. They couldn't find her, but their investigation revealed something potentially significant: Fugate had been seen with one Charlie Starkweather at around one-thirty the same day that the cops had entered the house through the basement and decided nothing looked unusual. Fugate and Starkweather both had suitcases. An all-points bulletin was issued for the couple, along with Starkweather's 1949 black Ford hot rod, and word issued that Fugate was likely with him.

Charlie Starkweather, also known as "Little Red," was a five-foot five-inch nineteen-year-old weighing around 140 pounds. When provoked, he had the personality of a wolverine. He was known in the area as a fierce fighter, someone you shouldn't mess with, who would stab you as sure as he would look at you. He had three interests in life: hot rods, comic books, and guns. He wore very thick glasses but was still a crack shot.

As it happened, police would not catch up with Starkweather and Fugate until they had cut a bloody swath across America that got international attention. When the two were captured, police pieced together what happened through their own investigations and the statements of Fugate and Starkweather. It all started at the house at 924 Belmont.

Reflex: Murder

Charlie Starkweather had come to see Caril Ann Fugate at the house on Saturday afternoon and got into an argument with her mother, Velda. Velda didn't like Starkweather, and she intensely disliked her pretty daughter going out with him, and at one point she slapped Starkweather in the face. Starkweather slapped her back, and then her husband, Marion, interceded. Starkweather responded by shooting him to death and "cutting him up a little," as Starkweather said later, "then doing the same to Velda. During this ordeal the baby was crying, so he used the butt of his rifle to smash her head; to make sure she would stop, he cut her throat. What precise role Caril Fugate played is not known, but she certainly didn't intercede on her parents' behalf.

After the murders, an interior door was taken down and used as a stretcher to carry the bodies out: Marion to the chicken coop, Velda and the baby, dumped in the box, to the outhouse.

Top photo—Caril Fugate, left, team killer
(Author's Collection)

Charlies "Little Red" Starkweather, the other half of the team and killer of thirteen people.
(Author's Collection)

Like Man and Wife

Charlie and Caril Ann didn't leave the house right away. In fact, they lived in the house for six days while the bodies of Caril's family froze just outside. Charlie had called Marlon's job and told one of the managers that Marlon wouldn't be in—he had the flu. They also put a note on the door which warned people not to come into the house because everyone in it had the flu. But then the relatives started knocking on the door, and the police followed.

Just a few hours before the brother-in-law discovered Marion's body, Fugate and Starkweather took off in his 1949 black Ford with the red-painted grill and headed south on Route 77. The house was getting too hot for them. Apparently, before they made their fourth kill, they encountered two people who were very lucky. Starkweather didn't shoot them.

One was a man who owned a gas station about seven miles from the Fugate house. He sold Starkweather two boxes of .22 shells and a box of shells for a .410 shotgun. The man saw the shotgun in the back of the truck.

The second lucky man owned a farm in Bennet, which was about thirteen miles south of Lincoln. He was driving his pickup when he came upon Starkweather and Fugate trying to push their car out of some mud near the storm cellar of an abandoned school. The man knew Starkweather from Starkweather's hunting in the area, and the man pulled the Ford out with his pickup. Why Starkweather didn't kill him is anyone's guess.

Another Victim

On Wednesday morning, another man who knew Starkweather reported seeing the black Ford parked in the driveway of the farm of seventy-year-old August Meyer. But there was no sign of life from the house, not even smoke from the chimney, an odd thing in the winter. Police quickly gathered and prepared for an assault on the house, aware that Starkweather was well armed and a good shot. The assault began with tear gas grenades being fired through the windows, and when there was no response, police stormed the house.

They found Gus Meyer on the living room floor, dead from a shot to the head. Later it was learned that Meyer had armed himself when he saw Starkweather coming, but Starkweather had gotten the drop on Meyer. The police now figured that

Starkweather and Fugate had killed four people. They were wrong—there were six victims. It was just that the bodies of the other two had not been discovered. They were to be found a few hours later in an old storm cellar.

Good Samaritans Killed

Robert Jensen, seventeen, was on a date with sixteen-year-old Carol King. As it happened, they had stopped on the evening of January 27 to help Starkweather and Fugate, who apparently had car trouble. Starkweather and Fugate marched them down to the cellar, where Starkweather sodomized Carol and then shot each of them in the head with a .22 long gun.

After the discovery of Meyer and the two high school kids, panic clutched the countryside. Now it was clear that police were after mad-dog killers who slaughtered at random. That image was reinforced on Wednesday, January 29, when Starkweather invaded the house of C. Lauer Ward on 24th Street in a posh section of Lincoln. Ward was an important politico in the state of Nebraska who just the day before had been to visit Governor Victor Anderson on business. Ward missed an appointment on Wednesday, and no one could contact him by phone, so a relative went over to investigate. Both the front and rear doors were locked, but something was amiss: instead of Lauer's 1956 Packard in the driveway, there was a blue 1950 Ford. The relative called the police.

When the police arrived, the blue Ford set off alarm bells. They checked the license plates and then they were sure. The blue Ford belonged to Robert Jensen, the seventeen-year-old murder victim. Again they surrounded the house, and when they were ready, they took the door down and rushed inside.

They almost tripped over the body of Lauer Ward. He was lying on the foyer floor. He had been stabbed in the back and shot in the head. There were more grisly discoveries upstairs. They found Ward's wife, Clara, and housekeeper, Lillian Fencl, tied up and gagged. They were covered with blood and both women had been stabbed to death. A nation that was already shocked by the killings was given another big jolt.

Stopping the Slaughter

The police were desperate to stop Charlie Starkweather and Caril Fugate; it was highly likely that they would continue to kill. Every available officer was put on the job. At one point, there were over a thousand people patrolling Lancaster County, and there were roadblocks—over a hundred—everywhere. Governor Anderson also offered a $1,000 reward (a hefty sum in the 1950s) on the deadly couple's heads and, additionally, he called out two hundred National Guardsmen.

They had Lancaster County locked up, as one lawman said at the time, "as tight as a clam's ass."

The problem was that Starkweather and Fugate were nowhere near Lancaster County. After killing Ward, his wife, and their housekeeper, they had sped north toward Wyoming, covering five hundred miles a day. They were driving Ward's Packard for awhile, but soon figured it was best to get a new car. The opportunity presented itself when they spotted a car parked by the side of the road on the highway about fourteen miles west of Douglas, Wyoming. There was a man sleeping behind the wheel. Starkweather woke the man up and told him to get out of the car. The salesman resisted and Starkweather shot him nine times.

Starkweather and Fugate now had a problem: They couldn't get the emergency brake released to start the car. Then Joseph Sprinkle, an agent for an oil company, was driving along and saw Caril Fugate in the back of the Packard, crying. Sprinkle, a big man, got out and approached the car. Starkweather emerged from behind the car, leveled a .22 long at Sprinkle, and said: "Help me get this emergency brake off or I'll kill you."

Sprinkle obeyed and leaned into the car to work on the brake and saw the bloodied body of the shoe salesman. He realized he was in mortal danger, and when Starkweather leaned near him as if to help, Sprinkle grabbed the rifle, and Starkweather smashed him in the jaw. The big man tripped Starkweather and then they were on the ground. Sprinkle knew that if Starkweather got the rifle, he was dead. They grappled furiously, and then lady luck smiled on Sprinkle: Deputy Sheriff Bill Romer came along, saw the fight, and stopped.

As Romer got out of his car, Caril Fugate ran toward him, yelling at him to stop Starkweather, that he had already killed ten people. She hugged Romer as if he were her savior—and it was just the moment Starkweather needed. Without the rifle, he bolted to the Packard, started it up, and the next thing Romer knew, Starkweather was heading away at high speed.

Romer ran to his car and radioed ahead to the state highway patrol at Casper to set up roadblocks. He also notified Douglas cops Sheriff Earl Hetlin and Police Chief Robert Ainslie that Starkweather was fleeing west. Romer and Sprinkle attended to the dead man—his name was Merle Collison—and, with Caril Fugate in back of the patrol car, headed toward Casper. As they went, Fugate, half hysterical, tried to convince the men that she was an unwilling hostage of Charlie Starkweather. It didn't sound convincing.

They had gone about twenty miles when the Packard, Starkweather behind the wheel, flashed by them from the opposite direction. It was going in excess of a hundred miles an hour. The roadblocks, Romer thought, were working. Shortly thereafter, Heflin and Ainslie, heading west, spotted Starkweather heading east back toward Douglas. They brought their car to a screeching halt, made a U-turn, and were in pursuit.

Desperate Chase

The chase was right out of a Hollywood movie. Starkweather was going one hundred miles per hour in the Packard, but the patrol car was doing 115 and caught up to Starkweather, who was just outside the Douglas city limits. The cops rammed the rear of Starkweather's car, locking bumpers, but a dip in the road jolted them free just as they entered downtown Douglas. They went through Douglas at speeds in excess of a hundred miles an hour. Unbelievably, no one was hurt.

Outside the town, the cops started to fire at Starkweather, trying to take out his tires, but the cops were unsuccessful. Then they simply fired at the car, peppering it with bullet holes and shattering the rear window. Suddenly, about five miles outside of Douglas, the Packard came to a screeching stop in the middle of the road and Starkweather emerged. He was crying and holding his ear, which was bleeding. "Help me," he yelled, "I'm dying, bleeding to death." The cops told him to get his hands up—and he did. He was taken into custody.

The Making of a Murderer

It's difficult to discern what produced the homicidal rage in Charlie Starkweather. His parents, Guy and Helen Starkweather, lived in Lincoln and, though poor, they were not destitute. Guy was a handyman, Helen a homemaker. Charlie was the third child in a family of seven boys and one girl. He was small and bowlegged, and this certainly didn't help his self-image. When he was a kid, other children would make fun of him.

His mother was apparently a sweet woman who was the anchor of the family, while his father was dominant and had a temper and drank. On at least one occasion the father physically attacked Charlie, but one doesn't get a sense of systematic abuse in their relationship. Charlie seemed to love his mother very much, but there was no love lost between him and his father. During his trial, however, both parents supported him. Still, people who knew Charlie knew him as a person who was oozing anger, and one friend characterized him as a "three-dollar bill": weird.

Caril Fugate, whose background is cloudy, continued to claim she was a captive of Charlie Starkweather during their murderous odyssey, but the facts of the case indicated differently, including one key: she had had numerous opportunities to escape. She was sentenced to life imprisonment. Charles "Little Red" Starkweather was sentenced to die in the electric chair. Fugate begged him to tell authorities that she was a captive rather than a collaborator, but Starkweather's response was quite clear. "If I go to the chair," he said, "she should be sitting on my lap."

On July 25, 1959, Charles Starkweather, swaggering to the end, went to the chair with no one on his lap.

Chapter 15
Arson

Q&A

Q: What is arson?

A: The malicious and willful burning of property. A fire is legally determined to be arson if it meets three qualifications:

1. The property is burned. This must be shown in court to be actual destruction, at least in part, not just scorching or creating soot.
2. The fire is intentionally set.
3. The fire was started with malice.

Car set on fire. (Dave Green)

Q&A

Q: According to FEMA, how many arson fires are there in the U.S. every year?

1. 50,000
2. 75,000
3. 200,000
4. 300,000
5. 500,000

A: About 500,000

The Power of Fertilizer

Years ago when Hawaii Five O was a popular TV show, one of the authors (Tom Philbin) concocted a plot where an extortionist, who also happened to be a volcanologist, an expert on how volcanoes worked, threatened to make one of Hawaii's volcanoes erupt—something he knew he could do if he could blow a hole in the side of one of the island's volcanoes. He knew that the resulting hole would then allow the lava cooking inside to flow out, something like what would happen if someone were to puncture the side of a pressure cooker.

The problem, though, was to find an explosive that was not only cheap, but powerful enough to blow a hole in a mountain.

Figuring they might know, the author called the DuPont Chemical Company, which, at the time, made explosives, and got one of their chemists on the line. In these non-terrorist times, the conversation was free and easy.

"So," Tom said, "is there a cheap explosive that is very powerful."

"Sure," the chemist said, "ammonium nitrate fertilizer."

"Fertilizer."

"Sure."

"How powerful is it?"

"More powerful that nitroglycerine," he said, "In the Forties, a ship docked in the harbor in Texas City, Texas, went up and they later found its anchor about two miles away."

"Wow! So how would this volcanologist make a bomb."

And then the chemist told me, something that cannot in good conscience be reported here.

But that same formula was used, many years later, by Timothy McVey, who parked a van outside the Murrah Building in Oklahoma City, Oklahoma, and detonated it, killing many people in the process and making the concrete building look like someone had used a giant ice cream scoop on it.

Q&A

Q: How many people are arson victims every year?

A: Arson kills more than 700 Americans a year and is the second leading cause of residential fire deaths.

One of the Deadliest Arsonists of All

For anyone interested in arson and arsonists, one of the best books available is *The Fire Lover: A True Story*, by Joseph Wambaugh.

The book is about a Los Angeles fire investigator named John Orr, who was fascinated by fires and set innumerable ones himself. At one point it was estimated that he set two thousand brush fires over a ten-year period. Such fires are incredibly dangerous, and all the homes that burned to the ground affirmed that.

Orr's fire setting caused a number of deaths, but even after being convicted, Orr denied that he had set any fires and that he was a victim of overzealous investigators, if not state and federal officials, and incompetent prosecutors and defense counsel.

All he asked Wambaugh in writing his book was that he be fair, that he go with the evidence in evaluating his guilt or innocence, and Wambaugh did. "There's a mountain of evidence," he said.

In his research into Orr's life, Wambaugh found that he was interested in firemen when he was young and he also wanted to be the one to notify firemen when a fire was discovered. But when he became a fireman, he was very critical of other firemen if they didn't extinguish a fire the way he thought they should.

Orr, who wanted to be a novelist, wrote a book about a fire investigator who had a good side and a bad side—just like him.

A Not So Good Joke

In the 1970s, I lived opposite a large restaurant known as Linck's Log Cabin that lay abandoned for years and that gradually got banged up and run down. There were various attempts to resuscitate the restaurant, all without success. Then, a man came in with a lot of money and proposed turning it into a country western club with big stars like Willie Nelson appearing. He appeared to have achieved that, but at the last minute, much to his chagrin, one of the neighbors who had promised to support him in his quest for the club betrayed him at a crucial town meeting and the project fell through.

The very next day, the first wisp of smoke appeared at the top of Linck's Log Cabin, and as it happened, being a journalist, I had a camera handy and photographed it as it burned to the ground.

The next day, the arson detectives were out in force, scrambling over the blackened husk this way and that, taking their own photos and gathering their evidence.

I figured that they might be interested in the pictures I had, so I went across and approached a particularly large and burly man who looked like he was one of the people in charge.

"Can I help you," he said as I approached.

"No," I said, "I just like to be around fires."

If looks could kill, I would have been prone.

Then I explained that I had the pictures. Later I found out that arson detectives often look for arsonists at the scene of a fire both before and during the event. Small wonder I got that look.

Understanding Arsonists

Forensic scientists have noted that there are generally two different types of arsonists. Arsonists may be divided into organized and disorganized.

Organized Arsonists:
- use elaborate incendiary devices (electronic timing mechanisms, or initiators)
- leave behind less physical evidence; if forced entry, it's skillful
- have a methodical approach (excessive accelerant use and a pattern in the attacks)

Disorganized Arsonists:
- tend to use the materials at hand
- use more common accelerants such as gasoline
- leave behind more physical evidence (footprints, fingerprints, and so forth)

Q&A

Q: What government agency investigates arson?

A: The Bureau of Alcohol, Tobacco and Firearms (ATF).

Profile of an Arsonist

Most arsonists are young: 55 percent are under the age of eighteen, and a good number—26 percent—are only ten to fourteen years old. Nine out of ten times they are male, and 75% of the time, they are black. Usually they are from blue collar backgrounds and have low IQs ranging from 70 to 90, with some IQs below 70 (in the retarded range). Family history is generally dysfunctional. The father is abusive or absent, and there are other emotional problems. Arsonists are usually held back in school and have learning problems.

Socially, the arsonist is usually a misfit, has problems with the opposite sex, and is physically and emotionally weak. They usually work at a subservient positions and resent authority figures, and they commit most of their offenses as children. Arsonists usually don't have drug or alcohol problems. While setting a fire, they go into a trancelike state. They feel no guilt, nor do they fret about the consequences of their actions, such as people getting killed.

Q&A

Q: How expensive is arson?

A: Arson is the most expensive crime in America, costing more than $2 billion a year in property loss.

Q: How many arsonists are convicted?

A: Only 16 percent of arson offenses ever lead to arrest, and only 2 percent of those arrested are convicted.

Q: Has there ever been a movie about a pyromaniac?

A: A number of them. One of the more interesting movies on this subject came out in 1995, when CBS aired a made-for-TV movie starring Neil Patrick Harris called Not Our Son, based on the life of Seattle's Paul Keller, who was America's most prolific serial arsonist at the time. Like many arsonists, Keller led a double life. No one would have suspected a man who was a successful advertising executive and practicing Christian who sang in his church choir, but when his reign of terror was over, there had been more than one hundred fires, seventy-seven buildings burned (with an estimated $35 million in damages), and three lives lost. Eventually turned in by his own father, Keller pled guilty and received a sentence of ninety-nine years. The TV movie had been inspired by a documentary entitled Portrait of a Serial Arsonist: The Paul Keller Story, which was considered the first real look into the mind and motivations of a serial arsonist.

Arson Jargon

Accelerant: Flammable substance used in the commission of arson.

Alligator Effect: The alligator-skin appearance of burned wood that has been doused with a liquid accelerant.

One way that arson investigators can tell if a fire is the work of an arsonist is to look for alligatoring. The fire burns deeper where gasoline or another accelerant has been poured, and the wood takes on the appearance of an alligator's skin.

Where There's Smoke . . .

Close to 75 percent of firefighters in this country are volunteers. In an ironic twist, hundreds of convicted arsonists have come from these ranks. In 2000, a volunteer fireman in Tennessee was killed during a blaze at an abandoned home. He did not die as a result of fighting the fire, however. He and six other volunteers had set the fire, and he was trapped while spreading gasoline in the attic.

Burn Patterns: The patterns created by the path a fire travels.

One way to determine if a fire has been caused by arson is to observe the site and see where the fire actually burned. For example, investigators will look to see if fire is "low burning," meaning the fire started at floor level; if it is, then arson is immediately suspected. A fire will not normally be "low burning" unless an accelerant was poured on the floor and lit. Investigators also examine wood that's been burned; this can show how long the fire was actually burning and whether an accelerant was used.

Jewish Lightning: On the east coast, some arson detectives describe arson this way. On the west coast it's known as "Mexican Lightning."

Pugilistic Attitude/Pose: This is the distorted position that commonly occurs when someone is burned to death, which looks like a person with their hands up in a boxing stance. One myth related to the pose is that the fire victim had his or her hands up to ward off the flames. In fact, says former homicide investigator Vernon Geberth in his book *Practical Homicide Investigation*, "the condition is caused by the natural contraction of the muscles as they are seared."

Pugilistic pose body takes when severly burned.
(Author's Collection)

Q&A

Q: How many arson fires occur outdoors?

A: About 50 percent.

Q: How many arson fires occur in vehicles?

A: About 20 percent.

Q: What is considered the peak time for intentionally set fires across the United States?

A: Halloween.

The Difference between Arsonists and Pyromaniacs

While society sometimes blurs the distinction, there is a difference between arsonists and pyromaniacs. Arsonists generally set fires as the means to an end—insurance fraud, revenge, a political statement, and so forth. Only a small percentage of them commit their crimes because of psychosis. Pyromaniacs, on the other hand, suffer from an impulse control disorder. The American Psychiatric Association characterizes a pyromaniac as someone who has deliberately set fires on at least two occasions, experiences tension and excitement before the act, feels relief and gratification afterward, and is obsessed with fire. It is a dangerous mental disorder because pyromaniacs often have no concern about the loss of property or life that can result from the fire. While behavior modification therapy and psychiatric counseling can be of help in some instances, the prognosis for pyromania is considered fair to poor.

Using the Internet to Catch Arsonists

The nation's largest web-based investigation system, known as L.E.A.D.S., is making it difficult for arsonists (as well as burglars and other types of criminals) to sell their stolen goods to pawn shops and other second-hand stores and get away with it. Over 2,500 businesses across the country (who buy used merchandise from customers) upload their daily sales records to a central data bank, which can then be viewed by some 500 law enforcement agencies. Dishonest homeowners attempting an insurance scam have been known to pawn their valuables, set fire to their home, and then claim it was all lost in the fire.

Unfortunately for them, a record of everything sold had already gone to L.E.A.D.S. online, so a simple comparison can spot the fraud. Before the power of the Internet, police had to go from store to store checking merchandise and receipts, which took huge amounts of manpower and time. Although it is estimated less than 1 percent of stolen goods come through stores, it still helps solve countless crimes each year.

Chapter 16
Celebrities
and Crime

Some Famous People Who Went To Jail

Chuck Berry. In 1962, rock and roll star Chuck Berry was convicted of transporting a fourteen-year-old girl across state lines for immoral purposes. He served two years in a federal penitentiary.

Ryan O'Neal. Served fifty-one days in a Los Angeles jail for assault.

Pete Rose. In 1990, the famous Cincinnati Red's catcher served five months for failure to report income from gambling and memorabilia sales.

David Crosby. In 1986, the singer served eleven months in prison for being caught with a loaded .45 pistol and marijuana.

Sean Penn. The actor served five days for reckless driving and assault, made a movie, then returned to jail to serve another twenty-eight days of his sentence.

O. Henry. Short-story writer served three years of a five-year sentence for embezzling funds from a Texas bank.

Kelsey Grammar. Failed to show up for alcohol program, but served only two weeks of the resulting thirty-day jail sentence because of jail overcrowding.

Sophia Loren. At the age of forty-seven, served seventeen days in prison on a tax evasion conviction for a crime committed eighteen years earlier.

Denny McLain. Major-league pitcher sentenced to twenty-three years for racketeering, extortion, and possession of cocaine. He served thirty months in prison.

Robert Mitchum. In 1949, the actor served seven weeks for possession of marijuana.

Stacy Keach. The actor served fifteen months in England's Reading Gaol for smuggling 1.5 ounces of cocaine.

Match Game

Hollywood Homicide

Match the circumstances of the murder with the murdered celebrity

1. Phil Hartman _____

2. Ramon Navarro _____

3. Dominique Dunne _____

4. Dr. Haing S. Ngor _____

5. Rebecca Schaeffer _____

6. Tupac Shakur _____

A. Shot in the chest by a stalker while standing in her doorway on July 18, 1989

B. On May 28, 1998, shot twice in the head, while sleeping, by his paranoid wife

C. Strangled to death at her West Hollywood apartment on November 4, 1982, by her jealous boyfriend

D. This romantic matinee idol in public but homosexual in private was found tied, tortured, and battered in his bedroom

E. The real-life Killing Fields doctor was shot to death by three young punks during a robbery on February 25, 1996

F. This seminal rap singer died on September 13, 1996, after being shot four times by four assassins

Answers: 1-B, 2-D, 3-C, 4-E, 5-A, 6-F.

Some Surprising Facts about Celebrity Murders

On June 5, 1968, assassin Sirhan Sirhan shot Presidential candidate Robert Kennedy in Los Angeles's Ambassador Hotel. Many people reported that the shot had been fired from a few feet away, but Coroner Thomas Noguchi's conclusion was that it had been fired from only three inches away. This gave rise to conspiracy speculation that there had been two shooters, but later Noguchi said he was positive that only one shooter, Sirhan Sirhan, was involved.

Sharon Tate, wife of director Roman Polanski, was a rising young actress when she and four friends were murdered on August 9, 1969, at a hillside estate in Bel-Air. (The slayings and subsequent conviction of Charles Manson were described in the best-selling book Helter Skelter by prosecutor Vincent Bugliosi.) Noguchi's office performed the autopsy on Tate and the other victims, and he helped tie the murder weapons to the later deaths of Leno and Rosemary La Bianca, also killed by the Manson Family. At the time she was murdered, Sharon Tate was eight-and-a-half months pregnant.

Singer Janis Joplin died of a heroin overdose in the Landmark Hotel in Hollywood. What few people know is that the cause was the strength of the heroin, which her body couldn't take. Less well

Death certificate of Janis Joplin
(Los Angeles County Coroner)

known is that eight other addicts died in the Los Angeles area that same night after using the same heroin, which was far too strong. If it has been ordinary heroin, the people—including Joplin—would likely not have died. Two weeks earlier, rock musician Jimi Hendrix had also overdosed and died from an injection of heroin.

Comedian Freddie Prinze shot himself in the head in front of his manager, Martin Snyder, on January 29, 1977. Prinze reportedly had been despondent, and the condition was exacerbated by the Quaaludes in his body. The coroner ruled suicide. But less well known is that Prinze's family later challenged the ruling and won, convincing a jury that Prinze was playing a prank and had not expected the gun to go off. The jury called the shooting accidental, and Prinze's family collected on his $200,000 life insurance policy.

Comedian John Belushi was only thirty-three when he died in bungalow #3 at the Chateau-Marmont Hotel on March 5, 1982. Less well known is that, earlier that evening, he had visited the Roy nightclub with Robert DeNiro and Robin Williams. Belushi's death was caused by an accidental overdose of cocaine and heroin, a combination sometimes called a "speedball." An acquaintance of Belushi's, Cathy Smith, was sentenced to prison because she supplied the drugs. Belushi was the last famous person to be autopsied by "coroner to the stars" Thomas Noguchi.

Other Celebrities in Trouble with the Law

On November 25, 2000, Robert Downey Jr. was arrested for cocaine possession and being under the influence of drugs. He did three years in rehab.

On July 6, 2005, the rapper Lil' Kim (aka Kimberly Jones) was sentenced to three years in jail for lying to a Grand Jury about a shooting. She was released in mid 2006.

In June 2000, Eminem (aka Marshall Mathers) was caught in Michigan and arrested for carrying a concealed weapon and displaying it. He escaped jail, receiving a year's probation.

On November 3, 1970, actress Jane Fonda kicked a police officer and was charged with assault. She was released on $5,000 bond and the charges eventually were dropped.

On September 11, 2002, actor Nick Nolte was charged with DUI for drugs and alcohol and ultimately received three years' probation. This arrest also produced the most talked-about mug shot in history.

On October 2, 1978, actor and comic Tim Allen was convicted of delivering a controlled substance (cocaine) in Detroit, and he ultimately served twenty-eight months. His past stayed hidden as he enjoyed success on television's successful series, Home Improvement, but someone dug it up and spread it all over the tabloids. Allen helped himself by being straightforward about his past.

On November 7, 2002, Bobby Brown, the troubled husband of Whitney Houston, was arrested in Atlanta for marijuana possession, speeding, and driving without a license. He served a few days in jail.

On March 5, 2005, Nick Carter, a Backstreet Boy, was convicted of a DUI for driving drunk in Huntington Beach, California.

On January 26, 2002, NYPD Blue star Kim Delaney was arrested for suspicion of drunk driving in Malibu.

On October 24, 1999, police answered a noise complaint at the actor Matthew McConaughey's Austin, Texas, home and found McConaughey playing bongos in the nude. He was charged with resisting arrest.

On March 9, 1990, actor Corey Feldman was charged with possession of heroin and cocaine with intent to sell, and the actor spent ten months in rehab.

On June 27, 1995, actor Hugh Grant was charged with lewd conduct—he picked up a hooker for sex—and was fined $1,180.

On September 3, 2004, *Growing Pains* star Tracey Gold rolled her SUV—with her husband and kids inside—and pled guilty to felony DUI charges.

On September 15, 2004, the animal-rights activist Edward Furlong was charged with public drunkenness after liberating a lobster from a tank in a Kentucky supermarket.

On January 22, 2003, singer R. Kelly was arrested on child pornography charges in Miami while already awaiting trial on 21 counts of child pornography in Illinois due to an incriminating sex video.

On November 24, 2003, singer Glen Campbell was charged with drunk driving and hit and run. He had fled the scene of a minor accident.

On November 3, 2003, singer Wynonna Judd was arrested for drunk driving in Nashville. Judd posted $500 bond and made a public apology.

On December 20, 1971, Larry King was charged with grand larceny for allegedly swindling a business partner. The case was dropped due to the statute of limitations having run out.

On February 16, 2005, performer Kid Rock was arrested in Nashville and charged with assaulting a disc jockey at a strip club.

On January 28, 2004, soul singer James Brown was arrested for allegedly beating his wife, Tommie Rae, with a chair.

On September 17, 2004, *Home Alone* star Macaulay Culkin was arrested for possessing controlled substances—sleeping pills, Xanax, and marijuana. He was jailed for a short time before posting a $4,000 bond.

On April 12, 2001, actor Vince Vaughn got into a bar fight in Wilmington, North Carolina, and was arrested for fighting in public. Charges later were dropped.

On December 10, 1997, Pam Anderson's ex-husband Tommy Lee was put under arrest for allegedly knocking over a security guard at a concert in Phoenix.

On July 26, 1991, Pee-Wee Herman (aka Paul Reubens) was dragged out of a porno movie theater and charged with indecent exposure. He received seventy-five hours of community service, was fined $50, and had to produce an anti-drug video.

On January 29, 2002, President Bush's niece, Noelle Bush, was charged with using a fake prescription to buy Xanax. She was ordered to do a sixteen-month stint in rehab.

On March 21, 1994, Dudley Moore was arrested for beating his then fiancée, Nicole Rothschild, but she did not press charges.

Death Outside the Ring

Sports announcer and boxing analyst Max Kellerman lost his brother, Sam, on October 2, 2004, to boxer James "The Harlem Hammer" Butler. As the story goes, Butler was living in Sam Kellerman's Manhattan home, and when Sam asked James to leave, James beat Sam to death with a hammer. Butler was a man who had always had a vicious temper. After one bout he lost, he took off his gloves, rushed over to his opponent's corner, and punched him in the face.

Top photo—Max Kellerman at funeral of his brother.
Bottom photo—James Butler, *left* who was convicted of killing Max Kellermans' brother.
Both photos (Dave Green)

On April 22, 1999, Chicago Bulls NBA star Scottie Pippen was arrested in Houston, Texas, for suspicion of driving while intoxicated. He failed a sobriety test but refused a Breathalyzer test, and later the charges were dropped.

On May 15, 1984, Memphis police said rocker Ozzie Osbourne was "staggering drunk" when they arrested him on Beale Street in Memphis and charged him with public drunkenness.

When he was twenty, actor Al Pacino was charged with carrying a concealed weapon in Rhode Island.

One of the most infamous killers of all is movie star Lillo Brancato Jr. He starred in *A Bronx Tale* with Robert DeNiro, and then went on to be one of the main players in the "The Sopranos." But one evening he and another man were confronted by an off-duty cop, and in the gunplay that followed the cop was shot dead. Brancato may well be executed.

Lillo Brancato Jr. of the "Sopranos" before he was charged with murdering a cop. (Dave Green)

Chapter 17
Kids Who Kill

Q&A

Q: In our society, how many kids are on psychotropic drugs?

A: Experts estimate that more than 900,000 kids are on antidepressants.

Characteristics of School Shooters

1. School shooters tend to kill and injure multiple victims in a single incident. They don't just target one person as part of an individual dispute, but rather they launch into a shooting spree that results in many deaths and injuries.

2. Their motive is to hurt, kill, and maim.

3. They tend to be very young: most young murderers are fifteen or over, but school shooters tend to be no older than fourteen.

4. They feel rejected and think others are out to get them.

5. They will try to hurt anyone who attacks their inflated image of themselves.

Q&A

Q: Do countries other than the U.S. have students who become homicidal?

A: Indeed, many school killings take place in areas of the world that we think of as safe, such as Japan. Many Japanese school killers use a knife as their weapon of choice, as opposed to the favored guns in the U.S. In general, boys tend to use a gun as a tool for murder more often than girls, who tend to use knives.

Q: How many parents are murdered by their kids every year?

A: Surprisingly, 300 parents a year are murdered by their children.

Characteristics of Children Who Kill Parents

Children who kill their parents usually have many of the following traits:

- Child is abused and thinks they have no other way out of their situation.
- Kids are mentally ill, though this is rare.
- Antisocial.
- Caucasian (almost all child killers are white).
- The murder weapon is a gun.
- Killers are passive—until the homicides occur.

- Kid feels isolated, alone.
- Professional help has been sought.
- Emotionally block out murders they commit.
- They are sorry for what they did.
- No criminal record.
- Amnesia reported after murder(s).
- Gun available in home.
- Attempts to run away or commit suicide.

Some Nasty Kid Killers

On the morning of April 20, 1999, life in Columbine High School began as it did on any other day. Kids went about their business, to class, to gym, their heads likely filled with the kinds of things that kids think: their studies, their futures, their boyfriends and girlfriends. However, this day was to be different—the lives of a number of them would end abruptly and violently because two of the young men in their midst, Eric Harris, eighteen, and Dylan Klebold, seventeen. On this, the anniversary of the birth of Adolph Hitler, Eric and Dylan planned to kill people.

The two young men, still considered children in many ways by the law, arrived dressed in black trench coats and entered through the back of the cafeteria. The trench coats were standard garb for a small group of students known as "the Trench Coat Mafia," of which Harris and Klebold were peripheral members. Then, amid shrieks of horror, they pulled out semi-automatic guns and started to fire. Students sought the only cover, jumping under tables and chairs.

In all, Harris and Klebold took the lives of thirteen others and wounded twenty-five more kids, after which they took their own lives by suicide. Why did they kill? There are various theories; probably the killings were the result of Harris and Klebold projecting rage from somewhere else onto people in the school. Typically this is the way mass murders work. Someone with pent up self-loathing and anger starts fantasizing about how others are to blame. Emotions build until they explode.

As with all murderers, the real answer to why they killed is we'll probably never know for sure. The bottom line is that answers almost always come from an analysis of the parent/child relationship. As someone said: "How many serial and mass murderers do you know of who came from happy homes?"

Starting in the spring of 1978, New York City's Willie Bosket had perpetrated more than two thousand crimes by the time he was fifteen, including knifing several people. He was a great admirer of his father, who was an incarcerated murderer, and, in Bosket's mind, killing was a very manly activity. Just before he turned sixteen, he committed murder for the first time himself. He killed another boy in a fight, and then he descended into the subway and started to rob and, ultimately, kill a couple of men. The motive, he said, was just to see what it felt like. Bosket knew the law, and knew he could more or less run wild while he was so young and the law couldn't touch him. However, Bosket miscalculated and gave his name to the "Willie Bosket Law," a law passed very rapidly in New York after his crimes that assured juveniles deemed dangerous could be tried as adults at the age of sixteen. Bosket did not commit any more murders, but a series of violent attacks on guards and other prisoners has guaranteed that he will spend the rest of his life in prison. He is known as New York's most dangerous inmate.

Shirley Wolf was fourteen and Cindy Collier was fifteen in 1983 when they started to knock on doors of condos in California. When they found an appropriate victim, an elderly woman, they talked their way into the apartment and decided to steal the woman's car. They grabbed her, and Shirley Wolf stabbed the older lady twenty-eight times while the woman begged for her life. Later, the duo called the event a "kick." Ultimately, both were sent to prison, where their age saved them. Cindy Collier was paroled in 1992 while Shirley Wolf, who is said to have attacked a guard, was sent to a prison in Fontana, California.

Mary Flora Bell, a young English girl, was raised in an abusive, dysfunctional home in Scottswood, a community 275 miles north of London, and as a result, she was constantly angry. By the spring of 1968, she was also constantly on the lookout for ways to vent this rage, and she found a willing partner in Nora Bell (no relation). When Mary was eleven, the body of four-year-old Martin Brown was found in her neighborhood. This was assumed to be an accidental death, until police found a note taking responsibility for the killing signed "Fanny and the Faggot." Three months after the Brown murder, another toddler, Brian Howe, went missing, and Mary suggested to police that she had seen the boy playing on a pile of concrete. When police investigated they found the boy's body. He had been cut with a razor and scissors and strangled. Police wondered why Mary knew about the boy, investigated her, and it led to Mary and Nora's arrests in 1968.

In 1998, the mother of fourteen-year-old Joshua Phillips noticed that there was something leaking beneath her son's waterbed. Under it was the body of Maddie, an eight-year-old neighbor. Phillips had accidentally hit her in the eye with a baseball; when she screamed, he panicked and dragged her to his house, where beat and stabbed her to death. He pled not guilty but the jury didn't believe him, and he was convicted of first degree murder.

Edmund Kemper. The horrific Edmund Kemper, whose career as a serial murderer was detailed earlier in the book, started his murderous activities with his grandparents. He had been seen as a psychological wreck, and he had been placed with his grandparents in order to hopefully restore some semblance of sanity to his life. When he was fifteen, he took a rifle and shot his grandparents to death. He was diagnosed as paranoid and psychotic, and he was placed in Atascadero State Hospital. While there, he worked in the psychology lab helping administer tests to others, something that gave him insight into what behavior doctors regarded as insane and sane. He mimicked sanity and got released five years later, when he embarked on a killing spree that resulted in him killing and dismembering eight females, including his mother and her best friend. (For more details on Kemper, see Chapter 4: Serial Murder.)

Q&A

Q: What is the murder of one's parents called?

A: Parricide.

Characteristics of Serial Murderers in the Making

The following are typical characteristics of most serial murderers:

- Morbid fascination (beyond normal for juvenile males) with violence and death.
- Cruelty to animals and smaller children.

- Tendency toward pyromania (likes to set fires).
- Talks about harming others.
- Considered weird by peers.
- Sociopath. Thinks that others have no rights.
- Temper tantrums at an early age.
- Bedwetting.

Chapter 18
Miscellaneous

Q&A

Q: When was the first murder shown on live TV?

A: On November 24, 1963. Lee Harvey Oswald, the alleged killer of President John F. Kennedy, was in a hallway being transferred to the county jail. A man in a fedora stepped out of the crowd of onlookers and shot Oswald in the stomach, a crime seen on television by millions of people. As a result, Oswald died. The killer was nightclub owner Jack Ruby (Rubenstein).

Miscellaneous Crime Jargon

Cover: Natural protection police officers hide behind when in danger.

People who specialize in survival tactics make a sharp distinction between cover and concealment. Concealment occurs when an officer is hidden from a suspect, but not protected against gunfire. For example, the officer may be hiding behind some cardboard boxes (and hence be concealed). If the suspect knows this, it would be very easy to simply riddle the boxes with gunfire and hit the officer. Cover is something that hides all or most of the officer's body and can't be penetrated by bullets, such as a brick wall, a fire hydrant, or a street mailbox.

One of the great myths perpetrated by television and the movies is that an officer is protected when he hides behind a car door. In fact, this is no protection at all—even .22 bullets will bore right through a car door's thin sheet metal.

Belt: The mind-altering effect caused by a drug, such as mood change, excitement, relaxation, pleasure, analgesia, stimulation, or sedation.

Mule: Person who transports drugs, sometimes swallowing plastic bags full of powdered material. Many times bags have broken or ruptured while inside a person, and the person has overdosed and died.

Bernie: In the New York area, a potential crime victim who may look like easy prey to criminals—but is emphatically not.

"Bernie" originated with Bernhard Goetz, a mild-looking, bespectacled man who was approached on a New York City subway train on December 22, 1984, by four youths—three of whom were brandishing long, sharpened screwdrivers—who asked for cigarettes and money. Goetz, who had been mugged twice before, reached into his pocket, and instead of coming out with money, produced a nine-millimeter automatic, which he used to shoot all four youths. He then retreated from the scene.

The climate in New York City at the time was such that, according to some polls, over 50 percent approved of Goetz's vigilantism, even though one of the youths, Darrell Cabey, was paralyzed from the waist down. Some suggested that Goetz had overreacted, firing at the youths when they were defenseless (and he used the nasty hollow point bullets that flatten on impact, become bigger and do much more damage than regular bullets).

Goetz subsequently gave himself up to Concord, New Hampshire, police. There followed a series of trials amid much furor that essentially resulted in Goetz receiving what amounted to a legal "slap on the wrist." One of the four youths sued Goetz for $50 million but lost the case.

Blanks: Low-quality drugs (also called lemonade and Lipton tea).

Drug buyers have no way of telling the quality or purity of the drugs they purchase on the street, except by the reputation of the dealer selling the drug. A regulated drug undergoes an average of ten years' testing by the U.S. government before being licensed for sale. Unregulated drugs require nothing.

Blizzard: A cluster of traffic summonses issued to one driver all at once (also called a package of summonses). Officers say that whether someone gets tickets—and how many—can depend to some degree on the attitude projected by the driver. "If the driver's snotty," says one officer, "you drop the hammer. If he's not, you might just let him drive away." And of course, most drivers are vulnerable to getting a blizzard of tickets, because at any given time most if not all cars are in technical violation of some traffic law, such as driving with slightly worn tires. Sometimes the driver has committed other offenses which the officer will learn about after doing a computer check.

Border rats: Customs and DEA agents who work the Mexican border.

Carolina pancake: A mixture of lye and Crisco or bacon grease blended together and used as a weapon.

One cop said of a Carolina pancake in *Cops: Their Lives in Their Own Words* by Mark Baker: "What happened was that this guy was involved in a family fight and some cops showed up. He had made a Carolina pancake. A Carolina pancake is a mixture of lye, Crisco or bacon grease. Fat and lye. They cook it up and then they throw it on you. The lye will burn right through you. You mix lye with grease and you can't wash it off. It happens a lot."

Bounty hunter: (1) A person who tracks down felons for reward money.

Those who do this for a living do it at their own peril, fiscal and physical. Bounty hunters are normally hired by bail bondsmen to track down clients who have skipped town on bail, putting the bail bondsmen at risk of losing the money they put up for the person. Bounty hunters must register with the police department in the jurisdiction where they operate, and they may carry licensed firearms. They usually pay their own expenses, and should they bring the felon back, they get a percentage of the money they save their client.

(2) A police officer who focuses on making arrests.

Officers who want to can make a lot of arrests, but not all of their arrests can be characterized as quality arrests. Arrests for such infractions as having the wrong license plates or carrying nunchakus (or "nunchucks") technically are classed as felony arrests, but they involve little or no risk to the officer. A large number of arrests look good on an officer's record and may require him to go to court and testify, which earns overtime pay. A lot of officers look down on this.

Dinosaur: A police officer who has been on the job for more than fifteen years. The term is also used to describe older officers who won't change their outmoded ways.

Attitude adjustment: Illegal brute force used to make a suspect or perpetrator comply with the demands of the police.

According to one cop, "When a cop says 'He needs an attitude adjustment,' he means the bad guy needs the crap knocked out of him."

Babe: Drug used for detoxification.

When an addict is trying to withdraw from drugs, doctors often administer other drugs to lessen the physiological impact on the body. The most common drug used to treat addicts is methadone, which is effective chiefly in heroin withdrawal.

In a planned treatment program, a drug like methadone is administered in a context of therapy and education and in conjunction with family or other support. Addicts, like alcoholics, are never considered cured.

The origin of *babe* is obscure, but the term does suggest warmth and support, just as a baby might receive from its mother.

Bag bride: A prostitute who smokes crack cocaine (also known as skeeger, skeezer, and coke whore).

The term most likely comes from the bags that drugs come in, as well as the disheveled and dilapidated look that prostitutes on drugs eventually assume.

Bender: Drug party. Classically, this term applies to a long alcoholic binge, but in recent years, it has come to be applied to drug taking as well.

Perp walk: When the police orchestrate showing a suspect or perpetrator to the media.

For publicity, police commonly arrange to have a perpetrator or suspect escorted past the media at a designated time, usually from a building entrance to a waiting vehicle. If the suspect/perpetrator is important enough, he or she will be walked around the block, followed by a horde of media. This is called "parading the perp."

Burnout: (1) Fatigue after using drugs. (2) A heavy abuser of drugs. (3) The collapse of veins from repeated drug injections. (4) Psychological collapse (in a police officer).

This is usually experienced by officers in high stress situations, such as undercover work. It also occurs when an officer is forced to shoot and kill someone. Contrary to officers like Dirty Harry (killing someone made his day), real officers often require psychological counseling before going back on the job after an event like that.

The daily grind of police work also can lead to burnout. Police are constantly in adversarial situations, may face danger, and have crazy hours that disrupt family life. These stressors can lead to alcoholism and a high rate of divorce.

(5) A dilapidated apartment building.

Black tar: Black tar is a very crude form of heroin that is sold on the street in quantities that are 40 percent to 80 percent pure. Sometimes it is diluted with burnt cornstarch; sometimes the tar is converted into a powder to which conventional diluents, such as mannitol or quinine, are added. It is usually taken by injection. Black tar is popular in the western United States.

Almost Assassinated

History is full of tragically assassinated leaders, from Julius Caesar to Anwar Sadat. But history is also full of near-misses. Here are a few famous leaders who were almost assassinated.

278

President Theodore Roosevelt. In October of 1912, while Roosevelt was at a campaign rally in Milwaukee, Wisconsin, a German immigrant named John Schrank shot at him with a .38. The bullet smashed Roosevelt's glasses and lodged in his chest, but Roosevelt was able to finish his speech. Schrank spent the rest of his life in an institution.

President Franklin D. Roosevelt. In February 1933, while at a campaign rally in Miami, Florida, Roosevelt was shot at by a man named Giuseppe Zangara. He missed but hit Chicago mayor Anton Cermak, who ultimately died of his wounds. Zangara was tried and executed within five weeks, on March 20, 1933. Whether justice was served is highly doubtful—there were only five weeks from arrest to death, and eyewitnesses have been wrong before.

King Hussein of Jordan. When he was sixteen, an assassin shot his grandfather Abdullah to death as they entered a mosque together. Hussein, only a few feet from his grandfather, was saved from death when the bullet intended to kill him smashed into a medal on his uniform. Hussein's father, King Talal, abdicated in 1952; Hussein became king in 1953 and ruled until his death in 1999.

President Gerald Ford. On September 5, 1975, Lynette "Squeaky" Fromme pulled the trigger on a gun she pointed at him as he reached to shake her hand in a Sacramento Hotel. Fortunately there wasn't a bullet in the chamber, and Secret Service agents wrestled her to the ground before she could fire another shot. Two weeks later, there was another attempt on Ford's life by a forty-five-year-old woman named Sara Jane Moore in San Francisco, but a bystander named Oliver Sipple deflected her shot. She was sentenced to life in prison and died there.

President Harry Truman. In 1950, while the White House was being remodeled, President Truman was living in Blair House, a state guest house in Washington. Two Puerto Rican terrorists assaulted Blair House, one from the front and one from the back. One guard was killed, as was one of the terrorists, Griselio Torresola. The other, Oscar Collazo, was wounded. He was captured and sentenced to death, a sentence which was commuted by President Truman himself in 1952 a week before Collazo was slated to die. In 1979, Collazo was freed by President Carter, and he returned to Puerto Rico.

President Charles de Gaulle was returned to power in 1958 when French military officers in Algeria threatened to mount a rebellion. However, de Gaulle gradually came to favor Algerian independence, and because of de Gaulle's politics, antindependence forces made a number of attempts on de Gaulle's life. One of the more well-known attempts was an attack on de Gaulle's car outside of Paris in August 1952, where the would-be assassins hit everything except de Gaulle and his wife. When de Gaulle got out of the car he commented: "They really are bad shots."

Governor George Wallace. While he was campaigning at a shopping center in Laurel, Maryland, on May 15, 1972, Alabama Governor Wallace was shot by Arthur Bremer. The end result was that Wallace was paralyzed from the waist down and Bremer was sentenced to prison until 2025. Bremer's diary indicated he wanted to kill either Wallace or Nixon—his motivation for the shooting was not political, he just wanted to be famous.

President Ronald Reagan. As the President was exiting the

Washington Hilton in March of 1981, he and three other men were shot with a .22 pistol fired by John Hinckley, Jr. Reagan almost died from his chest wound, and the shooting resulted in the creation of the Brady Bill for the Prevention of Handgun Violence (named after Regan's press secretary Jim Brady, who was crippled in the attack). Hinckley became obsessed with actress Jodie Foster and repeatedly watched her movie Taxi Driver, in which Foster played a twelve-year-old prostitute. Hinckley Jr. followed her around the country and apparently saw himself as Travis Bickle, the taxi driver in the movie who becomes obsessed with protecting Foster. Hinckley was institutionalized. On December 30, 2005, a federal judge ruled that Hinckley would be allowed visits, supervised by his parents, to their home outside of Washington, D.C.

Pope John Paul II. On May 13, 1981, Pope John Paul II was shot and badly wounded as he entered St. Peter's Square in the Vatican. The would-be assassin, Mehmet Ali Agca, was a member of a Turkish terrorist organization known as the Gray Wolves. After he recovered, Pope John Paul visited Agca in prison in 1983. The assassination attempt prompted the Pope to thereafter travel in a car with bulletproof glass (aka the Popemobile).

President Andrew Jackson. Jackson was shot on January 30, 1835, by house painter Richard Lawrence outside the U.S. Capitol building. Lawrence had two Derringers. One misfired, and he drew the other—which also misfired. Jackson survived the attack. Later the guns were examined and found to be in perfect working order. It was said that the odds against both Derringers misfiring were 125,000 to 1.

Andy Warhol. In 1968, Andy Warhol was shot in the abdomen by Valerie Solanas. Solanas was an acquaintance of Warhol's, a radical feminist and author of the outlandish S.C.U.M. Manifesto (S.C.U.M. supposedly standing for the "Society for Cutting Up Men"). Mentally unstable, Solanas was apparently angry at Warhol for ignoring a script she had given him the previous year. Warhol recovered, but the attack seemed to put an end to his creative years.

Adolph Hitler. Hitler met with staff members on January 20, 1944, in "the Wolf's Lair," his headquarters near Rastenburg. Halfway through the meeting, an explosion rocked the room; a bomb hidden in a briefcase had been set off. Four men were killed, but by chance the heavy oak conference table shielded the Fuhrer, leaving him with burns and punctured eardrums but otherwise very much alive. The bomb had been planted by Colonel Claus von Stauffenberg, a German officer who had become disillusioned with the Nazi regime. The Colonel and his co-conspirators were captured and shot.

Kidnapping

Beyond Belief

Some crimes are almost too strange and horrific to be believed. The in-house kidnapping, torture, and murder of Sylvia Likens in Indianapolis is one such case.

Sylvia was sixteen and her sister Jenny was fifteen in July of 1965, when they were entrusted to the care of a skinny, asthmatic, chain smoking—and as it turned out, psychotic—woman named Gertrude Baniszewski. Likens' parents had offered Baniszewski $20 a week to let their girls live with her while they traveled with a carnival, operating a concession stand.

Crime Can Be Funny

Not Quite DOA

My partner and I got a call to an apartment in the projects. This lady's nurse's aide had not been able to get in for days and didn't have a key. So I pounded on the door with my stick for a while and got no answer. I was thinking there was an obvious DOA inside. I called housing maintenance and they drilled the lock. I walked in slowly and looked in the kitchen; there was a pan with food in it that was obviously very old. I started to search the place and walked toward the bedroom. Sure enough, I saw someone in the bed, facing away, and I was absolutely sure the person was dead. So, like a good cop should, I tried to get an idea of how long she was there. I leaned over the bed to see her face, and all of a sudden she spun her head and yelled "What are you looking at!" I jumped back and fell into her dresser. I was useless for the rest of the day. It turned out the woman had been hearing voices for days and didn't want to answer the door. The EMS carted her away to the psycho ward.

Soon—and no one seems to know why—Baniszewski started to beat the girls, but then she focused her illogical rage on Sylvia. She also began to invite neighborhood kids, who hung out in Gertrude's house, to beat and torture Sylvia as well. Some kids would practice judo on her, and some would put out their cigarettes on her skin. On at least one occasion, Gertrude put Sylvia in scalding hot water to "cleanse her of her sins."

For a time Sylvia was allowed to leave the house, but eventually she became a kidnapping victim and was locked in the cellar and fed minimal food. Baniszewski used a needle to carve the words "I am a prostitute" onto her stomach.

On October 26, 1965, Sylvia died from brain swelling, internal bleeding, and shock. Baniszewski and the family members and neighbors who took part in the torture, kidnapping, and murder were tried and convicted of various degrees of crime.

Sylvia's parents were not charged. Her sister Jenny died in 2004 at the age of 54, and Baniszewski, who had been released from prison on parole in 1985, died of lung cancer in 1990.

Q&A

Q: Where does the word "kidnapper" come from?

A: The term "kidnapper" is a compound of two slang terms: "kid" (a child) and "napper" (one who steals, probably a variant of the word "nab"). The word was first used in the 1600s, a time when British children were being abducted and sold to sea captains, who brought them to the British colonies to work as slaves and laborers.

Q: Do parents kidnap their own children?

A: There are more than 350,000 cases of parental kidnapping in the U.S. each year. In 54 percent of the cases, the abductor is the mother, and in 46 percent of the cases, the abductor is the father.

Who Am I?

1. I was born in Germany in November 1899.

2. With only eight years of formal education, I went to trade school for two years to learn carpentry.

3. I served in the German infantry as a machine gunner in WWI.

4. Unable to find work after the war, I turned to crime. I was ultimately arrested and jailed twice for robbery and theft.

5. I entered the U.S. illegally in 1923 using a disguise and stolen identification card.

6. My wife and I lived in the Bronx, New York. She worked in a bakery and I was employed as a carpenter.

7. I was arrested and charged with murder for my involvement in a sensational kidnapping case that shocked the world.

8. Much of the evidence was compelling but circumstantial; however, I was tried, convicted and sentenced to death for the crime.

9. Maintaining my innocence to the end, I was executed in the electric chair on April 3, 1936.

10. Until her death in 1994 at the age of ninety-five, my wife carried on a six-decade crusade to exonerate me and clear my name. There are many people today who still believe an innocent man was executed.

A. I am Richard Bruno Hauptmann, kidnapper of the Lindbergh baby

The Kidnapping Capital of the World

Two to three thousand people are abducted in Columbia every year. In 1999, kidnappers burst into a church and kidnapped the entire congregation. Abductions are so common, in fact, that there's a weekly radio show called The Voice of Kidnapping, on which families can broadcast messages for abducted loved ones.

Look to the Parents

While thousands of children go missing each year, the vast majority fall under the category of "custodial interference," such as when a parent abducts a child or the child runs away. According to the FBI, there are only 100 to 120 criminal abductions per year.

Of the non-family abductions, 74 percent are girls.

The Worst Nightmare

In a study conducted by the Mayo Clinic on what parents worry about the most in relation to their children, almost three-quarters of them fear their children being abducted more than anything else. For the other third it ranked as a frequent worry, beating out other concerns including car accidents, sports injuries, and drug addiction.

Fewer Ransom Kidnappings

Today there are many fewer ransom kidnappings than there were decades ago—criminals are afraid that technology is so advanced that they will be easily trapped and caught.

Ancient Poisons

Ancient murderers did not have access to some of today's sophisticated poisons, but the ones they did have worked quite well. Some poisons were lethal, while some merely paralyzed their targets.

One ancient poison is the famous fugu poison, derived from the blowfish or puffer fish (so called because it puffs up its cheeks when annoyed or searching for food). In ancient times, it was simple to use a blowfish poison. All the person needed do was put a piece of the raw fish onto the plate of the intended victim. The poison attacks the respiratory center in the brain, paralyzing the muscles related to breathing. Even today, people in Japan are accidentally killed by this poison every year. In one recent year, for example, there were some 250 poisonings attributed to eating blowfish—and half of these people died.

Accidental poisoning by fugu is most common in the winter, when the puffer is at its tastiest. The poison is also at its most virulent at that time. Cooks are trained in not only preparing the puffer for eating, but also in removing the poison (they are licensed by the government). And it is not easy. The poison, technically known as tetradoxin, stays potent even though the fish is cooked, and only a small amount (eight to ten milligrams) is required to be fatal, and it can be found in any organ of the fish.

Another animal source of poison was the bufo marinus, an enormous toad, which also lays claim to being the world's largest type of toad—it has a body length (not counting legs) of up to nine inches. The toad's poison is extremely toxic; it causes high blood pressure, headaches, and paralysis. Its effect would be similar to taking uncontrolled amounts of the heart drug digitalis. The poison, which comes from glands behind the eyes, was used on spear tips, arrows, and darts. To extract the poison, the toad is impaled on a spit and roasted. Blisters form on the skin, and as the poison drips out from the glands. it is caught in containers and fermented.

Scorpions also were said to have been used to dispatch enemies. A relative of spiders, the scorpion has a pair of pincers it uses to dismember its victims and a long, curving tail that ends in a poisonous stinger. This stinger injects a venom that is, milligram for milligram, deadlier than snake venom. While the wound is not impressive, the sting actually goes deep, producing high fever, blurred vision, and an adverse effect on both the nervous system and the heart. If it doesn't kill, the venom can cause a kind of insanity in the victim.

Most Murderous Month
August (U.S. Department of Justice)

Legend has it that scorpions go out of their way to claim human victims. In one case related in several folk tales, a bunch of scorpions formed a chain from the ceiling to the face of a sleeping victim, and the last one on the chain made the bite. It is likely, however, that this is apocryphal because scorpions are not known to attack human beings.

While cyanide is thought of as a sophisticated, modern poison, it was commonly available in feudal times. People learned to extract it from various things such as the seeds of apples, apricots, cherries, plums and almonds; all of these are loaded with cyanide compounds, but the foods with these cyanide compounds have no effect on a person unless the compounds are given in large doses. One man, for example, was reputed to have saved a cupful of apple seeds—and then ate them all at once. He died within minutes. Cyanide, taken orally, works on the central nervous system and kills very quickly.

It's surprising that the seeds of common fruit, like apples and cherries, are poisonous, but the killing and/or paralyzing power of some other very common household plants and flowers is equally shocking. One deadly poison is found in ordinary tomato leaves; not the tomato itself, of course; just the leaves. Eat these and you create cardiac problems and, ultimately, cardiac arrest. It can be safely assumed that quite a few people throughout history dined to death on tomato leaves. They could simply be slipped into a salad or the like and, unless one knew of their poisonous potency, they would look totally harmless and be fully ingested before the person knew what hit him.

Another deadly leaf is on the rhubarb. It contains oxalic acid, and once a little is eaten, it generates all manner of abdominal cramps. If someone eats enough leaves, he could easily experience convulsions, coma, and death.

Another deadly poison people served each other was the so-called death-cap mushroom, technically the *amanita phalloides*. This ordinary-looking mushroom is well deserving of its reputation as the most lethal mushroom in the forest: Once ingested and in the bloodstream, it's fatal.

Bamboo is another poison widely used in ancient times. As noted in *National Geographic*: "Many bamboos have culm sheaths covered with a down of fine hairs. Beware of touching these. They will get under the skin and produce intense irritation." Indeed, this would have made an ideal poison. Bacteria on the hairs could even cause blood poisoning. In ancient times, sheath hairs were mixed with food to kill an enemy.

Declining Crime Rate

From 1994–2004, The United States has had a steadily declining rate of violent crime, reaching the lowest level ever in 2004. (National Crime Victimization Survey)

Sometimes ancient poisons acted quickly, other times slowly, becoming, over a long period of time, cumulatively fatal. Slow poisoning often could be useful. For example, in one Japanese town, there was one spy who reputedly was a mole—an enemy agent living as an ordinary citizen—who slowly but surely poisoned the "mayor" of that town over a period of months. The big advantage was that the spy drank the same green tea into which he had slipped the poison, so that it calmed some suspicions the mayor had about him. But each time after consuming the tea, the ninja had taken an antidote. Eventually, the mayor died a seemingly ordinary death, and the spy was never suspected.

Another "poison" of feudal times became known to American GI's during the war in Vietnam. The Vietcong would dip their knives or spears in horse manure and blood. When the blade was used to cut, the blood/dung concoction would cause an infection that could kill.

There are a variety of poisons, like curare, that leave very little indication that they kill. Even under the best conditions, and with a top-notch coroner, determining the cause of death is not as simple as television and the movies would have us believe. Coming up with some microscopic tracings of a poison only compounds the difficulty of detecting poisons.

The delivery of the poison is also, of course, much more sophisticated than it used to be. Ideally, a person will take it orally. But today, there are needles which could be dipped in poison and which are so fine that it would be virtually impossible for a coroner to detect the entrance wound, particularly if the wound is made in an out-of-the-way spot.

Also, while most of us think of poisons as being dramatic—like arsenic—ordinary household substances can be used (and have been used) with deadly effect. This includes not only material taken orally, but also deadly gases formed by combining common household substances, such as the classic bleach and ammonia, which creates a gas as potent as mustard gas. More than one political or military personage has died in this way.

The Most Dangerous States

Each year, various organizations measure which states are the most dangerous based on indexes to various kinds of crime: murder rate, rape rate, robbery, aggravated assault, and motor vehicle theft rates.

1. Nevada
2. Louisiana
3. Arizona
4. Maryland
5. South Carolina.

The Safest States

1. North Dakota
2. Vermont
3. Maine
4. New Hampshire
5. South Dakota

"Bleep You! Bleep You!"

In his book, *Soul of a Cop*, police officer Paul Ragonese tells the story of how one day a woman came into New York City's 23rd precinct and told the cops that her boyfriend was holding their

Crime Can Be Funny

Not a Silver Bullet

In his book, *My Life in the NYPD: Jimmy the Wags*, Patrick Picciarelli, tells this story involving a well-known celebrity: I was working in the ninth ward, the east village. Back then (in the 70s), it was referred to as the "Evil." It was a very busy night this night because it was the middle of a heat wave, and the natives were restless. We were on a midnight to eight tour and at about 4 a.m. things started to quiet down. Then right in front of us we see this Caddy weaving all over the street. So we decide to pull him over by Ave B and see what's up. I approach the driver side and my partner approaches the passenger side which is the proper tactic for car stops.

"Hi Officer," the driver managed to slur.

He looked familiar, but I couldn't put my finger on it. As he handed me his license he blurted out "I'm Tonto!"

With that he threw open the door and vomited all over the street. Sure enough I looked at his license and it read Jay Silverheels. I couldn't believe it. I grew up watching The Lone Ranger and here I was about to bust his faithful companion. I called to my partner on the other side of the car, "Hey Kenny, we got Tonto here."

He was a very happy drunk and a great guy and within ten minutes we had every working car in the command trading "Hows," taking pictures, and him signing autographs. He told us some great stories of the show and his life and how he loved Clayton Moore (the Lone Ranger) like a brother. After a few hours and some coffee he sobered up, so we put him back in his car and pointed him to the Brooklyn Bridge and watched him so we knew he was okay. As he drove away he stuck his head out the window and yelled, "Gettum up, Scout!"

Then my partner Kenny said, "Who was that man?"

"I don't know partner, but he left this," I said, pointing to the pile of Tonto's vomit in the street.

eight-year-old boy hostage in his apartment on 105 St. Immediately, uniformed cops went to the apartment and demanded that the guy open up.

The response, in a Spanish accent, was "Bleep You!" The detectives tried to convince the guy to open the door and all

Crime Can Be Funny

On the Table, Please

Back in the mid-1970s, I was part of a task force that conducted a raid on a gambling joint down on Crescent Street. It was run by wiseguys, and they usually didn't take much flack from anybody. They were always swaggering. However, we had one guy on the squad with us named Carl Benton who was one of the toughest guys I ever met, and he got off one of the best lines I ever heard when we made that raid.

We burst into the cellar where the game was going on, and everybody was told to freeze and put their hands in sight. Everybody cooperated except one guy, an enforcer without a neck named Tony Bol. It all happened in a split second, but he had his hands under the gaming table and one of the cops yelled for him to get his hands in sight; he didn't, so Carl ran up to him, cocked his Barretta, held it against his head, and said softly, "Put your hands or your brains on the table."

His hands came in sight real quick.

they got was the same "Bleep you! Bleep you!" so they called ESU (Emergency Service Unit). The thing played out for three hours, during which crowds had gathered, a helicopter hovered overhead, and the media was coming out of the woodwork. And over the three hours all the cops had gotten when they asked the guy to come out was "Bleep you!"

Finally, Ragonese said it was decided to take down the door and try to pull the kid out. So he and his partner used sledgehammers to take down the door and then other cops, armed with shotguns, rushed in, yelling "Freeze, Police!" They were met with yet another "Bleep You," coming from behind what was a closed bedroom door. The cops, fed up, yelled for the guy to come out—and again were told "Bleep you." They took the door down and discovered that the guy was gone, and staring at them was this innocent little dark brown, yellow-billed Mynah bird that again told them "Bleep you! Bleep you!" in a Spanish accent.

The Assassination of JFK

The murder of John Fitzgerald Kennedy ranks as one of the most horrific events of the twentieth century, but for people to claim that someone other than Lee Harvey Oswald was the shooter is truly off the wall. The Warren Commission investigated the assassination thoroughly, and no one yet has come forward with anything approaching a credible argument against Oswald

not being the lone killer. He had the rifle, he had the high ground and it was a very easy shot. History always tells us what people will do, and Oswald's history is filled with hatred for a father who abandoned his family and a boy who slept in the same bed with his mother until he was fifteen.

Lee Harvey Oswald, posing with the rifle he used to assassinate JFK.
(Warren Commission)

Minutes before the shooting.
(Warren Commission)

Reenactment showing how easy it was to shoot Kennedy with a high-powered rifle.
(Warren Commission)

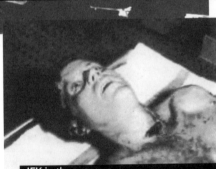

JFK in the morgue.
(Warren Commission)

Chapter 19
Mostly Gore
(Not Al)

Nicole Brown Simpson
(May 19, 1959–June 12, 1994)

Circumstances Surrounding Her Death

How someone is murdered can reflect who, in general, the murderer is. For example, if someone is shot in the head with a small caliber handgun such as a .22, chances are that a professional hit man was the "doer," as cops say. The pro knows that while a .22 doesn't have the velocity to go through the skull completely, it will penetrate one side and take a ricocheting path through the soft brain tissue, pinball-like, doing massive damage.

If internal organs are missing from a body, chances are a serial murderer is involved. Serial murderers commonly remove internal organs or heads and keep them as "trophies" of their success. If someone is poisoned, chances are that a female is the culprit. And if the victim is found to be stabbed many more times than is required to kill the person, he or she is a victim of "overkill," and chances are the person was killed by an enraged ex-lover or someone equally emotionally close.

Nicole Brown Simpson's autopsy report shows that there is no question the person wielding the knife (or knives) was experiencing extreme rage. Brown Simpson was stabbed multiple times, including one cut that was so deep that she was practically decapitated, the point of the knife nicking her spinal column. The young man with her, Ron Goldman, fought for their lives and also was stabbed many times.

A few hours before she was to die, Nicole hosted a dinner party at the Mezzaluna Restaurant in Los Angeles for her mother and father, who had driven in from Orange County. They had all gone to see Nicole's daughter, Sydney, who was in a dance recital at the Paul Revere School in Brentwood. After they parted company, Nicole's mother, Juditha Brown, discovered that her glasses were missing. She called the restaurant and learned that they had been found. Goldman, a waiter at the restaurant, agreed to take them over to the Simpson house and give them to Nicole. There was no indication that Goldman and Nicole had any romantic involvement. In fact, Goldman had a date scheduled for that evening, but deferred it so he could deliver the glasses. Goldman brought the glasses over to the rear entrance of the Simpson house, and it was probably the classic instance of someone being in the wrong place at the wrong time. The killer was lying in wait.

O.J. Simpson, found guilty in Civil Court of the murder of his wife, Nicole Brown Simpson. *Note: the murder scene photos were too gruesome to show.*
(Photofest)

Interestingly, the killer's rage also was demonstrated by his apparent unconcern with leaving clues around, such as bloody footprints and a bloody glove found near a fence that the killer had scaled. Then again, people who are enraged often don't think straight.

Autopsy Report: Nicole Brown Simpson

AUTOPSY REPORT 94–05136

I performed an autopsy on the body of BROWN-SIMPSON, NICOLE at the DEPARTMENT OF CORONER Los Angeles; California on June 14, 1994 @0730 HOURS

From the anatomic findings and pertinent history, I ascribe the death to: MULTIPLE SHARP FORCE INJURIES Due To Or As a Consequence of:

Anatomical Summary:

I. Incised wound of neck:

    A. Transection of left and right common carotid arteries.

    B. Incisions, left and right internal jugular veins

    C. Transection of thyrohyoid membrane, epiglottis, and hypopharynx.

    D. Incision into cervical spine, C3.

II. Multiple stab wound of neck and scalp (total of seven).

III. Multiple injuries of hands, including incised wound, ring finger of right hand (defense wound).

IV. Scalp bruise, right parietal.

NOTES AND PROCEDURES:

1. The body is described in the Standard Anatomical position. Reference is to this position only.

2. Where necessary, injures are numbered for reference. This is arbitrary and does not correspond to any order in which they may have been incurred. All the injuries are ante-mortem, unless otherwise specified.

3. The term "anatomic" is used as a specification to indicate correspondence with the description as set forth in the

textbooks of Gross Anatomy. It denotes freedom from significant, visible, or morbid alteration.

EXTERNAL EXAMINATION:

The body is that of a well-developed, well-nourished Caucasian female stated to be 35 years old. The body weighs 129 pounds and measures 65 inches from crown to sole. The hair on the scalp is brown. The irises are brown with the pupils fixed and dilated. The sclerae and conjunctive are unremarkable, without evidence of petechial hemorrhages on either. Both upper and lower teeth are natural, without evidence of injury to the cheeks, lips, or gums.

There are no tattoos, deformities, or amputations. Two linear surgical scars are found beneath each breast, transversely oriented and measuring 2 inches in length.

Rigor mortis is fixed at the time of autopsy examination

(please see form 1).

The body appears to the examiner as stated above. Identification is by toe-tag and the autopsy is not material to identification. The body is not embalmed.

The head is normocephalic and there is external evidence of antemortem injury to be described below. Otherwise, the external auditory canals, eyes, nose, and mouth are not remarkable. The neck shows sharp force injury to be described below, and the larynx is visible through the gaping wound.

No recent traumatic injuries are noted on the chest or abdomen; tan lines are seen on the lower abdomen (bathing suit). The genitalia are that of adult female with no gross evidence of injuries. Examination of the posterior surface at the trunk shows some excoriations compatible with postmortem injuries on the upper back, right side, on the medial aspect of the right scapula and on the lateral aspect of the right scapula (compatible with ant to insect bites). An abrasion above the left scapula measures 3/4 x 1/2 inch and is red-brown in color and appears antemortem. Otherwise, the lower back and remainder of the posterior aspect of the body shows no evidence or recent injuries.

Refer to available photographs and diagrams and the specific documentation of the autopsy protocol.

CLOTHING:

The decedent was wearing a short black dress, blood stained. Also, she was wearing a pair of black panties. To the unaided eye examination there was no evidence of cut or tear.

EVIDENCE OF INJURY:

DESCRIPTION OF INCISED WOUND OF NECK:

The incised wound of the neck is gaping and exposes the larynx and cervical vertebral column. It measures 5 1/2 x 2 1/2 inches in length and is found at the level of the superior border of the larynx.

After approximation of the edges, it is seen to be diagonally oriented on the right side and transversely oriented from the midline to the left side. On the right side it is upwardly angulated toward the right earlobe and extends for 4 inches from the midline. On the left side it is transversely oriented and extends 2 1/2 inches to the anterior border of the left sternocleidomastoid muscle. The edges of the wound are smooth, with subcutaneous and intramuscular hemorrhage, fresh, dark red purple, is evident.

On the right side, the upwardly angulated wound passes through the skin, the subcutaneous tissue, the platysma, passing under the ramus of the right mandible and upward as it passes through the strap muscles on the right, towards the digastric muscle on the right, and through the thyrohyoid membrane and ligament. Further dissection discloses that it passes posteriorly and transects the distal one-third of the epiglottis, the hypopharynx, and passes into the body of the 3rd cervical vertebra where it transversely oriented 3/4 inch incised wound is seen in the bone, extending it for a depth of 1/4 inch into the bone. The spinal canal and cord are not entered.

On the right side superiorly the wound passes towards the insertion of the sternocleidomastoid muscle, and then becomes more superficial and tapers as it terminates in the skin below the right earlobe.

On the left side the wound is transversely oriented and extends for 2 1/2 inches where the wound path intersects the stab wounds on the left side of the neck to be described below.

Dissection discloses that the right common carotid artery is transected with hemorrhage in the surrounding carotid sheath and there is a 1/4 incised wound 0; nick in the right internal jugular vein with surrounding soft tissue hemorrhage.

On the left side the left common carotid artery is transected with hemorrhage in the surrounding carotid sheath and the left internal jugular vein is subtotally transected with only a thin strand of tissue remaining posteriorly with surrounding soft tissue hemorrhage. The injuries on the left side of the neck intersect, and the pathways of the stab wounds on the left side to be described below.

There is fresh hemorrhage and bruising noted along the entire incised wound path.

Depth of penetration is not given because the neck can be either flexed or extended, and the length of the wound is greater than the depth.

Opinion: This is a fatal incised wound or sharp force injury, associated with transection of the left and right carotid arteries and incisions of the left and right internal jugular veins with exsanguinating hemorrhage.

DESCRIPTION OF MULTIPLE STAB WOUNDS:

There are four stab wounds on the left side of the neck over the left sternocledomastoid muscle; they extend to 3 inches below the external auditory canal.

1. This stab wound overlaps that of the incised wound of the neck described above. The wound measures 5/8 inch in length, is vertically oriented, and has a squared-off end inferiorly approximately 1/32 inch and a pointed end superiorly. The minimal depth of the penetration, from left to right, is 1 1/2 to 2 inches where it intersects the incised wound. Penetration is through the skin, subcutaneous tissue and muscle, and injury to the internal jugular vein or common carotid artery cannot be excluded.

2. Stab wound of left side of neck: This is a 1/8 inch superficial slit-like incision into the skin and dermis; no squared-off or dull end is evident.

This is a superficial slit-like wound of the skin, non-fatal.

3. Stab wound on left side of neck: This is a diagonally oriented stab wound measuring 1/2 inch in length; there is a pointed end on the posterior aspect and a squared-off end anterior less than 1/32 inch in length. The edges are smooth, and dissection disposes a depth of penetration for 1 1/2 to 2 inches where the stab wound intersects that of the incised wound of the neck; the stab wounds are approximately 1 inch from the left lateral termination of the incised wound. Fresh hemorrhage is noted along the wound path which goes through the skin, subcutaneous tissue and muscle.

Opinion: This stab wound cannot be distinguished from injuries caused by the incised wound of the neck and may have injured the left common carotid artery and/or the left internal jugular vein.

4. Stab wound of the left side of neck: This is a diagonally oriented stab wound measuring 7/8 inch in length; on the posterior aspect there is a pointed end and on the anterior aspect a squared-off or dull end approximately 1/32 inch in width; otherwise the edges are smooth. Subsequent dissection discloses the wound path through the skin, subcutaneous tissue and muscle where it intersects the incised wound of the neck. Depth of penetration is 1–1/2 inches.

Opinion: This stab wound may have injured the left common carotid artery and/or the left internal jugular vein as described above.

5. Stab wound of scalp, left parietal: This diagonally oriented stab wound is located on the left parietal scalp, which is shaved postmortem for visualization. It measures 1/2 inch in length and no definite squared-off or dull end is evident, both ends appearing to be rounded. Depth of penetration is through the scalp, to the galea, approximately 3/8–1/2 inch. There is deep scalp hemorrhage and a subgaleal bruise, measuring 1 1/2 x 1 1/2 inches; there is no cutting wound or injury to the skull and there is no penetration into the cranium.

Opinion: This is a superficial stab wound or cutting wound of the scalp, non-fatal.

6. Stab wound or cutting wound of scalp: This is transversely oriented and is found in the right posterior parietal-occipital region. The transversely oriented wound measures 1 1/2 inches in length and has a pointed end to the left and a fork or split into the right. Depth of penetration is 3/8–1 1/2 inches with fresh deep scalp bruising.

    Opinion: This is a non-fatal, stabbing or cutting wound of the scalp.

7. Stab wound or cutting wound of the scalp, right parietal-occipital: This is vertically oriented, measures 3/16 inch in length and involves the skin only. No squared-off or dull end is evident, both ends or spects being pointed or tapered. There is a small amount of deep scalp hemorrhage or bruising, no subgaleal hemorrhage.

    Opinion: This is a non-fatal superficial stabbing or cutting wound of the scalp.

8. Blunt force injury to head: On the right side of the scalp, 4 inches above the right external auditory canal there is a scalp bruise; this is revealed after postmortem shaving of the scalp. It measures 1 x 1 inches and is red-violet or purple in color. The skin is smooth, non-abraded or lacerated. Subsequent autopsy discloses fresh deep scalp hemorrhage and fresh dark red-purple subgaleal hemorrhage or bruising measuring 2 x 1 1/4 inches. Inferiorly the bruise extends to the superficial right temporal muscle. There is no associated skull fracture.

INJURIES TO HANDS:

Right hand: There is a 5/8 incised wound of the volar surface of the right index finger at the distal knuckle. This 5/8 inch incised wound is tangentially oriented or cut through the skin and dermis with the avulsed skin inferiorly indicating that the direction is from distal to proximal.

Further examination discloses that there is a split or forked end on the ulnar aspect and pointed end on the radial aspect. There is a small amount of dermal hemorrhage.

On the dorsal surface of the right hand, at the base of the ring finger, there is a 1/16 inch punctate abrasion.

Left hand: On the dorsal surface of the left hand, there is a punctate abrasion, red-brown in color at the base of the ring finger.

There is a 1/2 inch superficial incised skin cut; 1/2 inch in length, diagonally oriented, on the top of the left hand, midportion.

INTERNAL EXAMINATION:

The body is opened with the usual Y-shaped thoracoabdominal incision revealing the abdominal wall adipose tissue to measure 1/4—3/8 inch in thickness. The anterior abdominal wall has its normal muscular components and there is no evidence of abdominal wall injury. Exposure of the body cavities shows the contained organs in their usual anatomic locations with their usual anatomic relationships. No free fluid or blood is found within the pleural, pericardial, or the peritoneal cavities. The serosal surfaces are smooth, thin, and glistening and there are no intra-abdominal adhesions.

Marilyn Monroe
(June 1, 1926–August 4, 1962)

Circumstances Surrounding Her Death

To this day, there are many people who do not believe the conclusion of Los Angeles Medical Examiner, Dr. Thomas Noguchi, about what caused Marilyn Monroe's death. He called it "probable suicide." Some believe that she suffered an accidental overdose of medication, while others believe that she was murdered to ensure that she would never tell what she knew—whatever that might be—about high-ranking politicos, such as John F. Kennedy and his brother Robert.

Marilyn Monroe in all her natural beauty.
(Photofest)

Monroe had apparently spent all of Saturday, August 4, 1962, in her bedroom, the door locked. She did have a phone, though, and she made a number of calls during the day. One was to Joe DiMaggio, Jr., son of her ex-husband, who reported her to be upbeat, and another was to actor and Kennedy crony Peter Lawford, who said she seemed down.

It was the housekeeper, a woman named Eunice Murray, who first became suspicious that something was wrong. Before Murray went to bed at around 10:00 p.m., she looked at the door to Monroe's bedroom and could see a slit of light

305

under it. She assumed Monroe was still up. But when she awakened again at midnight to go to the bathroom and went past Monroe's door, she noticed the light was still on—which was unusual. She knocked at the door and called Marilyn, and when there was no answer she became alarmed. She called Monroe's psychiatrist, Dr. Ralph Greenson, who lived only a short distance away. He got to the house about 12:30 a.m. and also tried to get Monroe to answer the door. When she didn't, he went outside and looked through a bedroom window and saw her lying face down on the bed. He took a poker and broke the glass so he could unlatch the window and get in. Inside, he discovered that Monroe was dead.

The police were not notified until 4:25 a.m. Subsequent investigation determined that before calling the police Greenson, and then her physician, Hyman Engelberg, had called studio executives first. Just what they did to compromise what some observers thought was a crime scene is anyone's guess.

Marilyn Monroe in the morgue.
(Los Angeles County Coroner)

It was determined by Noguchi that Marilyn's death was caused by the ingestion of two drugs, a sleep aid and a tranquilizer. Police found an empty bottle of 100 milligram capsules of Nembutal, and ten capsules of chloral hydrate remained from a bottle of fifty that had been refilled on July 31.

In the years since Monroe's death, some observers contend that the empty and near-empty pill bottles were a ruse, that she was killed by a "hot shot" of barbiturate, and much was made of some unexplained bruises on her body that Noguchi supposedly was to later say were the result of "violence." Other observers say that it was accidental.

Still, her history would seem to indicate suicide. She was the child of a father who had deserted the family and a mother who had very serious mental issues. Monroe suffered frequent if not daily bouts of anxiety and depression, and had, in fact, attempted suicide by barbiturate a number of times. It hardly requires a mental leap to imagine that she killed herself.

Coroner Rules Monroe's Death a Suicide
(August 17, 1962)

STATEMENT BY THEODORE J. CURPHEY, M.D. CHIEF MEDICAL EXAMINER-CORONER, COUNTY OF LOS ANGELES

Now that the final toxicological report and that of the psychiatric consultants have been received and considered, it is my conclusion that the death of Marilyn Monroe was caused by a self-administered overdose of sedative drugs and that the mode of death is probable suicide.

The final toxicological report reveals that the barbiturate, previously reported as a lethal dose, has been positively identified as Nembutal by the toxicologist.

In the course of completing his routine examination, the toxicologist, Mr. Raymond Abernethy, discovered in addition to the Nembutal present a large dose of chloral hydrate.

Following is the summary report by the Psychiatric Investigative Team which has assisted me in collecting information in this case. This team was headed by Robert Litman, M.D., Norman Farbwow, Ph.D., and Norman Tabaohnlok, M.D.:

"Marilyn Monroe died on the night of August 4 or the early morning of August 5, 1962. Examination by the toxicology laboratory indicates that death was due to a self-administered overdose of sedative drugs. We have been asked, as consultants, to examine the life situation of the deceased and to give an opinion regarding the intent of Miss Monroe when she ingested the sedative drugs which caused her death. From the data obtained, the following points are the most important and relevant:

"Miss Monroe had suffered from psychiatric disturbance for a long time. She experienced severe fears and frequent depressions. Mood changes were abrupt and unpredictable. Among symptoms of disorganization, sleep disturbance was prominent for which she had been taking sedative drugs for many years. She was thus familiar with and experienced in the use of sedative drugs and well aware of their dangers.

"Recently, one of the main objectives of her psychiatric treatment had been the reduction of her intake of drugs. This has been partially successful during the last two months. She was reported to be following doctor's orders in her use of the drugs; and the amount of drugs found in her home at the time of her death was not unusual.

"In our investigation, we have learned that Miss Monroe had often expressed wishes to give up, to withdraw, and even to die. On more than one occasion in the past, when disappointed and depressed, she had made a suicide attempt using sedative drugs. On these occasional she had called for help and had been rescued.

"From the information collected about the events of the evening of August 4, it is our opinion that the same pattern was repeated except for the rescue. It has been our practice with similar information collected in other cases in the past to recommend a certification for such deaths as probable suicide.

"Additional clues for suicide provided by the physical evidence are: (1) the high level of barbiturates and chloral hydrate in the blood which, with other evidence from the autopsy, indicates the probable ingestion of a large amount of the drugs within a short period of time; (2) the completely empty bottle of Nembutal, the prescription for which was filled the day before the ingestion of the drugs; and (3) the locked door which was unusual.

"On the basis of all the information obtained, it is our opinion that the case is a probable suicide."

REPORT OF CHEMICAL ANALYSIS
LOS ANGELES COUNTY CORONER
Toxicology Laboratory
Hall of Justice
Los Angeles, California

File No. 81128   I

Name of Deceased   Marilyn Monroe

Date Submitted   August 6, 1962   Time   8 A.M.

Autopsy Surgeon   T. Noguchi, M.D.

Material Submitted:

Blood x	Liver x	Stomach x
Brain	Lung	Lavage
Femur	Spleen	Urine x
Kidney x	Sternum	Gall bladder
Drugs x	Chemicals	Intestines x

Test Desired: Ethanol, Barbiturates

Laboratory Findings:

Blood: Ethanol   Absent

Blood: Barbiturates   4.5 mg. per cent
         Phenobarbital is absent

Drugs:
(1) 27 capsules, #19295, 6-7-62, Librium, 5 mgm. #50
(2) 17 capsules, 20201, 7-10-62, Librium, 10 mgm. #100
(3) 26 tablets, #20569, 7-25-62, Sulfathallidine, #36
(4) Empty container, #20858, 8-3-62, Nembutal, 1½gr.#25
(5) 10 green capsules, #20570, 7-31-62, Chloral Hydrate, 0.5 gm. #50 (Refill: 7-25-62 - original)
(6) Empty container, #456099, 11-4-61, Noludar, #50
(7) 32 pink capsules in a container without label Phenergan, #20857, 8-3-62, 25 mg. #25

Examined By R.J. Abernethy Head Toxicologist. Date August 6, 1962

Autopsy report showing the drugs Marilyn Monroe was using and used to kill herself.
(Los Angeles County Coroner)

309

George Reeves
(January 5, 1914–June 16, 1959)

Circumstances Surrounding His Death

According to some people, there is still a mystery concerning the death of George Reeves, the handsome actor who became famous as TV's Superman in the 1950s. The autopsy report stated that he had committed suicide, but close friends including, ironically, actor Gig Young—ironic because he was to kill himself and his wife years later—stated that "he was in no way capable of bumping himself off." A staunch believer in the idea that he had been murdered was his mother, who hired private investigators to look into his death and who, until the day she died, believed her son had been murdered. What the motive for murder could have been is pure speculation, but it seems that Reeves had a romantic involvement with someone else's wife.

George Reeves aka Superman.
(Los Angeles County Coroner)

Another possible motive for suicide was his depression over his career. His *Superman* series had been wildly popular since its inception in 1951, but when it shut down production in 1957, Reeves found he was typecast and could not get the kind of meaty, dramatic roles that he craved. However, he did not have any money worries: he was constantly in demand for personal appearances as Superman.

On the night he died, George had gone to dinner with his fiancée, a New York showgirl named Leonora Lemmon, and a writer and houseguest named Robert Condon. Following dinner the three, all a bit tipsy, went back to Reeves' Los Angeles home, where they continued to drink.

Shortly after midnight they all went to bed, but they were awakened around 1:00 a.m. by two merrymakers and neighbors, Carol Von Ronkel and William Bliss. Leonora let them into the house and then Reeves, a man who normally enjoyed merrymaking, did something uncharacteristic: he came down from his bedroom and laid into them for showing up so late. But Reeves stayed around for a while and ended up apologizing for his behavior, then he went back upstairs.

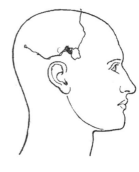

Before he did, however, it seemed clear to his fiancée, at least, that he was very depressed over his career, something that had been discussed earlier at dinner. So when he went upstairs she said, bizarrely, perhaps prophetically: "He'll probably go to his room and shoot himself." She was well aware that Reeves owned a 30 caliber Luger. This got everyone's attention, and they listened and heard him pulling open what was a dresser drawer. "He's getting the gun out now," Lemmon said, "and he is going to shoot himself."

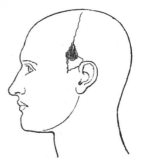

Then, they heard the loud report of a gun. Lemmon asked Bliss to check it out. He did, and found Reeves lying

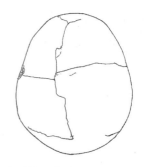

What a bullet from a Luger did to the head of Superman.
(Los Angeles County Coroner)

311

nude on his back across his bed. And he also saw, the autopsy report stated, "a large amount of blood on the body and head."

Bliss alerted the others to what he found, and Los Angeles homicide detectives were called. They found the Luger between Reeves' legs, and their investigation also revealed that the bullet had passed through his head and had lodged in the ceiling. There was also a shell casing under his body. There were a number of unresolved questions about Reeves' death, particularly some bruises on his body that gave rise to speculation that he had been murdered.

Death certificate of Georges Reeves.
(Los Angeles County Coroner)

JonBenet Ramsey Autopsy Report

JonBenet Ramsey Autopsy Report

Here is the complete text of the JonBenet Ramsey autopsy report, released by Boulder County Coroner John Meyer on August 13, 1997.

NAME: RAMSEY, JONBENET

DOB: 08/06/90

NAME: Ramsey, JonBenet

DOB: 08/06/90

AGE: 6Y

SEX: F

PATH MD: MEYER

TYPE: COR

AUTOPSY NO: 96A-155

DEATH D/T: 12/26/96 @1323

AUTOPSY D/T: 12/27/96 @ 0815

ID NO; 137712

COR/MEDREC# 1714-96-A

FINAL DIAGNOSIS:

I. Ligature strangulation

   A. Circumferential ligature with associated ligature furrow of neck

   B. Abrasions and petechial hemorrhages, neck

   C. Petechial hemorrhages, conjunctival surfaces of eyes and skin of face

II. Craniocerebral injuries

   A. Scalp contusion

B. Linear, comminuted fracture of right side of skull

C. Linear pattern of contusions of right cerebral hemisphere

D. Subarachnoid and subdural hemorrhage

E. Small contusions, tips of temporal lobes

III. Abrasion of right cheek

IV. Abrasion/contusion, posterior right shoulder

V. Abrasions of left lower back and posterior left lower leg

VI. Abrasion and vascular congestion of vaginal mucosa

VII. Ligature of right wrist

Toxicologic Studies
blood ethanol - none detected
blood drug screen - no drugs detected

CLINICOPATHOLOGIC CORRELATION: Cause of death of this six year old female is asphyxia by strangulation associated with craniocerebral trauma.

John E. Meyer M.D.
Pathologist
jn/12/27/96

The body of this six year old female was first seen by me after I was called to an address identified as 755 - 15th street in Boulder, Colorado, on 12/26/96. I arrived at the scene approximately 8 PM on 12/26 and entered the house where the decedent's body was located at approximately 8:20PM. I initially viewed the body in the living room of the house. The decedent was laying on her back on the floor, covered by a blanket and a Colorado Avalanche sweatshirt. On removing these two items from the top of the body the decedent was found to be lying on her back with her arms extended up over her head. The head was turned to the right. A brief examination of the body disclosed a ligature around the neck and a ligature around the right wrist. Also noted was a small area of abrasion or contusion below the right ear on the lateral aspect of the right cheek. A prominent dried abrasion was present on the lower left neck. After examining the body, I left the residence at approximately 8:30PM.

EXTERNAL EXAM: The decedent is clothed in a long sleeved white knit collarless shirt, the mid anterior chest area of which contains an embroidered silver star decorated with silver sequins. Tied loosely around the right wrist, overlying the sleeve of the shirt is a white cord. At the knot there is one tail end which measures 5.5 inches in length with a frayed end. The other tail of the knot measures 15.5 inches in length and ends in a double loop knot. This end of the cord is also frayed. There are no defects noted in the shirt but the upper anterior right sleeve contains a dried brown-tan stain measuring 2.5x1.5 inches, consistent with mucous from the nose or mouth. There are long white underwear with an elastic waist band containing a red and blue stripe. The long underwear are urine stained anteriorly over the crotch area and anterior legs. No defects are identified. Beneath the long underwear are white panties with printed rose buds and the words "Wednesday" on the elastic waist band. The underwear is urine stained and in the inner aspect of the crotch are several red areas of staining measuring up to 0.5 inch maximum dimension.

EXTERNAL EVIDENCE OF INJURY: Located just below the right ear at the right angle of the mandible, 1.5 inches below the right external auditory canal is a 3/8 x 1/4 inch area of rust colored abrasion. In the lateral aspect of the left lower eyelid on the inner conjunctival surface is a 1mm in maximum dimension petechial hemorrhage. Very fine,less than 1mm petechial hemorrhages are present on the skin of the upper eyelids bilaterally as well as on the lateral left cheek. On everting the left upper eyelid there are much smaller, less than 1mm petechial hemorrhages located on the conjuctival surface. Possible petechial hemorrhages located on the conjunctival surfaces of the right upper and lower eyelids, but livor mortis on this side of the face makes definite identification difficult.

Wrapped around the neck with a double knot in the midline of the posterior neck is a length of white cord similar to that described as being tied around the right wrist. This ligature cord is cut on the right side of the neck and removed. A single black ink mark is placed on the left side of the cut and a double black ink mark on the right side of the cut. The posterior knot is left intact. Extending from the knot the posterior aspect of the neck are two tails of the knot, one measuring 4 inches in length and having a frayed end, and the other measuring 17 inches in length with the end tied in multiple loops around a length of a round tan-brown wooden stick which measures 4.5 inches in length. This wooden stick is irregularly broken at both ends and there are several colors of paint and apparent glistening varnish on the surface. Printed in gold letters on one end of the wooden stick is the word "Korea". The tail end of another word extends from beneath the loops of the cord tied around the stick and is not able to be interpreted. Blonde hair is entwined in the knot on the posterior aspect of the neck as well as in the cord wrapped around the wooden stick. It appears to be made of a white synthetic material. Also secured around the neck is a gold chain with a single charm in the form of a cross.

A deep ligature furrow encircles the entire neck. The width of the furrow varies from one-eighth of an inch to five/sixteenths of an inch and is horizontal in orientation, with little upward deviation. The skin of the anterior neck above and below the ligature furrow contains areas of petechial hemorrhage and abrasion encompassing an area measuring approximately 3x2 inches. The ligature furrow crosses the anterior midline of the neck just below the laryngeal prominence, approximately at the level of the cricoid cartilage. It is almost completely horizontal with slight upward deviation from the horizontal towards the back of

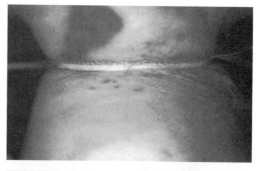

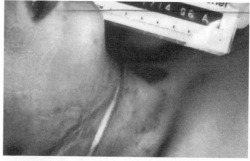

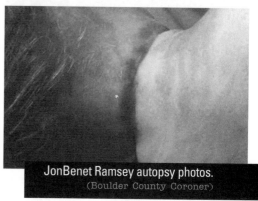

JonBenet Ramsey autopsy photos.
(Boulder County Coroner)

the neck. The midline of the furrow mark on the anterior neck is 8 inches below the top of the head. The midline of the furrow mark on the posterior neck is 6.75 inches below the top of the head.

317

The area of abrasion and petechial hemorrhage of the skin of the anterior neck includes on the lower left neck, just to the left of the midline, a roughly triangular, parchment-like rust colored abrasion which measures 1.5 inches in length with a maximum width of 0.75 inches. This roughly triangular shaped abrasion is obliquely oriented with the apex superior and lateral. The remainder of the abrasions and petechial hemorrhages of the skin above and below the anterior projection of the ligature furrow are nonpatterned, purple to rust colored, and present in the midline, right, and left areas of the anterior neck. The skin just above the ligature furrow along the right side of the neck contains petechial hemorrhage composed of multiple confluent very small petechial hemorrhages as well as several larger petechial hemorrhages measuring up to one-sixteenth and one-eighth of an inch in maximum dimension. Similar smaller petechial hemorrhages are present on the skin below the ligature furrow on the left lateral aspect of the neck. Located on the right side of the chin is a three-sixteenths by one-eighth of an inch area of superficial abrasion. On the posterior aspect of the right shoulder is a poorly demarcated, very superficial focus of abrasion/contusion which is pale purple in color and measures up to three-quarters by one-half inch in maximum dimension. Several linear aggregates of petechial hemorrhages are present in the anterior left shoulder just above deltopectoral groove. These measure up to one inch in length by one-sixteenth to one-eighth of an inch in width. On the left lateral aspect of the lower back, approximately sixteen and one-quarter inches and seventeen and one-half inches below the level of the top of the head are two dried rust colored to slightly purple abrasions. The more superior of the two measures one-eighth by one-sixteenth of an inch and the more inferior measures three-sixteenths by one-eighth of an inch.

There is no surrounding contusion identified. On posterior aspect of the left lower leg, almost in the midline, approximately 4 inches above the level of the heel are two small scratch-like abrasions which are dried and rust colored. They measure one-sixteenth by less than one-sixteenth of an inch and one-eighth by less than one-sixteenth of an inch respectively.

On the anterior aspect of the perineum, along the edges of closure of the labia majora, is a small amount of dried blood. A similar small amount of dried and semifluid blood is present on the skin of the fourchette and in the vestibule. Inside the vestibule of the vagina and along the distal vaginal wall is reddish hyperemia. This hyperemia is circumferential and perhaps more noticeable on the right side and posteriorly. The hyperemia also appears to extend just inside the vaginal orifice. A 1 cm red-purple area of abrasion is located on the right posterolateral area of the 1x1 cm hymenal orifice. The hymen itself is represented by a rim of mucosal tissue extending clockwise between the 2 and 10:00 positions. The area of abrasion is present at approximately the 7:00 position and appears to involve the hymen and distal right lateral vaginal wall and possibly the area anterior to the hymen. On the right labia majora is a very faint area of violet discoloration measuring approximately one inch by three-eighths of an inch. Incision into the underlying subcutaneous tissue discloses no hemorrhage. A minimal amount of semiliquid thin watery red fluid is present in the vaginal vault. No recent or remote anal or other perineal trauma is identified.

REMAINDER OF EXTERNAL EXAMINATION: The unembalmed, well developed and well nourished caucasian female body measures 47 inches in length and weighs an estimated 45 pounds. The scalp is covered by long blonde hair which is fixed in two ponytails, one on top of the head secured by a cloth hair tie and blue elastic band, and one in the lower back of the head secured by a blue elastic band. No scalp trauma is identified. The external auditory canals are patent and free of blood. The eyes are green and the pupils equally dilated. The sclerae are white. The nostrils are both patent and contain a small amount of tan mucous material. The teeth are native and in good repair. The tongue is smooth, pink-tan and granular. No buccal mucosal trauma is seen. The frenulum is intact. There is slight drying artifact of the tip of the of tongue. On the right cheek is a pattern of dried saliva and mucous material which does not appear to be hemorrhaic. The neck contains no palpable adenopathy or masses and the trachea and larynx are midline. The chest is symmetrical. Breasts are prepubescent. The abdomen is flat and contains no scars. No palpable organomegaly or masses are identified. The external genitalia are that of a prepubescent female. No pubic hair is present. The anus is patent. Examination of the right extremities is unremarkable. On the middle finger of the right hand is a yellow metal band. Around the right wrist is a yellow metal identification bracelet with the name "JonBenet" on one side and the date "12/25/96" on the other side. A red ink line drawing in the form of a heart is located on the palm of the left hand. The fingernails of both hands are of sufficient length for clipping. Examination the back is unremarkable. There is dorsal 3+ to 4+l livor mortis which is nonblanching. Livor mortis is also present of the right side of the face. At the time of the initiation of the autopsy there is mild 1 to 2+ rigor mortis of the elbows and shoulders with more advanced 2 to 3+ rigor mortis of the joints of the lower extremities.

INTERNAL EXAM: The anterior chest musculature is well developed. No sternal or rib fractures are identified.

Mediastinum: The mediastinal contents are normally distributed. The 21 gm thymus gland has a normal external appearance. The cut sections are finely lobular and pink-tan. No petechialhemorrhages are seen. The aorta and remainder of the mediastinal structures are unremarkable.

Body Cavities: The right and left thoracic cavities contain approximately 5 cc of straw colored fluid. The pleural surfaces are smooth and glistening. The pericardial sac contains 3-4 cc of straw colored fluid and the epicardium and pericardium are unremarkable. The abdominal contents are normally distributed and covered by a smooth glistening serosa. No intra-abdominal accumulation of fluid or blood is seen.

Lungs: The 200 gm right lung and 175 gm left lung have a normal lobar configuration. An occasional scattered subpleural petechial hemorrhage is seen on the surface of each lung. The cut sections of the lungs disclose an intact alveolar architecture with a small amount of watery fluid exuding from the cut surfaces with mild pressure. The intrapulmonary bronchi and vasculature are unremarkable. No evidence of consolidation is seen.

Heart: The 100 gm heart has a normal external configuration. There are scattered subepicardial petechial hemorrhages over the anterior surface of the heart. The coronary arteries are normal in their distribution and contain no evidence of atherosclerosis. The tan-pink myocardium is homogeneous and contains no areas of fibrosis or infarction. The endocarium is unremarkable. The valve cusps are thin, delicate and pliable and contain no vegetation or thrombosis. The major vessels enter and leave the heart in the normal fashion. The foramen ovale is closed.

Aorta and Vena Cava: The aorta is patent throughout its course as are its major branches. No atherosclerosis is seen. The vena cava is unremarkable.

Spleen: The 61 gm spleen has a finely wrinkled purple capsule. Cut sections are homogeneous and disclose readily identifiable red and white pulp. No intrinsic abnormalities are identified.

Adrenals: The adrenal glands are of normal size and shape. A golden yellow cortex surmounts a thing brown-tan medullar area. No intrinsic abnormalities are identified.

Kidneys: The 40 gm right kidney and 40 gm left kidney have a normal external appearance. The surfaces are smooth and glistening. Cut sections disclose an contact corticomedullary architecture. The renal papillae are sharply demarcated. The pelvocaliceal system is lined by gray-white mucosa which is unremarkable. Both ureters are patent throughout their course to the bladder.

Liver: The 625 gm liver has a normal external appearance. The capsule is smooth and glistening. Cut sections disclose an intact lobular architecture with no intrinsic abnormalities identified.

Pancreas: The pancreas is of normal size and shape. Cut sections are finely lobular and tan. No intrinsic abnormalities are identified.

Bladder: The bladder is contracted and contains no urine. The bladder mucosa is smooth and tan-gray. No intrinsic abnormalities are seen.

Genitalia: The upper portions of the vaginal vault contain no abnormalities. The prepubescent uterus measures 3 x 1 x 0.8cm and is unremarkable. The cervial os contains no abnormalities. Both fallopian tubes and ovaries are prepubescent and unremarkable by gross examination.

Gallbladder: The gallbladder contains 2-3 cc of amber bile. No stones are identified and the mucosa is smooth and velvety. The cystic duct, right and left hepatic duct and common bile duct are patent throughout their course to the duodenum.

G.I. Tract: The esophagus is empty. It is lined by gray-white mucosa. The stomach contains a small amount (8-11cc) of viscous to green to tan colored thick mucous material without particulate matter identified. The gastic mucosa is autolyzed but contains no areas of hemorrhage or ulceration. The yellow to light green-tan apparent vegetable or fruit material which may represent fragments of pineapple. No hemorrhage is identified. The remainder of the small intestine is unremarkable. The large intestine contains soft green fecal material. The appendix is present.

Lymphatic System: Unremarkable.

Musculoskeletal System: Unremarkable.

Skull and Brain: Upon reflection of the scalp there is found to be an extensive area of scalp hemorrhage along the right temporoparietal area extending from the orbital ridge, posteriorly all the way to the occipital area. This encompasses an area measuring approximately 7x4 inches. This grossly appears to be fresh hemorrhage with no evidence of organization. At the superior extension of this area of hemorrhage is a linear to comminuted skull fracture which extends from the right occipital to posteroparietal area forward to the right frontal area across the parietal skull. In the posteroparietal area of this fracture is a roughly rectangular shaped displaced fragment of skull measuring one and three-quarters by one-half inch. The hemorrhage and the fracture extend posteriorly just past the midline of the occipital area of the skull. This fracture measures approximately 8.5 inches in length. On removal of the skull cap there is found to be a thin film of subdural hemorrhage measuring approximately 7-8 cc over the surface of the right cerebral hemisphere and extending to the base of the cerebral hemisphere. The 1450 gm grain has a normal overall architecture. Mild narrowing of the sulci and flattening of the gyri are seen. No inflammation is identified. There is a thin film of subarachnoid hemorrhage overlying the entire right cerebral hemisphere. On the right cerebral hemisphere underlying the previously mentioned linear skull fracture is an extensive linear area of purple contusion extending from the right frontal area, posteriorly along the lateral aspect of the parietal region and into the occipital area. This area of contusion measures 8 inches in length with a width of up to 1.75 inches. At the tip of the right temporal lobe is a one-quarter by one-quarter inch similar appearing purple contusion. Only very minimal contusion is present at the tip of the left temporal lobe. This area of contusion measures only one-half inch in maximum dimension. The cerebral vasculature contains no evidence of atherosclerosis. Multiple coronal sections of the cerebral hemispheres, brain stem and cerebellum disclose no additional abnormalities. The areas of previously described contusion are characterized by purple linear streak-like discolorations of the gray matter perpendicular to the surface of the cerebral cortex. These extend approximately 5mm into the cerebral cortex. Examination of the base of the brain discloses no additional fractures.

Neck: Dissection of the neck is performed after removal of the throacoabdominal organs and the brain. The anterior strap musculature of the neck is serially dissected. Multiple sections of the sternocleidomastoid muscle disclose no hemorrhages. Sections of the remainder of the strap musculature of the neck disclose no evidence of hemorrhage. Examination of the thyroid cartilage, cricoid cartilage and hyoid bone disclose no evidence of fracture or hemorrhage. Multiple cross sections of the tongue disclose no hemorrhage or traumatic injury. The thyroid gland weights 2 gm and is normal in appearance. Cut sections are finely lobular and red-tan. The trachea and larynx are lined by smooth pink-tan mucosa without intrinsic abnormalities.

MICROSCOPIC DESCRIPTION: (All sections Stained with H&E)

(Slide key) - (A) - scalp hemorrhage, (B) sections of vaginal mucosa with smallest fragment representing area of abrasion at 7:00 position, (C) - heart, (D-F) - lungs, (G) liver and spleen,(H) pancreas and kidney, (I) - thyroid and bladder, (J) - thymus and adrenals, (K-L) - reproductive organs, (M) - larynx, (N-T) - brain.

Myocardium: Sections of the ventricular myocardium are composed of interlacing bundles of cardiac muscle fibers. No fibrosis or inflammation are identified.

Lungs: The alveolar architecture of the lungs is well preserved. Pulmonary vascular congestion is identified. No intrinsic abnormalities are seen.

Spleen: There is mild autolysis of the spleen. Both red and white pulp are identifiable.

Thyroid: The thyroid gland is composed of normal-appearing follicles. An occasional isolated area of chronic interstitial infiltrate is seen. There is also a small fragment of parathyroid tissue.

Thymus: The thymus gland retains the usual architecture. The lymphoid material is intact and scattered Hassall's corpuscles are identified. Mild vascular congestion is identified.

Trachea: There is mild chronic inflammation in the submucosa of the trachea.

Liver: The lobular architecture of the liver is well preserved. No inflammation or intrinsic abnormality are identified.

Pancreas: There is autolysis of the pancreas which is otherwise unremarkable.

Kidney: the overall architecture of the kidney is well preserved There is perhaps mild vascular congestion in the cortex but no inflammation is identified.

Bladder: The transitional epithelium of the bladder is autolyzed. No significant intrinsic abnormalities are seen.

Reproductive Organs: Sections of the uterus are consistent with the prepubescent ages. The ovary is unremarkable.

Adrenal: The architecture of the adrenal is well preserved and no intrinsic abnormalities are seen.

Brain: Sections from the areas of contusion disclose disrupted blood vessels of the cortex with surrounding hemorrhage. There is no evidence of the inflammatory infiltrate or organization of the hemorrhage. Subarachnoid hemorrhage is also identified. Cortical neurons are surrounded by clear halos, as are glial cells.

Vaginal Mucosa: All of the sections contain vascular congestion and focal interstitial chronic inflammation. The smallest piece of tissue, from the 7:00 position of the vaginal wall/hymen, contains epithelial erosion with underlying capillary congestion. A small number of red blood cells is present on the eroded surface, as is birefringent foreign material. Acute inflammatory infiltrate is not seen.

EVIDENCE: Items turned over to the Boulder Police Department as evidence include: Fibers and hair from clothing and body surfaces; ligatures; clothing, vaginal swabs and smears; rectal swabs and smears; oral swabs and smears; paper bags from hands; fingernail clippings; jewelry; paper bags from feet; white body bag; samples of head hair, eyelashes and eyebrows; swabs from right and left thighs and right cheek; red top and purple top tubes of blood.

Index

.22-caliber Marlin, usage, 101
.35-caliber Marlin carbine, usage, 101
.44-caliber killer, 52–63
274Cover273-274, Belt
596 Club, 36

A

Abuser, identification (likelihood), 175–176
Accardo, Tony (nickname), 32
Accidental poisoning, 287
Acetone, usage, 7–8
Acquaintance rape, 156
Adelman, Howard, 111
Adler, Pearl "Polly," 39–40
Adonis, Joe, 26
Aggressive behavior, kinds, 52
Ainslie, Robert, 240–241
Airbags, theft, 187
Alcohol, usage, 205–206
Algor mortis, definition, 145
Allen, Tim (Conviction), 260
Alligator effect, 250
Amanita phalloides. See Death-cap mushroom
American Gigolo (movie), 41
American prostitution, 44–45
Amityville Horror, 95–113
Ammonium nitrate fertilizer, explosive, 244

Ammons, Leland, 134
Amurao, Corazon, 120–123
    confession, 124–125
    terror, 124
Anastasia, Albert, 26
    nickname, 32
Ancient poisons, 287–291
Anderson, Pam, 262
Angel of Death, 225, 227–228
Appel, George (last words), 192
Arsenic, usage, 151–152
Arson
    cost/expense, 249
    definition, 243
    investigation, ATF (involvement), 248
    jargon, 250–251
    movies, 249
    questions/answers, 248–249, 251
    victims, number, 245
Arson fires
    frequency, 244
    occurrence. See Vehicles
    outdoor frequency, 251
    peak time, 152
Arsonists. *See* Disorganized arsonists; Organized arsonists
    catching, Internet (usage), 252–253
    characteristics, 248
    conviction rate, 249

pyromaniacs, contrast, 252
ranking, 245–246
understanding, 247–248
Asphalt gypsies, 20
Assassinations, 278–282
Atkins, Susan, 230
Aum Cult, 181–182
Auto theft, 187
facts, 188–189
recovery rates. See Stolen cars
Avenal Diagnostic Treatment
Center, 153, 157

B

Baader-Meinhof Gang, 182
Babe, 277
Bad apple postal worker, 8
Bag bride, 277
Bag the hands, terminology, 145
Bailey, F. Lee, 66
Baker, Mark, 275–276
Bamboo, poison, 289
Baniszewski, Gertrude, 282–284
Bank robberies, 15
average haul, 15
Banks, Delma, 197
Bank statements, examination, 8
Bardo, Robert John, 221–222
Barfield, Margie Velma, 227
Barrow, Clyde, 229–230
Bartlett, Marion (murder), 234
Bartlett, Velda (murder), 234
Starkweather, argument,
235–236
Beck, Martha, 230
Bell, Mary Flora, 269
Belushi, John, 259
Bender, 277
Berkowitz, David, 52–63
calming, 55–56
locations, 54
murder, decision, 62

Bernandin, Joseph, 167–168
Berry, Chuck (jail sentence), 255
Berry, Jason, 167, 168
Best Little Whorehouse in Texas
(movie), 41
Bibi, Mukhtaran, 162
Big jab, 191
Big Units, 153
bin Laden, Osama, 184
Birmingham Church Bombing, 182
Black Liberation Army, 184
Blackman, N., 52
Black tar, 278
Black Widow, 225–227
Blair House, assault, 280
Blanks, 275
Bliss, William, 311
Blitz rape, 156
Blizzard, 275
Bloch, Robert, 83–86
Blue-eyed devils, 185
Blue Oyster Cult, 148
Bonanno, Joe, 26
Borden, Lizzie, 149
Border rats, 275
Borrelli, Joseph (Berkowitz letter),
59–60
Bosket, Willie, 268
Boss of all bosses. See Capo di
tutti di cappi
Boston Strangler. See DeSalvo
Botts, Cheryl, 131–132
Bounty hunter, 276
Bouyeri, Mohammed, 182
Bradley, Dana, 181
Brady, Jim, 280
Brady, Patrick, 195
Brady Bil for the Prevention of
Handgun Violence, 280
Brady Bunch, The, 52
Brancato, Jr., Lillo (murderer), 263
Bremer, Arthur, 280
Bridgewater State Hospital, 66

Brigante, Michael, 103, 105, 109

Brinks, robbery (FBI investigation), 16

Bronx Tale, A (movie), 263

Brooks, David Owen, 82

Brown, Bobby (arrest), 260

Brown, Debra, 232

Brown, Juditha, 296

Brown, Martin, 269

Brown, Mary, 67

Brudos, Darcie, 79

Brudos, Jerry, 79–80
    places, abduction/murder, 81

Brunner, Mary, 230

Brussel, James, 185

Buchalter, Louis "Lepke," 26

Budd, Albert, 63–65

Budd, Delia/Albert, 143

Budd, Grace, 63–65
    murder trial, 92–94

Bufo marinus (poison), 287–288

Bugliosi, Vincent, 258

Bundy, Carol, 232

Bundy, Ted, 68–69, 196–197

Bunko (con game), 10

Bunko squad. See Los Angeles bunko squad

Bureau of Alcohol, Tobacco, and Firearms (ATF), involvement. See Arson

Burglaries
    cops, response, 24
    involvement, 4
    occurrence, timing, 14

Burglars. See Cat burglars; House burglars
    characteristics, 17–18

Burglars on the Job (Wright/Decker), 14

Burke, Elmer "Trigger," 16

Burke, Jimmy (nickname), 32

Burnout, 278

Burn patterns, 250

Bush, Noelle (drug charge), 262

Busywork, 143

Butler, James "The Harlem Hammer" (murder conviction), 262

Button man, 28

Buxton, Philip R., 115

Buy Back plan, 21

C

Caesar, Julius (assassination), 278

Campbell, Glen (drunk driving charge), 261

Campus rape, facts, 160

Capo di tutti di cappi (boss of all bosses), 28

Capone, Al "Scarface," 31
    nickname, 32
    tax evasion, conviction, 30

Capote, Truman, 117, 195

Carjacking
    action, 188
    commonness, 187
    prevention, 187–188

Carlos the Jackal, 182

Carolina pancake, 275–276

Carriages (false bottoms), usage, 12

Carter, Nick (DUI conviction), 260

Car theft, city ranking, 189

Cashman, Edward, 176

Castellano, Paul, 24, 26

Castle Keep (movie), 102

Cat burglars, 18

Celebrities
    crime, 255
    law, trouble, 259–263
    murder, facts, 258–259

Cermak, Anton (murder), 279

Chalk fairy, 144

Chapman, Mark David, 222

Charter Arms .44-caliber Bulldog, purchase, 54

Check kiter, 10–11
Check kiting, derivation, 11
Checks
    washing, 7–8
    writing, gel ink (usage), 8
Chicken hawks, 164
Chickens, 45–46
Child molesters, prison release, 201
Child prostitutes
    age, 47–48
    attention/affection, desire, 48–49
    depression, 47
Child prostitution, 46–49
    alcohol, usage, 47
    exploitation, 49
    homelessness/poverty, 47
    long-term dangers, 46–47
Children
    molestation, reaction, 173
    murderers, 265
        characteristics. See Parents
        examples, 267–270
        parent kidnappers, frequency, 284
    sexual abuse, devastation, 174–175
Church, relationship. See Pedophilia
Clark, Doug, 232
Class I misdemeanor, 146
Clutter, Bonnie, 196
Clutter family, murder, 117
Codd, Michael, 59
Coffman, Cynthia, 233
Coleman, Alton, 232
Collazo, Oscar, 280
Collier, Cindy, 268–269
Collison, Merle, 240
Colombian necktie, 30
Columbine High School, 267–268
Columbo, Joe, 26

Complainant, terminology, 147
Complaint, terminology, 147
Condemned, last words, 191–192
Condon, Robert, 311
Connecticut Consumer Affairs Department, 23
Consigliere, 28
Contract, execution, 27–28
Cook, Steven, 167
Coonan, Jimmy, 34–37
Co-op City, 53–54
Cops: Their Lives in Their Own Words (Baker), 275–276
Corona, Juan, 76
Coroner, role, 144
Corpus delicti, definition, 144
Corrallo, Anthony "Tony Ducks," 29
Coryll, Dean, 82–83, 95
Costello, Frank (nickname), 32
Council of Better Business Bureau, home repair complaints, 19
Counting Room, entry, 16
Coutant-Peyre, Isabelle, 182
Covenant House, 167
Crack-addicted prostitutes, sex, 44
Crankcase-oil brigade, 21
Crime
    jargon, 273–278
    rate, decline, 289
    women, responsibility, 224
Criminal history, 207
Criminal investigations, 141
Cromarty family, 97
Crosby, David (jail sentence), 255
Crotch walking, 5
Crum, Allen, 135–136
Culkin, Macaulay (arrest), 261
Cumminsky, Eddie, 34
Cunanan, Andrew, 147
Curare, poison, 290
Curphey, Theodore J., 307

Custodial interference, 286
Cyanide, poison, 288–289
Cyberstalking, 219–220

D

Date rape drugs, 155
Davidge, Frank, 104, 107
Davy, Charlene, 120
Davy, Gloria, 120, 122
    appearance, importance, 128
    date, return, 124
Dead Man Walking (movie), 196
Death-cap mushroom (Amanita
    phalloides), poison, 289
Death row, 191
    freedom, number, 198
    jargon, 191
Death wish, 196–197
Decker, Scott, 14
DeFeo, Allison (murder), 100
DeFeo, Dawn, 105
    murder, 100
DeFeo, John (murder), 100
DeFeo, Jr., Ronald "Butch," 97–98
    admission, 102–104
    alarm, 98
    cooperation, 101
    murder, reason, 103–105
    sentencing, 111–112
    St. Jerome, expulsion, 106
    trial, 109–111
    violence/guns, appreciation,
      107–108
DeFeo, Louise (death), 99–100
DeFeo, Mark (murder), 100
DeFeo, Sr., Ronald (death), 99–100
DeFeos, occurrence, 96
de Gaulle, Charles (assassination
    attempt), 280
Delaney, Kim (arrest), 260
Deliverance (movie), 76
DeMasi, Donna, 56–57

DeMeo, Roy, 24
Denaro, Carl, 56
DeNiro, Robert, 259, 263
DeSalvo, Albert (Boston Strangler),
    65–68
    background, 68
Dewey, Alvin, 196
Diagnostic Treatment Center, 153
DiMaggio, Jr., Joe, 305
Dinosaur, 276–277
Dip, pickpocket technique, 11
Disorganized arsonists, 247
Dlement, Del, 149
Do a piece of work, 28
Documents, alteration (scam), 7
Doing the Dog, 166
Doin' the Houdini, 30, 34
Dolman, Denver, 133
Downey, Jr., Robert (arrest), 259
Doyle, Thomas, 167
Drug addicts, cash desperation, 4
Dunne, Dominique (homicide), 257
DuPont Chemical Company, 244

E

E.F. Hutton and Co. Inc. (guilty
    plea), 10–11
Elderly, scamming, 22–23
Electric chair, nicknames, 193
Electrocution, painlessness, 194
Electronic security systems,
    beating, 6–7
Elliot, Robert G., 198
Ellis, Edward (last words), 191
Emergency Service Unit (ESU), 293
Eminem (Marshall Mathers),
    arrest, 260
Emotionally disturbed person
    (EDP), 170
Esau, Alexander, 59–60
Evidence, chain, 143

F

Falini, Louis, 101
Fallen off a truck (stolen item), 12
Fanny and the Faggot, signature, 269
Farbwow, Norman, 307
Featherstone, Mickey, 36
Federal Bureau of Investigation (FBI). *See* Uniform Crime Reports
Federal prison, attending (chances), 207
Federal prison inmates
    characteristics, 204
    state prison inmates, comparison, 204
Feldman, Corey (drug charge), 261
Fernandez, Raymond, 230
Ferrario, Joseph, 167
Fertilizer, impact, 244–245
Firefighters, volunteer status, 250
Fire Lover, The (Wambaugh), 245
Fish, Albert, 64–65, 142, 163
    psychiatric analysis, 92–94
    sexual career, 93–94
Fleiss, Heidi (questionnaire), 42–43
Fleming, Mary, 40
Fonda, Jane (assault charges), 260
Ford, Gerald (assassination attempt), 279–280
Ford, Larry C., 184
Foster, Jodie, 281
Framer, help, 15
Fratianno, Jimmy (nickname), 32
Fremont County, prison capitol, 200
French, James (last words), 192
French fries, last meal (request frequency), 192
Freund, Christine, 57, 58
Fromme, Lynette "Squeaky," 279–280
Fugate, Caril Ann, 223, 233–242
    captive, claim, 242
    escape, 236–237
    police search, 235
    Starkweather, visit, 235–236
    stopping, police desire, 238–241
    surrender, 240
Fugitive, The (show), 66
Fugu poison, 287
Furlong, Edward (drunkenness charge), 261

G

Gabour, Mark, 132
Gabour, Mary Frances, 132
Gacy, John Wayne Michael, 51, 70–71
    boys, murder, 95
    childhood, 75–76
Galante, Carmine, 26
Gallego, Charlene, 231
Gallego, Gerald, 231
Gallo, Joey "Crazy Joe," 26, 27
Gambino, Carlo, 26
Gamma hydroxybutyric acid (GHB), 155
Gang bang, 157
Gang rape. *See* Group rape
Gang-related homicides, 33
Gargullo, Merlita, 122
Garrett, Johnny Frank (last words), 191
Gas chamber, concept, 198
Gauthe, Gilbert, 167
Geberth, Vernon J., 144, 251
Gein, Ed, 83
    custody, 84
    hangup, 85
Geisha Disease, 150
Gemini Lounge Clubhouse, 24
Genovese, Vito, 27
Geoghan, John, 168
Giancana, Sam, 26
    nickname, 32
Giardella, Bill, 63

Gigante, Vincent (nickname), 32
Gilligan, Amy, 226
Gilmore, Gary, 148
    ad idea, 193
Glass, Jimmy (last words), 192
Glatman, Harvey, 80
Glothe, Glenn, 72–74
Goetz, Bernhard, 274–275
Gold, Tracey (DUI charges), 261
Goldman, Ron, 296
Gold Rush, prostitution (increase), 49
Gore, Al, 219–220
Gotti, John, 26
    nickname, 32
Graham, Gwendolyn, 233
Grammar, Kelsey (jail sentence), 256
Grant, Hugh (lewd conduct charge), 261
Gravano, Sammy (nickname), 32
Gray rape, 158
Greeley, Andrew, 168
Greenson, Ralph, 306
Grillo, Danny, 36
Grooming, 164–165
Grounder, terminology, 145–146
Group rape (gang rape // pack rape), 157–158
Growing Menace, The (Norris), 91
Gruesome Gert (electric chair), 192
Gunness, Belle (Lady Bluebeard), 226

H

Hahn, Anna Marie, 229
Halberstam, David, 3
Hall, Robert, 119
Hambali, 182
Hamilton Avenue, murders, 138–139
Hands, bagging. See Bag the hands

Hansen, Robert, 72–74
Harris, Eric, 267–268
Harris, Neil Patrick, 249
Harris, Robert Alton (last words), 192
Hartman, Phil (homicide), 257
Hauptmann, Richard Bruno, 284–285
Hearst, Patty, 183
    See also Patty Hearst Story
Heirens, William, 199
Hellman, D.S., 52
Helter Skelter (Bugliosi), 258
Henley, Wayne, 95
Herman, Pee-Wee (Paul Reubens) (indecent exposure charge), 262
Hetlin, Earl, 240–241
Hickock, Dick, 117
    execution, 195–196
Hillside Strangler, 71
Hinckley, Jr., John, 281
Hit-and-run, accident definition, 145
Hitler, Adolph, 267
    assassination attempt, 282
Hollywood, suicides, 257
Hollywood Slasher, 232
Home improvement contractors
    theives, percentage, 19
    theiving behavior, 18–19
Home Show (ABC), bank manager story, 22
Homicidal triangle, 52
Homicides. See Gang-related homicides; Justifiable homicide
Honor Thy Father and Mother (movie), 152
Hoover, J. Edgar, 51, 147
Houdini. See Doin' the Houdini
House burglars, 18
House spiking (scam), 22–23
Houston, Whitney, 260
Howard, Frank, 142
Hoyt, Waneta, 226

Huberty, James Oliver, 118
Hullet, Mark, 176
Human bomb, 13
Human Rights Watch report. *See* No Escape

I

I Cheated the Law (movie), 114
Incest, 156–157
In Cold Blood (Capote), 117
   killers, execution, 195–196
Infantophilia, 172
Instant messages (IMs), 219
Internal organs (trophies), 295
Inventory shrinkage, 10
   cost. *See* U.S. retailers
Investigative jargon, 143–147

J

Jackal. *See* Carlos the Jackal
Jackson, Andrew (assassination attempt), 281
Jack the Ripper, 224
Jacobs, Jesse DeWayne (last words), 191
Jail, contrast. *See* Prisons
Jay, Jerry, 135
Jeffrey Manor (murders), 118–128
Jensen, Robert, 238
Jewish Defense League, 185
Jewish Lightning, 250
Jimmy the Wags. *See* Picciarelli
Johnson, Earl (last words), 192
Jones, Genene, 227
Jones, Kimberly. *See* Lil' Kim
Joplin, Janis, 258–259
Jordan, Mary Ann, 121
Judd, Wynonna (arrest), 261
Julius Caesar (play), 178
Justifiable homicide, 2–3

K

Kaczynski, Ted (Unabomber), 183–184
Kahane, Meir, 185
Karpis, Alvin "Creepy," 110
Keach, Stacy (jail sentence), 256
Keller, Paul, 249
Kellerman, Max, 262
Kelly, Carl (last words), 191
Kelly, Daniel, 119–120
Kelly, R. (arrest), 261
Kelske, Bobby, 98, 107
   police interview, 102
   Suffolk County Police call, 99
Kemper, Edmund, 86–90, 270
   rope, breakage, 88
   stabbing, 88–89
Kennedy, John F. (assassination), 294
Kennedy, Robert (assassination), 258
Kesabian, Linda, 230
Ketamine hydrochloride (special K), 155
Kidnapper, etymology, 284
Kidnapping, 282–284. *See also* Ransom kidnappings
   world capital, 286
King, Carol, 238
King, Larry (grand larceny charge), 261
King, Will, 141–142
King Hussein of Jordan (assassination observation), 279
King Talal, abdication, 279
Klausner, Lawrence D., 61
Klebold, Dylan, 267–268
Krenwinkel, Patricia, 230
Kriesle, Leonard, 137
Krumm, Victor, 72–74

L

La Bianca, Leno/Rosemary, 258
Lady Bluebeard. *See* Gunness
Lady Gambles, The (movie), 114
Lamport, William, 132
Lansky, Meyer, 26
Lauria, Donna, 54–56
Lawrence, Richard, 281
L.E.A.D.S., usage, 252–253
Lead Us Not Into Temptation
   (Berry), 168
Lee, Tommy (arrest), 262
Lemmon, Leonora, 310–311
Lennon, John (murder), 222
Lethal cocktail, 196
Likens, Sylvia (kidnapping/torture/murder), 282–284
Lil' Kim (Kimberly Jones), sentence, 260
Linck's Log Cabin, arson, 246–247
Lindbergh baby, kidnapping, 285
Little John, punishment, 75
Lolita syndrome/complex, 164
Lonely Hearts Killers, 230
Long, Bobby Joe, 90–92
   masturbation, 90
Loren, Sophia (jail sentence), 256
Los Angeles bunko squad, 22–23
Lot lizards, 46
Love obsession group, 218
Low burning, 250
Lucas, Henry Lee
   childhood, 76–78
   serial murderer, prolificness,
      78
Lucas, Viola, 77–78
Lucchese, Thomas (nickname), 32
Luciano, Charles (nickname), 32
Luciano, Lucky, 26
   Schultz, friend, 39
Lumbaghi, Peter, 18
Lupo, Salvatore, 60

Lutz, George Lee, 95
   house, searching, 96
Lutz, Kathleen, 95
   house, searching, 96
Lutzes, local media, 96–97

M

Mad Bomber, terror, 143, 185
Madonna/prostitute complex, 127
Mafia-endorsed weaponry, 33
Mafia nicknames, 32
Mafioso
   deaths, 26–27
Mafioso, fear, 25
Mail, direct delivery, 8
Make My Day law, 1–2
Males
   female rape, possibility, 158–159
   male rape, possibility, 160–161
Manson, Charles, 110, 229
   family, 230
   slayings, 258
Marital rape, 156
Market Diner, Grillo/Stein meeting, 36
Marlow, James, 233
Married to the Mob (movie), 12
Martha, Inc. (movie), 152
Martin, Rhonda Bell, 226
Martinez, Romero, 135, 136
Marty, Specks, 84
Mary Ann (Kemper murder), 88–90
Mass murder, 95
   contrast. See Serial murder
Mathers, Marshall. *See* Eminem
Matusek, Patricia, 122
Mayo Clinic study, 286
McConaughey, Matthew (arrest charge), 260
McCoy, Houston, 135
McCrary, Carolyn, 230–231
McCrary, Daniel, 230–231

McCrary, Sherman, 230–231
McCrary Family, The, 230–231
McElroy, Ken Rex, 147–149
McKenzie, D., 28
McLain, Denny (jail sentence), 256
McVeigh, Timothy, 180–181
Meagher, Eddie, 141
Mercy killing defense, 229
Metesky, George, 143, 185
Metropolitan Los Angeles, bank robberies (maximum), 15
Mexican Lightning, 250
Meyer, August (Gus), 237–238
Midnight Cowboy (movie), 41
Miles, C.A., 134
Mitchum, Robert (jail sentence), 256
Money laundering, 11
Monroe, Marilyn, 305–309
    examiner-coroner statement, 307–308
Moore, Blanche Taylor, 227
Moore, Dudley (arrest), 262
Moran, Thomas "Butterfingers," 15
Moskowitz, Stacy, 61, 62
Mule, 274–275
Mullen, Mary, 67–68
Murder
    assembly line, 24
    committing, 149–150
    month, frequency, 288
    rate
      country rank, 149
      ranking, 290
Murder in New Hampshire (movie), 152
My Life in the NYPD (Picciarelli), 292
My Siste Sam (show), 221

N

Nassar, George, 66
National Catholic Reporter, 167
National Check Fraud Center, 8
National Maritime Union, 125
National Retail Security Survey, 10
Navarro, Ramon (homicide), 257
Neelley, Alvin, 231–232
Neelley, Judith, 231–232
Nelson, Willie, 246
Nepiophilia, 172
New York Police Department (NYPD) Ballistics Unit, 58–59
New York Private Chauffeurs Benevolent Association (NYPC-BA), 142
Ngor, Haing S. (homicide), 257
Nichols, Sue, 23
Night Rider and Lady Sundance, The, 231–232
Nitroglycerine, explosive, 245
Nitti, Frank, 26
    nickname, 32
No Escape (Human Rights Watch report), 161
Noguchi, Thomas, 259, 305–306
No Legs (Lucas father), 76
Nolte, Nick (SUI charge), 260
Norris, Joel, 78, 91
Nosair, El-Sayid, 185
Not Our Son (movie), 249
Npguchi, Thomas, 258
Nunchakus (nunchucks), 276

O

O. Henry, jail sentence, 255
O'Hara, Bridget, 40
O'Keefe, Specs, 16
Old Smokey (electric chair), 193
Old Sparky (electric chair), 192
Olsen, Jack, 82
O'Neal, Ryan (jail sentence), 255
Organized arsonists, 247
Organized crime/gangs, 25
    crime jargon, 27–30
Orr, John, 245–246

Osbourne, Ozzie (arrest), 263
Oswald, Lee Harvey, 294
Overkill victim, 295
Oxalic acid, poison, 289

P

Pacino, Al (weapons charge), 263
Pack rape. *See* Group rape
Palestinians
    hatred, 178
    homicide bombers, 184
Pancuronium bromide, lethal
    injection, 196
Panic Room (movie), 4–5
Panzram, Carl (last words), 192
Parents, children murderers
    (characteristics), 266–267
Parker, Bonnie, 229–230
Parole, 207
Parris, Suzanne, 121
Paslon, Valentina, 121
Patriarca, Raymond, 26
Patty Hearst Story, The (movie), 152
Pedophile activism, 175
Pedophiles, 157
    birth, 176
    definition, 163
    desire, 172
    identification, ability, 169
    number, 169
    rapists, contrast, 165
    recovery, percentage, 165
    sex drive (reduction), drugs
        (impact), 172
    strike, reduction (possibility),
        172
    term, coinage, 163–164
Pedophile victims, examples, 175
Pedophilia
    Church, relationship, 167–168
    incurability, understanding,
        173

occurrence, frequency,
    173–174
    prevalence. See Priests
    problem, impact, 169
Penn, Sean, 196
    jail sentence, 255
Perfect Husband, The (movie), 152
Perkins, Anthony, 83
Perp walk, 277–278
Persico, Carmine (nickname), 32
Phillips, Joshua, 269
Picciarelli, Patrick (Jimmy the
    Wags), 292
Pickpockets, techniques, 9. See
    also Dip
Pile-Up-Pick, 9
Pimps, Department of Justice
    estimates, 44
Pino, Anthony "Fats," 16
Pippen, Scottie (arrest), 263
Poison, 287–291
    delivery, 290–291
    usage, 151–152
Polanski, Roman, 258
Ponne, Leonard, 120–123
Pope John Paul II, 168
    assassination attempt, 281
Popova, Madame, 228
Portrait of a Serial Arsonist: The
    Paul Keller Story (documentary),
    249
Positively True Adventures of the
    Alleged Texas Cheerleader
    Murdering Mom, The (movie),
    152
Potassium chloride, lethal injec-
    tion, 196
Practical Homicide (Geberth), 251
Practical Homicide Investigation,
    144
Preppie Murder, The (movie), 152
Pretty Baby (movie), 41
Pretty Woman (movie), 41

Priests, pedophilia (prevalence), 173

Prinze, Freddie, 259

Prisons, 199
  capitol. See Fremont County
  conduct, rules, 215
  jail, contrast, 200
  jargon, 208–213
  medical problems, 202–203
  questions/answers, 199–200
  race, predominance, 199
  rape, 161
  sentence
    length, ranking, 199
    record, 200
  worldwide populations, 206

Prison state inmates, injury, 202

Profaci, Joe, 26

Prostitutes
  customers, pornography (usage), 45
  demographics, 44
  fortunes, decline, 45
  Illinois legislature, proposal, 44
  juveniles/runaways, percentage, 45
  movies, 41–42
  murder weapon, 40
  sex charges. See Street prostitutes
  sexual abuse, percentage, 45
  virginity, loss, 44–45

Prostitution, 39. See also American prostitution; Child prostitution
  arrests, 44
  increase. See Gold Rush
  jargon, 45–46
  seasonal problem, 48
  trend, 49

Public-order crimes (victimless crimes), 206

Puente, Dorothea, 229

Pugilistic attitude/pose, 251

Pulling train, 30

Pyromaniacs, contrast. See Arsonists

R

Rachals, Terri, 228

Rae, Tommie, 261

Rafferty, Dennis (interrogation), 102

Ragonese, Paul, 291–293

Ramsey, JonBenet
  autopsy report, 313–327
  clinicopathologic correlation, 314–315
  evidence, 327
  external examination, 315
  remainder, 319–320
  final diagnosis, 313–314
  injury, external evidence, 316–319
  internal examination, 321–325
  microscopic description, 325–327

Ransom kidnappings, 286

Rape, 153
  crime, viewpoint, 155
  facts, 159
  fantasies, 162
  law, knowledge, 159–160
  legal definition, 159
  punishment, 162
  sexual torture, 161
  time, serving, 201
  types, 156–158

Rapists
  contrast. See Pedophiles
  motives, 154
  victims, knowledge (number), 154
  weapons, usage, 155

Rathel, Otis, 123
Reading Gaol, 256
Reagan, Ronald (assassination attempt), 280–281
Recidivism, 205
Redstone, David, 115
Reeves, George, 310–312
Reles, Abe, 26
Restraining order, obtaining (wisdom), 221
Retail stores, theft (percentage), 5
Reubens, Paul. See Herman
Rhubarb, poison, 289
Ride the Lightning, 191
Ritter, Bruce, 167
Roach, importance, 141–143
Robberies. See Bank robberies
Robbers, purse theft (allowance), 9–10
Robbery, 1
Rock, Kid (arrest), 261
Rohypnol (flunitrazepam // roofies), 155
Romer, Bill, 240
Roosevelt, Franklin D. (assassination attempt), 279
Roosevelt, Theodore (assassination attempt), 279
Rose, Pete (jail sentence), 255
Rosenbaum, Ron, 76
Rossetti, Stephen, 172
Rothschild, Nicole, 262
Rudolph, Eric, 184
Ruppert, Charity, 138
Ruppert, James, 95, 138–139
Ruppert, Leonard, 138

S

Sadat, Anwar (assassination), 278
Schaeffer, Rebecca, 220–221
homicide, 257
Schmale, Nina, 121

School shooters, characteristics, 265–266
Schrank, John, 279
Schultz, Dutch, 26
protection, 39
Schwartz, Daniel, 109–111
Scorpions, poison, 288
Scrutton, Hugh, 183
S.C.U.M. See Society for Cutting Up Men
Serial killers, women (percentage), 224
Serial murder, 51
mass murder, contrast, 95
Serial murderers. See Women
characteristics, 270–271
psychiatrists, opinion, 91–92
Sex offenders
guide, 200–202
victimization, 202
Sex Slave Murderers, 231
Sexual abusers, victims' parents, 169
Sexual perversions, 163
jargon, 164–165
questions/answers, 172–176
Shakur, Tupac (homicide), 257
Shankill Butchers, The, 184
Sheen, Charlie, 42
Sheppard, George, 135
Sheppard, Sam (conviction), 66
Shirvell, Jack, 101–102
Shoplifters
cashiers, quality, 7
children, assistance, 12
males/females, commonness, 6
solo work, 12
techniques, 5
technology, advantage, 7
umbrella, assistance, 13
Shotaro complex, 164
Shotgun teams, disbanding, 6

Siegel, Benjamin (nickname), 32

Siegel, Bugsy, 26

Silence of the Lambs, The (Gein), 83

Simple obsession group, 219

Simpson, Nicole Brown, 295–296

   anatomical summary, 297–298

   autopsy report, 297–304

   external examination, 298–299

   hands, injuries, 303–304

   injury, evidence, 299–301

   internal examination, 304

   multiple stab wounds,

     description, 301–303

Simpson, O.J., 295–296

Sirhan, Sirhan (murderer), 258

Site, chalking, 143–144

Sixteenth Street Baptist Church, 182

Sizzlin' Sally (electric chair), 193

Skyjacking, chronology, 180

SLA. *See* Symbionese Liberation Army

Smith, Cathy, 259

Smith, James (murder), 194–195

Smith, Leroy, 126

Smith, Perry, 117

   execution, 195–196

Smith, Susan, 225

Snyder, Martin, 259

Society for Cutting Up Men (S.C.U.M.) Manifesto, 282

Sodium thiopental (Pentathal), lethal injection, 196

Solanas, Valerie, 282

Son of Sam, 59–62

   handwriting, 63

Sopranos, The (show), 263

Soul murder, 174

Soul of a Cop (Ragonese), 291–293

South Side Community Hospital, 118

Spanish Llama .45 automatic, usage, 2

Speck, Richard Franklin (murderer), 126–127

Speck, Shirley, 127

Speed, Billy, 134

Speedball, usage, 259

Spenkelink, John (last words), 192

Spiking (scam). *See* House spiking

Spree Killers (Redstone), 115

Sprinkle, Joseph, 239–240

St. Louis Globe Democrat, dip report, 11

Stalkers, violence rate, 220

Stalking, 217–219. *See also* Cyberstalking

   example, 222

   gender, commonness, 217

   questions/answers, 220–221

Standard Time Burglar. *See* Welch Jr.

Starkweather, Charles "Little Red," 223, 233–242

   custody, 241

   escape, 236–237

   homicidal rage, 241–242

   stopping, police desire, 238–241

Starkweather, Guy, 241–242

Starkweather, Helen, 241–242

State prison, attending (chances), 207

State prison inmates

   characteristics, 203–204

   violent offenders, percentage, 204

   women, percentage, 203

States

   danger, ranking, 291

   safety, ranking, 291

Statutory rape, 156

Stein, Ruby, 35–36

Stolen cars

   ranking (2004), 190

   recovery rates, 189

Street prostitutes, sex charges, 44
Struckman-Johnson, Cindy/David (research), 161
Students, homicidal tendencies, 266
Sturiano, Jack, 99
Subway Peep Show, 170
Sudden Infant Death Syndrome (SIDS), claim, 226
Suicides. *See* Hollywood
Sullivan, Gerard, 100
Sunset Slayer, 232
Suriana, Valentina, 59–60
Sutton, Willie, 1
Swayze, John Cameron, 193
Symbionese Liberation Army (SLA), 183
Syosset house, finished basement, 96

T

Tate, Sharon, 258
Taylor, Ginger, 230–231
Taylor, Ray, 230–231
Team killers, 229–233
    example, 233–242
Ten Most Wanted List, 147
Terrorism, 177
    copycat action, 178
Terrorists, acts (chronology), 181–185
Three Card Monte, 10
Tiny Terror, 233–242
Toppan, Jane, 224
Torresola, Griselio, 280
Townsley, Edna, 132
Trench Coat Mafia, 267
Troubles gang, 184
Trueblood, Lydia, 226
True crimes
    miscellany, 273
    movies, 152

Truman, Harry (assassination attempt), 280
Tylenol Murderer(s), 185

U

Unabomber. *See* Kaczynski
Uniform Crime Reports (FBI), 188
University of Texas (murders), 128–138
Unruh, Howard
    characteristics, 113–115
    Luger, usage, 116
    mass murderer, 115–116
U.S. retailers, inventory shrinkage cost, 10

V

Van Gogh, Theo (murder), 182
Van Houten, Leslie, 230
Vaughan, Vince (arrest), 262
Vehicles, arson fires (frequency), 251
Victimless crimes. *See* Public-order crimes
Violante, Robert, 61, 62
Violent offenders, percentage. *See* State prison inmates
Von Busch, Bob
    complaint, 233
    suspicions, 234
von Krafft-Ebing, Richard, 163
Von Ronkel, Carol, 311
Voskerichian, Virginia, 58–60

W

Walden, Don, 131–132
Wallace, George (assassination attempt), 280
Wallets
    female thieves, tricks, 9

theft, tricks, 9–12
Wambaugh, Joseph, 245
Ward, C. Lauer, 238
Warhol, Andy (assassination
    attempt), 282
Warlord, murder, 149–150
Watson, Charles, 230
Weather Underground, 184
Weinstein, Jack, 97
Welch Jr., Bernard C. (Standard
    Time Burglar), 2–4
Wertham, Frederic, 92
Westies gang, 34
Whitehead, Harold, 34
Whitman, Charles
    acting out, 130
    hatred, 137–138
    murders, 128–137
    police, standstill, 135
    preparations, 128–129
    university arrival, 130–132
weaponry, 129
Whitman, Kathy, 130
Whitney, Jay, 79
Whore (movie), 41
Whore stroll, 46
Wilie Bosket Law, passage, 268
Wilkening, Pamela, 121
Williams, Robin, 259
Williamson gang, 20–21
Windmiller, Freda, 119
Wire man, 29
Wolf, Shirley, 268–269
Women
    killers, 223
        questions/answers, 223, 224
        uniqueness, 225–228
    murder
        motives, 225
        weapons, selection, 225
    offenders, 206
    percentage. See Serial killers
    responsibility. See Crime

serial murderers, 228–229
Wood, Catherine May, 233
Worden, Beatrice, 83–86
Work, do a piece of. See Do a
    piece of work
Working Girls (movie), 42
World Trade Center (WTC)
    attack, 178–179
    towers, description, 179
Wright, Richard, 14
Wuornos, Aileen, 228

Y

Yellow Mama (electric chair), 192
Young, Gig, 310
Young, Lila, 228–229

Z

Zangara, Giuseppe, 279
Zebra Killers, 185
Ziporyn, Marvin, 127–128
Zolan, Harold, 109, 111

About the Authors

Tom Philbin and his brother Mike have been close to crime (and its consequences) for many years. Tom is a long-time freelance writer who has written nine cop novels. He lives in New York.

Michael Philbin is a musician, and this is his first book. He lives in South Tamworth, New Hampshire.